Victorian Chester

LIVERPOOL HISTORICAL STUDIES
published for the
Department of History, University of Liverpool

1. Patrick J. N. Tuck, *French Catholic Missionaries and the Politics of Imperialism in Vietnam, 1857–1914: A Documentary Survey*, 1987, 352pp. (**Out of print**)

2. Michael de Cossart, *Ida Rubinstein (1885–1960): A Theatrical Life*, 1987, 244pp.

3. P. E. H. Hair, ed., *Coals on Rails, Or the Reason of My Wrighting: The Autobiography of Anthony Errington, a Tyneside colliery waggon and waggon-way wright, from his birth in 1778 to around 1825*, 1988, 288pp.

4. Peter Rowlands, *Oliver Lodge and the Liverpool Physical Society*, 1990, 336pp.

5. P. E. H. Hair, ed., *To Defend Your Empire and the Faith: Advice on a Global Strategy Offered c. 1590 to Philip, King of Spain and Portugal, by Manoel de Andrada Castel Blanco*, 1990, 304pp.

6. Christine Hillam, *Brass Plate and Brazen Impudence: Dental Practice in the Provinces 1755–1855*, 1991, 352pp.

7. John Shepherd, *The Crimean Doctors: A History of the British Medical Services in the Crimean War*, 1991, 2 vols, 704pp.

8. John Belchem, ed., *Popular Politics, Riot and Labour: Essays in Liverpool History 1790–1940*, 1992, 272pp.

9. Duncan Crewe, *Yellow Jack and the Worm: British Naval Administration in the West Indies, 1739–1748*, 1993, 352pp.

10. Stephen J. Braidwood, *Black Poor and White Philanthropists: London's Blacks and the Foundation of the Sierra Leone Settlement 1786–1791*, 1994, 336pp.

11. David Dutton, *'His Majesty's Loyal Opposition': The Unionist Party in Opposition 1905–1915*, 1992, 336pp.

12. Cecil H. Clough and P. E. H. Hair, eds., *The European Outthrust and Encounter: The First Phase c.1400–c.1700: Essays in Tribute to David Beers Quinn on His 85th Birthday*, 1994, 380pp.

13. David Dutton, ed., *Statecraft and Diplomacy in the Twentieth Century: Essays Presented to P. M. H. Bell*, 1995, 192pp.

14. Roger Swift, ed., *Victorian Chester: Essays in Social History 1830–1900*, 1996, 263pp.

Victorian Chester

ESSAYS IN SOCIAL HISTORY
1830–1900

edited by
ROGER SWIFT

Published for the
Department of History
University of Liverpool

LIVERPOOL UNIVERSITY PRESS
1996

Liverpool Historical Studies, no. 14
General Editor: C. H. Clough

First published 1996
by Liverpool University Press
Senate House, Abercromby Square, Liverpool, L69 3BX

British Library Cataloguing in Publication Data
A British Library CIP record is available
ISBN 0–85323–661–5

Typeset in 10½/12½ point Times by
Wilmaset Ltd, Birkenhead, Wirral
Printed in the European Union by
Redwood Books, Trowbridge, Wiltshire

Preface

This edited collection of essays has arisen largely from recent research conducted by staff and postgraduate students associated with the Centre for Victorian Studies at University College Chester. Indeed, several of the essays derive from dissertations submitted by students who completed the Master of Arts degree programme in Victorian Studies at the College between 1992 and 1995.

In editing this collection, I am especially indebted to Mary Glazier, Research Assistant in the Department of History at University College Chester, whose patience, efficiency, and word–processing skills enabled the project to develop smoothly from inception to completion. I would also like to thank Cecil Clough, of the University of Liverpool, for his encouragement and support throughout the duration of the project. Thanks are also due to my colleague, Dr Peter Gaunt, who read and commented helpfully on some of the drafts, and to the staff of the Cheshire County Record Office, the Chester City Record Office, and the Grosvenor Museum for their unstinting efforts in offering invaluable advice and assistance. Above all, my greatest debt is to the contributors, whose commitment and forbearance helped to translate this project from image to reality.

Roger Swift
Chester, 1996

Contents

List of Tables

The Contributors

Mary Glazier is a graduate of the University of Liverpool, where she was awarded the degree of MA in Victorian Studies in 1995, and was Research Assistant in the Department of History at University College Chester, from 1993–95.

John Herson is Head of History at the Liverpool John Moores University, and a Fellow of the Institute of Irish Studies at the University of Liverpool. His research interests and publications lie primarily in the field of nineteenth-century Irish immigration, urban history and transport history.

Kristina Jeffes is a graduate of the University of Manchester, where she was awarded the Warren Kinsey History Prize. She lives in Chester, where she has embarked on a management career in the National Health Service.

Jacqueline Perry is a graduate of the University of East Anglia, and was awarded the degree of MA in Victorian Studies by the University of Liverpool in 1994. A civil servant in Chester, she is currently conducting postgraduate research on domestic service in late–Victorian Cheshire.

Julian Reed-Purvis is a graduate of the University of Nottingham and was awarded the degree of M.A. in Victorian Studies by the University of Liverpool in 1994. He is a History Master at Bradford Grammar School, where he teaches modern British and European history.

Roger Swift is Director of the Centre for Victorian Studies at University College Chester, and a Fellow of the Institute of Irish Studies at the University of Liverpool. His research interests and publications lie in the general field of Victorian social history, notably in the context of Irish immigration, crime and social protest.

Chris Walsh is Head of English at University College Chester. He has published numerous articles and reviews on Victorian literature, and is co-editor of *Studying Literature: A Practical Introduction* (Harvester Wheatsheaf, 1995). Currently, he is writing a book on the history and theory of the English novel.

Introduction

Roger Swift

The Victorian period marked a significant phase in the development of the city of Chester, for not only did it witness a rapid increase in the size of the population—from 23,029 in 1831 to 47,975 in 1901—but also much of Chester's physical growth took place in the Victorian period and many of its present-day streets and buildings are a legacy of that age. In particular, the mid-Victorian years witnessed the renovation of the city centre. Half-timbered gabled buildings of Stuart origin were refurbished and new buildings, indicative of the 'black and white' revival, were erected in Eastgate Street, St Werburgh Street, and Northgate Street. Impressive public buildings, the epitome of civic pride, were constructed, including the General Railway Station, constructed by Thomas Brassey and opened in 1848, and the Town Hall, erected in 1869 after a fire had demolished its predecessor, and which reflected the influence of the Gothic revival, whose chief exponent in Chester was James Harrison. Old churches were restored and new churches and chapels were built for Anglicans, Roman Catholics, Presbyterians, Wesleyan Methodists and Baptists. Moreover, the old street pattern of central Chester was transformed by the construction of new roads, including Grosvenor Street and City Road, whilst the physical expansion of the city was reflected in both the development of predominantly working-class suburbs in Boughton, Newtown, Hoole and the Garden Lane-Sealand Road area, and in the emergence of new middle-class estates at Queens Park and Curzon Park.[1] Indeed, as Nikolaus Pevsner has observed, 'If one tries to make up accounts, Chester is not a medieval, it is a Victorian city'.[2]

Yet in contrast to other contemporary cathedral cities such as

York, Lincoln and Exeter,[3] Victorian Chester has received a poor academic press, as the dearth of publications on the social, economic, political and religious history of the city during the period illustrates, and references to Chester are conspicuous by their absence from some of the finest scholarly studies of Victorian cities.[4] Moreover, with the notable exception of John Tomlinson's excellent collection of contemporary photographs,[5] the Victorian phase in the development of the city has only merited relatively superficial treatment in recent general histories of Chester, which have been designed primarily with the needs of the tourist in mind.[6] In some respects this is surprising, for a wealth of primary source material pertaining to the Victorian period, much of it relatively untapped, is deposited in the Chester City Record Office and the Cheshire County Record Office.[7] In contrast, the historical study of this ancient city has, to date, focused overwhelmingly on the Roman, medieval and early modern periods, although it is to be hoped that the forthcoming volume, *The Victoria History of the County of Cheshire: Vol. V, The City of Chester*, edited by Alan Thacker,[8] and the research being undertaken by postgraduate students in the newly-established postgraduate Centre for Victorian Studies at University College Chester, will stimulate further scholarly interest in Victorian Chester. In this context, this collection of essays does not seek to present either a comprehensive or a definitive history of Chester during the Victorian period, for a substantial body of research needs to be conducted before such a venture can even be contemplated. Rather, it presents the results of recent research into some selective yet important aspects of the social history of Chester during the period and, since the local history of a community does not exist in a vacuum, each of the themes explored in this volume is placed firmly in its wider Victorian context. As such, this volume seeks not only to break new ground but also to illustrate the potential for further research on the development of Chester during a key period in its history.

John Herson's introductory essay, which provides a contextual framework for those which follow, explores the ways in which Chester's economy and population reacted to the changing circumstances of the Victorian period and, by reference to contemporary census data, explores the extent to which the process of demographic change was influenced by patterns of migration to and from the city. Herson also examines the impact of changing demographic patterns on the city's economic structure and illustrates the light which local business records and commercial directories can shed on both the weakening of Chester's traditional economy and the expansion of Chester's emerging regional role as a centre for transport, administration, retail and service industries, and tourism. Yet by charting the fluctuating economic fortunes of Victorian Chester, Herson's essay is of wider relevance, for it illustrates not only the potential, but also the problems of basing an economy, local or national, on shopping, services and tourism. Moreover, by examining the far-reaching implications of economic change for urbanization in a local context during a period when British economy and society became more extensively and intensively urbanized than ever before,[9] Herson provides further evidence to support the revisionist thesis that the development of Victorian cities was characterized more by differentiation rather than by homogeneity.[10]

Of course, there were also great contrasts within Victorian cities,[11] and the reality of life in Victorian Chester was often very different from the prosperous image which the city conveyed to middle-class visitors. Whilst Chester avoided the worst excesses of the Industrial Revolution, the working-class districts of the city exhibited all the hallmarks of urban squalor and the problems of poverty, disease and insanitary living conditions presented a constant challenge to the city authorities. During the early and mid-Victorian years, when state intervention in social policy was gradual and piecemeal, the responsibility for dealing with these problems rested primarily in the hands of the Chester Corporation, reformed by the Municipal Corporations Act of 1835, and the Improvement Commissioners, established in 1762, whose powers in regard to lighting, watching and cleansing the streets were extended by the local Improvement Acts of 1845 and 1884.[12] In this context, the essays by Mary Glazier, Kristina Jeffes and Jaqueline Perry break new ground by analysing local attitudes and responses to some of the most pressing social problems which faced Victorian Chester. They also provide a local perspective on one of the broader themes which has informed the recent study of urban history, namely the issue of centralization versus local autonomy at a time when many argued that central government should take a more coercive line against inefficient local authorities who seemed incapable of tackling the problems of urban growth.[13]

In her study of common lodging houses in the city, Mary Glazier employs the Council Assembly Books and the Improvement Committee Minute Books in order to examine the perceptions and policies of the Chester authorities in regard to this issue during the 1830s and 1840s. Moreover, by detailed analysis of the Minutes of the Lodging House Committee, she explores the impact of mandatory central government legislation—in the form of the Common Lodging Houses Act of 1851—on both the monitoring of conditions in lodging-houses and the extension of control over the lodging-house population.

The condition of such houses was but one aspect of urban squalor, which was illuminated and magnified in Chester, as elsewhere, by Irish immigration during the late 1840s and early 1850s in the wake of the Irish Famine. Although Irish settlement in Chester had ancient roots, many of these famine migrants settled in St John's Parish in the poor working-class suburb of Boughton, notably in Steven Street and its surrounding courts and alleys, a poverty-ridden district which had earned the unenviable description of 'the St Giles of Chester' during the early decades of the nineteenth century. However, by the mid-nineteenth century the area was widely regarded as 'the Irish district' and it was popularly held that poverty and insanitary conditions were themselves a product of Irish immigration, which provides the context for the essay by Kristina Jeffes. This original micro-study, which has wider implications for the general debate in regard to Irish settlement in Victorian cities,[14] employs contemporary census data and the voluminous files of the *Chester Chronicle* in order to ascertain how far the Boughton Irish formed an outcast ghetto community, locked together in defensive ethnicity in face of popular prejudice, during the early Victorian period.

Many of the social problems experienced by the Irish poor also formed part of the reality of daily life in Chester for the English poor. These included low standards of public health, which were compounded by overcrowding, poor ventilation, inadequate water supply, poor drainage, lack of refuse collection and general squalor. Inevitably, endemic diseases such as typhus, typhoid fever, measles, scarlet fever, influenza and tuberculosis were present in Chester's working-class districts. Low standards of public health in Chester were further highlighted by the cholera epidemics of 1831–32, 1848–49, 1853–54 and 1865–66. Indeed, these were years of crisis in regard to sanitary interventions in many English towns,[15] and the most serious cholera epidemic—that of 1848–49—provides the context for Jacqueline Perry's essay. Drawing on the records of the City Council and the Improvement Commissioners, Perry examines the reasons why the municipal authorities preferred to respond to the epidemic by establishing a local Sanitary Committee under the terms of the Nuisance Removals and Disease Prevention Acts of 1848 (which allowed for the adoption of emergency measures during epidemics), rather than by taking advantage of the permissive clauses of the Public Health Act of 1848, which empowered municipal authorities to establish a local Board of Health. Indeed, Perry's essay suggests that the city authorities frequently sought local and often temporary solutions to problems pertaining to public health, responses which not infrequently bred confusion, inefficiency and complacency. Thus, when cholera returned in 1853–54 and, again, in 1866, the city was as ill-prepared to cope with these epidemics as it had been in 1832 and 1848. Even in 1879, Chester was one of numerous boroughs still lacking piped water,[16] and in 1905 it was reported that there were some 2,500 people living in insanitary conditions in 122 squalid courts.[17]

However, in an essentially laissez-faire age, when philanthropy was widely believed to be the most wholesome and reliable remedy for the nation's ills,[18] philanthropic endeavour and religious zeal also often combined, in the form of voluntary agencies, to address social issues. Indeed, Chester took great pride in its charitable provisions, which included the Bluecoat Hospital, the Chester General Infirmary, and a profusion of Almshouses, and Kelly's *Directory of Cheshire* reported in 1892 that the annual value of Chester charities, for distribution in money and kind, and excluding parochial gifts, amounted to almost £1,500.[19] Education provided a significant focus for philanthropic effort, as Roger Swift's essay on the work of the Chester Ragged School Society during the mid-Victorian period illustrates. Founded in 1851, and supported by the elite of local society, the Society sought to address the problem of Chester's street-children on the grounds of compassion and social expediency in an attempt to integrate into society those who would otherwise have turned to crime. The Society established three schools in the city and Dr Swift shows how the Annual Reports and Minutes of the Society can shed light on contemporary attitudes to the education and welfare of these deprived children in the years preceding the 1870 Education Act and beyond.

Yet even in the general realm of popular education, which witnessed substantial state intervention during the late-Victorian period, Chester clung to its traditions and, as a county borough, did not build elementary or secondary schools until the early twentieth century; unlike some towns of equivalent size, it did not establish a school board in the late-nineteenth century, on the grounds that charitable and religious bodies were providing sufficient school places.[20] Indeed, as the essays by Glazier, Jeffes, Perry and Swift suggest, Chester's response to social problems was frequently characterized by localism, paternalism and voluntaryism, all of which exercised a powerful influence on social relationships and social discipline in a city whose political life was dominated for much of the Victorian period by the Grosvenor family. Chester was a two-member parliamentary constituency until 1885, when it lost one member due to boundary revisions, but between 1832 and 1874 the Grosvenors—temperamentally Whigs and generally supportive of reforming governments—nominated one of these members, and the election of 1874 was the first for over 150 years not contested directly by the family.[21] Political radicalism made little headway in the city, as the virtual absence of both Chartist activity and large-scale popular disorders in Victorian Chester indicate, yet the working-class populace did not always accept constraints on its culture with impunity and attempts to moralize to the poor were sometimes resisted, as Julian Reed-Purvis shows in his study of the so-called 'Boughton Riot' of March 1882. This disturbance arose from an attack by a large crowd of 'roughs', including some Irishmen, on a Salvation Army procession in Boughton and was perceived by some Cestrians to be symptomatic of a religious conflict between Roman Catholics and Salvationists. However, Reed-Purvis challenges this interpretation by exploring the complex roots of the riot with particular reference to correspondence in local newspapers and, in so doing, illustrates local attitudes to such issues as religious toleration, freedom of speech and law enforcement at a time when the use of riot as a vehicle for the expression of working-class grievances was in decline in British towns and cities.[22]

Thus several of the essays in this collection indicate that there was a downside, a darker and less-familiar side of Victorian Chester which offered a sharp contrast to the lighter and more familiar image which attracted large numbers of visitors to the city during the period. The Chester Races, the Regatta, and the Market—not to mention the attractions of a visit to Eaton Hall or a trip along the River Dee in a pleasure boat—drew people of all classes from far afield to Chester, whose bustling streets were depicted in contemporary photographs and in the paintings of Louise Rayner.[23] The city—visited by Princess Victoria in 1832, when she opened the Grosvenor Bridge—was also renowned for, and took great pride in, its role as a provincial cultural centre. Charles Dickens visited Chester in 1867, reading from his own work at the Music Hall,[24] and the city's wide-ranging cultural provisions included the Mechanics Institute, founded in 1835;[25] the teacher-training College in Cheyney Road, established in 1839, whose foundation stone was laid by William Ewart Gladstone in 1842;[26] and the Chester Society of Natural Science, Literature and Art, founded by Charles Kingsley, then a Canon of the Cathedral, in 1871.[27] Moreover, as in other Victorian towns, the culture of urbanism, with its emphasis on those cardinal 'Victorian values' of progress, growth and improvement, was manifest in a variety of ways in Victorian Chester, including a profusion of guidebooks, directories, engravings, histories and public buildings, all of which served to both reinforce and celebrate the city's local and provincial identity.

However, then as now, the greatest tourist attraction was 'Historic Chester' itself, the ancient city described by Hemingway[28] with its Roman remains, its Castle, Cathedral, medieval buildings, and Rows. Writing in 1856 in probably the best-known contemporary local guidebook, *The Stranger's Handbook to Chester and its Environs*, Thomas Hughes remarked that 'The eye of the stranger, be he Englishman or foreigner, European or American, will here find an ample and luxuriant field for admiration: the man of taste, who may linger within its walls, will not depart ungratified; nor will the antiquary search here in vain for some rich and profitable treasures of investigation'.[29] Henry James, the American novelist, who visited the city in May 1872, was one such 'man of taste'. James was fascinated by what he found in Chester and subsequently recorded his impressions in an essay, published in July 1872, which provides the context for the final essay, by Chris Walsh. Conducting the reader on a grand tour of the Roman walls, the Rows, and the Cathedral (where he witnessed, but was not impressed by Charles Kingsley's preaching), James remarked that 'Chester is probably the most romantic city in the world . . . an antique town, and Medieval England sits bravely under her gables'.[30] Although many of these gables were, in fact, Victorian, Dr Walsh shows how James used Chester as a vehicle for exploring late–Victorian English urban civilization as well as providing an intelligent, sensitive observer's sense of Chester's (and England's) Victorian present measured against its past.

Thus the themes of continuity and change loom large in this study of Victorian Chester, a city of contrasts where past and present were inextricably linked. Yet one is conscious of the fact that Cestrian society during the Victorian period remains in many respects opaque, and it will be the duty of future historians to continue to lift that veil of anonymity by exploring some of the themes which did not fall within the parameters of this selective collection of essays. In particular, fruitful areas for further research include the growth of municipal administration; the development of municipal politics; social structure and social relationships; the nature of, and responses to social problems such as poverty, crime, and housing; the influence of religion; patterns of employment, and of leisure and recreation; changes in popular culture; the development of specific industries, including tourism; the changing roles of women; and the rise of the middle-class. If substantial research on these, and other themes is forthcoming in the near future then the production of a comprehensive history of Victorian Chester will become a distinctly feasible proposition.

Notes

1 For further details of the development of the city centre during this period, see especially B. Harris, *Chester* (Edinburgh and London, 1979), 30–36.

2 N. Pevsner and E. Hubbard, *The Buildings of England. Cheshire* (London, 1971), 131.

3 See, for example, Charles Feinstein (ed.), *York, 1831–1981* (York, 1981); Francis Hill, *Victorian Lincoln* (Cambridge, 1974); Robert Newton, *Victorian Exeter* (Leicester, 1969).

4 These include A. Briggs, *Victorian Cities* (London, 1963); H. J. Dyos and M. Wolff (eds.), *The Victorian City: Images and Realities* (2 vols, London, 1973); R. J. Morris and R. Rodger (eds.), *The Victorian City: A Reader in British Urban History 1820–1914* (London, 1993).

5 J. Tomlinson, *Victorian and Edwardian Chester* (Chester, 1976).

6 See, for example, P. Carrington, *The English Heritage Book of Chester* (Bath, 1994); R. Morris and K. Hoverd, *The Buildings of Chester* (Stroud, 1993).

7 For further details, see Caroline M. Williams (ed.), *Guide to the Cheshire Record Office* (Chester, 1991); Annette M. Kennett (ed.), *Archives and Records of the City of Chester: A Guide to the Collections in the Chester City Record Office* (Chester, 1985).

8 A. T. Thacker (ed.), *The Victoria History of the County of Cheshire: Vol. V, The City of Chester* (Oxford, in press, 1996).

9 R. J. Morris and Richard Rodger, 'An Introduction to British Urban History, 1820–1914', in Morris and Rodger, *The Victorian City*, 1–39.

10 See, for example, Briggs, *Victorian Cities*, 11–58; D. Cannadine, 'Victorian Cities: How Different?', *Social History*, 2 (1977), 457–87; P. J. Waller, *Town, City and Nation: England, 1850–1914* (Oxford, 1983), 1–23.

11 F. M. L.Thompson, 'Town and City', in F. M. L. Thompson (ed.), *The Cambridge Social History of Britain, 1750–1950, Vol. 1, Regions and Communities* (Cambridge, 1990), 1–86.

12 For administrative developments in Cheshire, including Chester, during the period, see B. Harris, 'Administrative History' in *The Victoria History of the County of Cheshire* (Oxford, 1979), Vol. II, 1–82.

13 Derek Fraser, 'Municipal Reform in Historical Perspective', in D.Fraser (ed.), *Municipal Reform and the Industrial City* (Leicester, 1982), 2–14.

14 See, for example, Roger Swift and Sheridan Gilley (eds.), *The Irish in*

the Victorian City (London, 1985); Graham Davis, 'Little Irelands', in Roger Swift and Sheridan Gilley (eds.), *The Irish in Britain, 1815–1939* (London, 1989); Graham Davis, *The Irish in Britain, 1815–1914* (Dublin, 1991), 51–82.

15 Michael Sigsworth and Michael Worboys, 'The public's view of public health in mid-Victorian Britain', *Urban History*, 21,2 (Oct. 1994), 240.

16 Waller, *Town, City and Nation*, 302.

17 B. Harris, *Chester*, 30.

18 For the role of charity during the period, see especially F. K. Prochaska, 'Philanthropy', in Thompson, *Cambridge Social History, Vol. 3, Social Agencies and Institutions*, 357–94.

19 J. Kelly, *Directory of Cheshire* (1892), 187.

20 D. Wardle, 'Education before 1903', in B. Harris (ed.), *VCH: Cheshire* (Oxford, 1980), Vol. III, 209.

21 J. S. Morrill, 'Parliamentary Representation', *VCH: Cheshire* (Oxford, 1979), Vol. II, 98–166.

22 J. Stevenson, *Popular Disturbances in England, 1700–1870* (London, 1979), 275–300.

23 Louise Rayner was born in Derby in 1829 and lived in Chester from 1871 to 1886. A popular topographical artist who worked almost exclusively in watercolour, she exhibited at major exhibitions in London, including the Royal Academy. The Grosvenor Museum holds twenty-one Raynor water-colours—the largest number in any public collection—of Chester street-scenes and buildings. Little has been written about Raynor, although her work was applauded in Ellen C.Clayton, *English Female Artists* (1876). For further details, see *Louise Raynor 1829–1924* (Grosvenor Museum Cata-logue, Chester, 1978).

24 P. Ackroyd, *Dickens* (London, 1990), 1102.

25 For further details on the development of the Chester Mechanics Institute, see especially K. M. Peate, 'A Survey of Provisions for Adult Education in Chester and Birkenhead during the Victorian Period', (unpub-lished MA dissertation, Chester College of Higher Education, 1993).

26 For the origins and development of Chester College, see J. L. Bradbury, *Chester College and the Training of Teachers* (Chester, 1975).

27 For further details, see J. D. Siddall, *The Formation of the Chester Society of Natural Science, Literature and Art* (Chester, 1911); H. Robinson, *The Chester Society of Natural Science, Literature and Art, 1871–1971* (Chester 1971).

28 J. Hemingway, *A History of the City of Chester* (Chester, 1831).

29 T. Hughes, *The Stranger's Handbook to Chester and its Environs* (Chester, 1856), 110.

30 See also D. M. Palliser, *Chester: Contemporary Descriptions by Residents and* (Chester, 1980), 31–33.

1

Victorian Chester:
A City of Change and Ambiguity

John Herson

'The modern history of the trade of Chester is rather the history of its decay.'[1]

This jaundiced comment on Chester's fortunes was made in 1860, and it illustrates a contemporary view that the city had failed to benefit from the economic transformation of north-west England which we now call the Industrial Revolution. Its aberrant performance is perhaps the reason why Chester has rarely attracted the attention of historians of this period.[2] As the heartland of the early Industrial Revolution, the development of the industrial north-west has been studied intensively and, indeed, the region could be regarded as the proto-typical case of industrialization.[3] North-east Wales, geographically important for Chester, was also significant in early industrial history and has attracted its share of historians.[4] There were substantial changes outside the core industrial areas, for example the rise of Liverpool, the modernization of farming in Cheshire and the growth of the seaside resorts, all of them charted to some degree.[5] There is also now some interest in the decline and deindustrialization which affected regions of the British Isles by-passed by industrial and urban development.[6]

Chester in the Victorian era does not fit neatly into any of these 'typical' situations. It was an ancient and formerly important city which lay close to industrializing areas but was not clearly part of them. As such, it could throw light on how places close to the mainstream fared during that period of dynamic growth. The evi-

Table 1.1: Population and Net Migration, Chester Suburbs, 1821–1911

Year	Population	% Change	Estimated Net Migration in Previous Decade
1821	21 516	na	na
1831	23 029	+7.0	−1379
1841	25 039	+8.7	−1089
1851	29 216	+16.7	+810
1861	34 209	+17.1	+1913
1871	39 757	+16.2	+1636
1881	42 246	+6.3	−2454
1891	44 002	+4.2	−2842
1901	47 975	+9.0	−453
1911	50 220	+4.7	−2713

Note: Chester and Suburbs covers Chester City and the parishes of Great Boughton, Hoole, Upton, Newton and Bache. Saltney is not included because of boundary problems, but its presence would not decisively alter the trends shown.
Source: Census 1821–1911 and Herson, *VCH V*

dence suggests that the responses in Victorian Chester were ambiguous in a number of ways. The city's economy and population grew, but both at the beginning and at the end of Victoria's reign its growth rate was slow (Table 1.1).

Chester lost out during the canal and turnpike revolutions, and it was finished as a port, but the coming of the railways put new life into the city. That stimulus proved to be limited in the longer-term, however. Although Chester consolidated as a major market, shopping and service centre, any pivotal role it had played in national trading patterns was lost. Some new manufacturing industry arrived—it is wrong to say Chester had no industry—but the relative importance of manufacturing declined. The city avoided the worst excesses of the Industrial Revolution, but there was, nevertheless, appalling slum housing, industrial pollution, poverty and social polarization. There was also a lack of entrepreneurial dynamism. In other words, Chester occupied a position between the extremes of growth and decay in Victorian Britain, but its position on the continuum between the two varied over time.

The explanation for this can be sought both in terms of the specific responses to change exhibited by Chester's landowning and political elite, and also in Chester's relationship to the structural economic changes occurring in the Victorian era. This period was pivotal in the process of transmitting the full effects of the Industrial Revolution throughout the economy. Urban and regional specialization brought about by the Industrial Revolution was at its most extreme in the middle 40 years of the 19th century,[7] and those towns, like Chester, which failed to develop any clear industrial strength or specialism were bound to be disadvantaged. It would be misleading, however, to assume that industrialization permeated all aspects of the economy equally and simultaneously. Substantial areas of production in towns like Chester remained in the hands of local handicraft and workshop producers until they were driven out by the competitive edge of centralized production. Similar pressures also affected the distribution of goods and the provision of services. These processes occurred at different times for different products and services, and the trend to integration within the industrial economy was therefore uneven and long drawn out.

This essay charts how Chester's economy and population reacted to the changing circumstances of the Victorian era. It is suggested that the city went through three main phases in this period. In the first phase, the dawn of the Victorian age, Chester was still trapped in a stagnation which reflected fundamental and adverse shifts in the economic geography of the region which had begun in the 18th century. The arrival of the railways in 1840 ushered in a second phase during which the city's elite was forced to respond to new opportunities. Considerable prosperity ensued, but the responses were often ambiguous, conflicting or impractical. The third phase began around 1870 when, despite the continuation of a superficial gloss, the underlying weaknesses of Chester's situation were exacerbated by problems in the hinterland and a more complete integration within the national economy.[8]

At the beginning of the Victorian era Chester was a city with substantial problems. In the previous hundred years key parts of its economy had withered away[9] as the economic geography of Britain and north-west England changed. These developments had, firstly, undermined the city's manufacturing base. By the 1830s traditional manufacturing trades, such as the making of gloves, clay tobacco pipes and clocks, were more or less extinct.[10] Shipbuilding was also in terminal decline,[11] and ropemaking only survived in a small way. The water-powered Dee Mills, a feature of the Chester scene since the 12th century, were also in decline. It had been observed in 1814 that 'in this city, although we mark the infancy of several manufactures, few arrive at maturity',[12] and this continued to be true in the 1830s. A pottery had been established in the mid-18th century, but it was isolated from the dynamic trade of the Potteries and failed to make the necessary transition to high quality products. It only survived 20 years.[13] There were two cotton mills in the early 19th century, but both had closed by the 1820s.[14] The reasons for closure are unknown but the very fact is significant. The leading industry of the Industrial Revolution could not establish itself in Chester. At the very least this suggests that the lack of cheap coal, abundant water power or any real tradition of textile production were disadvantages, but it is also possible that a social environment hostile to entrepreneurship was equally to blame. There was some iron-founding, but it was mostly small-scale and served the needs of the surrounding countryside.[15] Only the emergence of steam corn milling and the leadworks, founded in 1800, offset the ingrained decline of Chester's manufacturing in the early 19th century.[16]

The second problem lay in Chester's communications. The leadworks and corn mills proved to be the last industries attracted to Chester by its waterways. By 1830 the port had long been eclipsed by Liverpool, and dwindling numbers of boats now struggled up the shallow, neglected channel of the River Dee to the city's wharves.[17] The canal, opened to Nantwich in 1779, had been intended to open up links to the hinterland, but the plan was a miserable failure. The link opened in 1805 between Chester and the Mersey at Ellesmere Port revived the canal, but ironically proved the port's *coup de grace* by diverting yet more of Chester's trade through the Mersey.[18] Nor were things much better on the roads. Although turnpiking had improved Chester's links with its immediate hinterland, the city's national importance in the road network dwindled, and its 'golden age of coaching' was over by 1832 because of the rise of Liverpool and the diversion of the Irish traffic through Shrewsbury and Telford's Holyhead Road.[19] The last through Royal Mail service to London from Chester was abandoned in 1829.[20]

The decline in Chester's role as a national transport centre reflected a third problem, the city's dwindling significance in national trade, above all that in linen. In the 18th century the city's fairs had been dominated by Irish linen, a trade which peaked in the 1760s. By 1830 it was dead.[21] Its demise was due to an inter-connected set of factors. There was competition from Liverpool, the penetration of the Irish manufacturing areas by English merchants, and an increase in orders placed directly with Irish manufacturers.[22] It also reflected, however, the decline of the rural Irish linen industry orientated to the Dublin–Chester route, and its shift north to mills around Belfast. This move resulted, in turn, from the competition of machine-spun English and Scottish yarns and substitution by cheap cotton goods.[23] In other words, a traditional Chester trade was destroyed as an indirect result of industrialization elsewhere in Britain.

The decline of the port, traditional manufactures and Chester's national trading function had left a large hole in the city's economy by the 1830s, and the economic difficulties were reflected in physical and social problems. Areas away from the commercial heart of Eastgate and Bridge Streets were increasingly decrepit. The Stanley Palace in Watergate Street was 'a decayed mansion' in 1831, despite having been 'a place of general resort for the carriages of gentlemen' during the races in the mid-18th century.[24] Gamul House and its outbuildings in Lower Bridge Street were 'divided into several dwellings of inferior grade'.[25] Worse, the demand for housing from a rising population meant piecemeal infilling on cramped sites behind the city centre streets. By the 1830s Chester had a problem of appalling slum courts which, in relative terms, was as bad as that in the region's industrial towns.[26] The courts functioned as a pool of cheap housing for the poor, many of them in-migrants forced out of the countryside by enclosure, unemployment and poverty. This exacerbated Chester's polarized social character. The city's gentry and bourgeoisie were clearly prosperous, and Chester's contemporary historian,

Joseph Hemingway, thought there were few places where the gentry formed such a high proportion of the community. He was glad that the lack of factories meant the absence of 'the crowds of the lowest rabble they engender'.[27] His social analysis was faulty, however. The poor state of industry meant a large and impoverished working class overdependent on jobs in dying manufactures and in the unskilled service sector.[28]

Chester's difficulties in the 1830s were offset by some positive developments. The corn mills, leadworks and foundries provided at least a foothold in growth industries. More importantly, the city was strengthening its role as a regional service centre. The old fairs still retained some importance, but they were being upstaged by retailing from permanent shops. Hemingway observed in 1831 that:

> at present the shops . . . are equal in elegance to those of Manchester or Liverpool; and there is at least one in Eastgate Row, that of Messrs. William and Henry Brown, silk mercers and milliners, lately built, which would not suffer by a comparison with the magnificence of Regent-street.[29]

The number of shops and other businesses in Chester nearly doubled between 1781 and 1834,[30] but this trend was not, of itself, an indicator of general economic success; it was to be found in old market towns elsewhere as the pattern of goods distribution moved from periodic fairs and markets towards permanent shops.[31] The increasing importance of shops was, nevertheless, paralleled by the development of other services such as hotel and inn keeping, banking, printing and publishing.[32] The city also continued to derive trade from its role as county town, garrison town and bishopric.

Despite these developments, Chester in the 1830s had major problems which reflected its decline from earlier splendour. G.L. Fenwick, looking back to this period from the late Victorian era, concluded that:

> for a long time [Chester] lay almost motionless upon the great tidal wave of progress which was sweeping past, but at length a movement became apparent, and even ancient Chester . . .

could no longer withstand the onward rush of events. The turning point dates from the accession of Queen Victoria.[33]

Fenwick was correct with his timing, but he implied a greater shift than actually occurred. In 1837 the city's elite groups were faced with strategic questions on what sort of city they wanted, on whether they wished to act to achieve it, and on what types of action they needed to take. These questions were to be answered, but in negative as well as positive ways, in the first three decades of the Victorian era.

In 1847, during a bitter debate in the Town Council on the city's future, it was suggested that 'Chester must henceforth depend on the introduction of manufactories and not on her attractions as a place of genteel residence'.[34] This proposition illustrates how some members of Chester's elite were prepared, verbally at least, to grasp the nettle of the city's problems and propose solutions. Chester did indeed enjoy its most successful period in the 19th century during the first thirty years of Victoria's reign, but its economic success was not outstanding and a clear resolution of the city's difficulties was not achieved. A number of factors conspired to produce this mixed picture.

The railways were the first factor in the equation. Great things were anticipated of the railways, and the Town Council embraced their arrival with enthusiasm. It was hoped Chester's greatness might be recreated, and Alderman Brown asserted in 1837 that 'if they make Chester a great thoroughfare, they must make it the centre of business. . . . [These developments] are all calculated to bring Chester once again into the grand line of communication'.[35] The railway age began in 1840 with the opening of the lines to Birkenhead and Crewe. In the next 30 years Chester became a focus of the regional rail network, with main lines radiating from the city in six directions.[36] Despite a carping note from one councillor in 1845 that 'railways have done Chester little good so far',[37] their impact was undoubtedly substantial, most directly on employment and on the physical geography of the city. By 1861 at least 500 men worked on the railways, over 5 per cent of the male labour force, and the two main companies were the biggest employers in the city.[38] Most of these workers were incomers and were a large element in the wave of migrants attracted to Chester in the mid 19th century.[39] They added new spending power to the Chester economy, even though many were unskilled and relatively poorly paid. The railways also drastically altered Chester's physical appearance, something the city fathers seemed to accept with equanimity, despite concerns voiced on other occasions about the city's visual heritage. The tracks formed a major barrier to movement north east of the city centre, and the line to Wales then sliced through the north-west corner of the City Walls before striding across the edge of the Roodee and the river on an obtrusive viaduct.

The railways were widely expected to revive Chester's fortunes as a port, and this is the second factor to be considered in Chester's early Victorian history. Dominant interests in the city were obsessed with the problems of the port and the River Dee. It was hoped that the railways would connect Chester effectively to its hinterland, something the canal had signally failed to do, and that 'ultimately, no doubt, the improvement of the Dee will follow so that . . . as a shipping port Chester may again become celebrated.'[40] The problem was, however, to get the Dee improved. Large vessels were unable to reach Chester at all due to the inadequate depth and dangerous state of the river, and plans ranging from dredging to the construction of ship canals were put forward between the 1820s and the 1860s to rectify the situation.[41] They all foundered on the refusal of the River Dee Company, proprietors of the navigation, to do anything except add to their lucrative estate of reclaimed land in the estuary.[42] The River Dee Co. was criticized frequently and bitterly in the press, the Town Council and at public inquiries. In 1839, for example, the *Chester Chronicle*' accused it of being an enterprise 'with whom territory is the sole object and who care no more for the trade of Chester than for the trade of the moon'.[43]

This furore can be seen, however, as symptomatic of a refusal in Chester to address contemporary problems realistically, and to seek refuge instead in trying to turn the clock back. It was, moreover, only too tempting for town councillors and others to give an impression of action by lambasting the River Dee Co., thereby sloughing off responsibility for doing something about Chester's problems on to others. It is clear that the River Dee Co. did neglect its statutory duties in favour of land reclamation, and this weakened the development of the outports—Saltney, Connah's Quay and Mostyn—further down the estuary. One can only conclude, however, that its neglect of Chester itself was based on a realistic, if cynical, view that the port was beyond revival. The fundamental nature of the Dee estuary was unfavourable, and, without massive investment to produce approaches and a dock system comparable to the Mersey, there was nothing Chester could offer shippers to entice them away from the upstart rival. The Chester and Crewe Railway, whose chairman, John Uniacke, was mayor of Chester in 1839/40, proposed initially to build a dock at Chester. It abandoned the plan in 1839 following complaints in the city that this would throw an undue preponderance of the trade of the port into the hands of one company.[44] It might be expected that city interests would have been glad *any* company was willing to build a rail-connected dock at Chester but, again, it seems that an obsession with glories past clouded a realistic appraisal of the opportunities of the present. The Town Council did agree to ask the railway company to reconsider the decision,[45] but, even then, objections were raised to the proposed site of the dock. The railway forthwith passed the poisoned chalice to a prospective River Dee Navigation Co., also chaired by Uniacke, but, despite much optimistic talk, the proposals again came to nothing.[46] Chester never got its dock, and despite a critical report by the Tidal Harbours Commission in 1846,[47] a public inquiry into improvement of the river in 1849,[48] legislation to enforce a minimum depth in 1851,[49] and further abortive schemes in the 1860s,[50] the port continued to slip into oblivion. The hated River Dee Co. was finally expropriated by the River Dee Conservancy Act of 1889, but by then it was too late for Chester.[51]

Not all interests in Chester were fixated on the port, however. Some argued that the city's salvation would be through new manufacturing industry. The acid test of this proposition, and the city's response to it, came in June 1847 when an approach was made to the Council to build a locomotive works on corporation land immediately west of the Walls and adjacent to the newly-opened railway to Wales. The immediate response from some councillors was enthusiastic. The Town Clerk noted that the site was opposite the infirmary and that the noise would be inconvenient, but Councillor French's terse riposte was 'never mind the infirmary. We want hammering and banging in Chester and I for one would be very glad to hear it',[52] whilst Councillor Turner argued that 'Chester ought to look to manufactories, for as a place of genteel residence its day was long gone by. Gentlemen of £4–5,000 a year would not come down to the country to live as they used to and they must depend on the extension of trade as the support of the city'.[53]

The application was referred to the Corporate Estates Committee, which agreed to lease the land to John Gray and partners, the proposers of the works. It was then, however, that opposition emerged. By the time the matter was referred back to the full Council, petitions for and against the scheme had been received, the opponents being the Infirmary authorities and the residents of exclusive Stanley Place close by. A bitter row then ensued. Those councillors backing the venture argued that creating new jobs would produce 'clean, orderly workpeople', reducing the poverty, misery, crime and other privations which the current lack of employment produced. Councillors should not, they said, repeat the mistakes of their predecessors by obstructing new industry in the hope that gentlemen would come to live in the city. Besides, new industry would help reduce the rates. The site proposed was excellent, close to the river, the canal and railway and the area was already less salubrious because of the gasworks. Gray's locomotive works would, they argued, be the nucleus of similar developments, and they clearly saw it as Chester's opportunity, perhaps never to be repeated, to make a new start in the industrial age.[54]

It was this the opponents feared. Their arguments depended heavily on the environmental damage the proposal would do. Although some claimed to agree that new industry was desirable, the proposed site was wrong. It was, in any case, worth more than the offer price. It would bring intolerable nuisance to the infirmary, local residents and even to the prisoners in the City Gaol. The beautiful promenade of the Walls would be destroyed and the city's antiquities undermined. But the objections ran deeper. Chester's hopes of being the abode of gentlemen would be extinguished and a thousand such people already living in the city, and paying rates, would be driven out to be replaced by a thousand impecunious workmen. If the locomotive works' trade stagnated, the city would be burdened with its unemployed workers. Chester, they argued, should not have manufactories 'at any price', and if this one came everyone, except 'those deriving a pecuniary advantage', would regret it.[55]

The polarization was clear, and the debate remarkably similar to conflicts over economic development and the environment in the late 20th century. A struggle was on for the soul of Chester, and superficially it was the 'modernizers' who carried the day. A majority on the Council backed the scheme at the end of the debate. Referral back to the Corporate Estates Committee delayed the matter, just as it was probably intended to do, and in September 1847 Gray and his partners wrote demanding an immediate decision. This raises the suspicion that the proposal was never really serious, although Gray did already operate the Roodee Iron Foundry and had a clear stake in the city. The 'offensive and indecent' ultimatum was, in any case, rejected and the scheme abruptly died.[56] It was later reported that the investment had gone to Bradford instead.[57]

It *was* a poor site. Chester's subsequent inhabitants were probably fortunate that an area of heavy industry did not develop so close to the historic core. The feeling lingers, however, that key elements in Chester's elite looked back fondly to the city's golden age and reacted with hostility to contemporary developments. This is revealed too in the Town Council's harassment of existing manufacturers against whom complaints of nuisance were laid. Foundries, breweries, chemical works, a tannery and the gasworks were all pursued in the 1840s and 1850s.[58] The Roodee was a particularly sensitive location. A low-lying area of around 90 acres immediately to the south west of the city centre, and partly encircled by a meander of the Dee, the Roodee formed a key element in the visual setting of the city. Horse racing began there around 1539. The corporation owned the land, controlled the racing and owned the Roodee Race Course Co.[59] This meant that racing interests had substantial power in the council and ensured that most of the Roodee was saved permanently from development. Even here, however, the policies were contradictory. By the early 19th century the scene had been spoilt by allowing an iron foundry, a shipyard and the workhouse to develop along the Roodee's north-west river frontage, whilst the railway viaduct followed in the 1840s. Nevertheless, in the 1840s the foundry, then occupied by John Gray, was frequently harried by the Town Council over allegations of smoke nuisance, and the suspicion is that some councillors wanted rid of it altogether.[60] A ropewalk renting part of the Roodee was summarily given notice to quit in 1859 because it was encroaching on the racecourse and allegedly damaging the drains.[61]

It would be easy, therefore, to castigate the Council for hostility to industry, and accuse its members of reflecting a backward-looking mentality on the part of Chester's elite. Other evidence suggests the picture is not so clear cut and that the city's fortunes were only influenced by the Council to a limited extent. The fact is that significant manufacturing activity *did* develop in Chester in the mid 19th century which helped diversify the city's base, although it is also clear that some of this growth was transitory and could not be sustained in the face of growing integration within the wider economy.

Chester at this time provides clear evidence that the Industrial Revolution did not mean the rapid demise of local, small-scale, craft and workshop production, even in a region which was in the forefront of industrialization. For a time, indeed, it increased.[62] The traditional handicraft activities which grew in Chester during the mid 19th century reflected a rising population and increased demand which was not, as yet, satisfied fully by factory products made in the industrial centres. The most important trades were tailoring and shoemaking. Both occupied a blurred area between retailing and manufacturing, since many tailors and shoemakers retailed their goods directly to the general public as well as making them. Many, on the other hand, were probably outworkers working either for middlemen wholesalers or directly for retailers.[63]

Although handicraft employment grew, other traditional industries continued to decline, a symptom of structural change brought about by increasing centralization and mechanization of production nationally. The number of tanneries dropped from seven to two, whilst Chester's breweries reached their peak and then began to dwindle.[64] The mid 19th century also saw the final demise of shipbuilding when the shipyard closed in the slump which followed the national banking crisis of 1866.[65]

The decline of some industries was, nevertheless, counterbalanced by growth elsewhere. Chester benefited in the prosperous 'high farming' era of the mid 19th century from an intermediate stage in the history of milling. This was when medium-sized steam mills in market towns were superseding wind or watermills in the countryside, but the age of massive mills at the seaports had not yet dawned.[66] Steam mills were built along the canal, notably the Milton Street (Cestrian) Mill in the 1850s and the Albion Mill in 1868/9.[67] The old water-powered Dee Mills were increasingly undermined by these developments but they nevertheless lingered on for a few more decades.[68]

The leadworks of Walkers, Parker and Co. continued to grow and prosper. Chester's gain was North Wales' loss, since the Chester works was increasingly favoured for lead production over older works at Bagillt, probably because the growing amount of pig lead imported from overseas could be sent more conveniently to Chester by rail or boat from the Liverpool and Birkenhead docks.[69]

The arrival of the railways may have helped the development of new activities in Chester, as they did elsewhere, by reducing the cost of imported raw materials and making access to external markets cheaper and/or faster. A classic example of the latter trend in this period was the expansion of Chester as a centre for market gardens, plant nurseries and seed merchants. The city's site at the geographical centre of the British Isles, together with its good rail connections and mild climate, made it an ideal location to serve the national market. Despite the saga of Gray's locomotive works, the mid 19th century saw an expansion of engineering in Chester which could also be evidence of these processes. In 1850 there were only three engineering enterprises within the city,[70] but by 1870 there were eleven. They were located in two main areas. The first lay on the edge of the old city centre between the canal and the railway around Brook Street, Egerton Street and George Street, but none of the general engineering firms here was actually on the canal side itself or had a railway siding. Most occupied restricted sites hemmed in by housing; in essence they were small firms with little ultimate growth potential. Two wagon repair shops in the same area were, of necessity, linked to the railway, and reflected Chester's nodal position in the railway network.[71]

Chester's other industrial zone grew on a greenfield site at Saltney on the edge of the city and straddled both sides of the border with Wales. Its development began at almost the same time as the controversy over Gray's locomotive works, but in Saltney the Town Council took a more positive stance towards industrialization. The area became rapidly the city's most vibrant district, making a major contribution to diversifying the economy. The trigger to Saltney's growth was its emergence as a transport node in 1846. The Shrewsbury and Chester Railway built a wharf on corporation land beside the Dee, a site which was also adjacent to the junction with the Chester and Holyhead line.[72] Although Saltney Wharf was always too far up the Dee to be the port of Chester's salvation, the location was an immediate magnet for Henry Wood and Co., a firm of chainmakers from Stourbridge, who opened an anchor, chain and general engineering works in 1847. It was an altogether more 'modern' industrial development than the back-street concerns in central Chester. A number of other firms followed Woods to Saltney. Lloyd's Cambrian Chain and Anchor Testing Co., a firm symbiotically related to Woods, was set up next door in 1866,[73] and three oil refineries were in operation by 1870. They used crude oil extracted from the distinctive Flintshire 'cannel coal', and were part of an industry which boomed in the district from 1858 to the 1880s.[74] A chemical works was operating in the area as early as 1843, and in 1856 another firm, Proctor and Ryland, moved to Saltney from Birmingham and opened a bone manure works on the riverside.[75] All of these industries developed on private land on the Welsh side of the border, but the Town Council owned a finger of land extending southwards from the Dee along the English side of the boundary.[76] The Council was clearly keen to exploit the development value of this land, and part was occupied after 1847 by the locomotive and carriage works of the Shrewsbury and Chester Railway.[77] The council then sold building leases for other sites on which a rash of Victorian terraces was built to accommodate workers attracted to Saltney. Here at least, Chester spawned as a 'child of the old city'[78] an industrial area indistinguishable from that in many other British towns and cities.

Saltney's advantage to Chester's elite was clearly its location. Here the industry people desired could develop well away from the old city in a low-lying, flat and dull landscape unattractive for high class residential development. The city's ratepayers could, furthermore, benefit directly through the accretion of value to the corporate estate at Saltney. By 1869 it was bringing in over £2500 a year in ground rents.[79] Chester did, therefore, embrace the industrial age to some extent in the mid 19th century even though the signals emanating from the Town Council were mixed, and its handling of development issues dilatory and full of wrangling.

The Council was, however, only one of the bodies able to influence development and, in areas outside its own corporate estate, its influence was much less than that of other landowners. It is necessary, therefore, to consider whether the policies of other landowners were a factor in Chester's development, or the lack of it, at this pivotal point in its history.

The built up area of Chester in the 1840s was surrounded by a number of large estates, and on none of them did any industrial development take place in the mid 19th century. Throughout the century the Grosvenors assiduously acquired large land holdings south of Chester from Handbridge to the family seat at Eaton, the aim being mainly to control and landscape the area in the vicinity of the hall and its various 'approaches'.[80] Although Grosvenor land at Saltney was developed for industry, none was allowed in this area to the south of Chester. Nearby the large estate of Lord Howe, across the river from the Roodee, was developed, albeit lethargically, into the exclusive housing suburb of Curzon Park.[81] To the north of the city much of the land was owned by the Cathedral Dean and Chapter, later the Ecclesiastical Commissioners, who from 1845 began to sell it for housing development with covenants designed to ensure high quality building. In Hoole and Newton the large estates of the Earl of Shrewsbury, Rev. Peploe William Hamilton and the Earl of Kilmorey began to be built up with solid suburban housing later in the century and after, again with restrictive covenants.[82] Even near the railway station, in Flookersbrook, land in other private hands was sold with covenants designed to prohibit industrial development.[83] The evidence suggests, then, that the big estate owners were anxious to prevent anything but good quality house building on their land, and even then they were prepared to bide their time. Only to the east of the city, in Great Boughton, was the land more fragmented amongst smaller owners. They were perhaps keener to reap quick profit from any suitable development,[84] and it is significant that a belt of mixed uses, including industry, the waterworks and meaner terraced housing, developed in parts of this area in the 19th century.

The landowners and, perhaps more actively, the substantial numbers of Chester's solicitors, land agents, surveyors, managers and others who derived income from them, formed a group of people who may have adopted a conservative stance towards alien development. They and the landowners also possessed what Garrard describes as 'a reputation for power' which probably ensured that some issues could be kept off the agenda altogether in a 'non-decisional' form of politics.[85] The Grosvenors were the only big landowning family with a local main residence, but their influence as landowners and politicians was pervasive,[86] and it is likely they opposed drastic industrial development in the city.[87] Chester's freeman borough franchise in fact opened up council membership to the commercial and industrial middle classes,[88] to many shopkeepers and also to the occasional better-off craftsman.[89] This meant a diverse council in which the landowner interest was not necessarily dominant in numerical terms, but it was also an often divided council in which landowner power may been exercized through influence, patronage and divide and rule tactics.[90] Many councillors derived substantial business from the rich and influential of the district and were likely to adopt suitably deferential policies. Families such as the Browns, Potts and Gamons (solicitors), the Wardells (bankers) and Jones (land agents) played central roles in civic and commercial life, and members of all the first four were to be found on the Town Council in 1847 voting against the Gray locomotive works.[91] Even in this group the motives were probably mixed, however. Charles Potts, for example, may have opposed the site of the locomotive works as much for pecuniary as for environmental reasons. Seeing the development potential of Saltney, he and his relatives were acquiring land there in the late-1840s, and in the following years they were quite happy to resell sites for industrial development, presumably at a good profit.[92]

Although there was an active debate about Chester's future and the need for industry in the 1840s, the issue died away in the 1850s. This is almost certainly because, by then, the railways had helped to reinvigorate the city's role as a service centre, promoting a prosperity which, temporarily at least, removed the incentive for a more drastic adaptation of the economy. The railways undoubtedly brought new trade to the city. The adjacent areas of Flintshire were traditionally Chester's strongest market, but the proportion of Chester's trade from wider areas of north and mid Wales seems to have grown markedly with the opening of the lines to Wrexham, Shrewsbury and the North Wales coast.[93] Farming in central and west Cheshire was prosperous in the mid 19th century, and trade from this area also seems to have grown in both absolute and relative terms.[94] Chester annexed the trade of other local markets and strengthened its position as the main centre in West Cheshire, a trend exhibited by larger market towns elsewhere after the advent of the railways.[95] The railway into the Wirral peninsula seems to have increased that area's significance in Chester's trade too, but the city's influence does not seem to have stretched farther than a line running from Parkgate to Eastham. Beyond that the pull of Liverpool and the growing commercial weight of Birkenhead were too strong. The railways brought more tourists and long-distance customers to Chester, but they still contributed a relatively small proportion of the trade.[96]

Although Chester's rural hinterland became generally more prosperous, wealth was not evenly distributed. Farm labourers lost work as agriculture became more capital intensive, and the relative importance of liquid milk increased at the expense of crops demanding more intensive, if seasonal, labour. Many farm workers, their families or their children were forced off the land and moved into Chester to find work, much of it in domestic service, transport and unskilled, casual, trades.[97] Many Irish also came to the city.[98] Skilled workers came from all over the region and beyond, and, for some employers, such recruits may have been a necessity given the city's own limited skill base.[99]

Thus the mid-century boom meant an infusion of newcomers into Chester society. It meant, too, another wave of in-migrants crowding into the reeking courts, and the court population probably reached its maximum in the 1860s, at about 5500 people or 17 per cent of the city's inhabitants.[100] The boom also produced a demand for new housing. In the 1850s Chester's housing stock increased by nearly one fifth, the sharpest rise of the century, and building continued at a relatively high level in the 1860s.[101]

Chester's boom in the mid-century put new life into its shops and other services. Between 1840 and 1878 the number of businesses in Chester rose by 46 per cent. Food and clothing shops fell in relative importance, whilst those associated with a growth and broadening of consumer spending power expanded. The city centre became increasingly populated with furniture shops, jewellers, china shops and hardware dealers, and the city could now support the specialized services of seven photographers, a bird dealer, an art dealer and a taxidermist. The number of accountants, solicitors, auctioneers and property agents nearly trebled, whilst there was a dramatic rise in the number of insurance agents in the city, an example of how national firms could now tap local business using the services of the GPO and the railways.[102] Individual businesses also found new prosperity. Browns, for example, built the gothic extension in 1858 which still dominates Eastgate Street today. In the 1860s the firm diversified into furniture and furnishing fabrics and they opened a furniture factory in Newgate Street. This was a good example of how, in this period, goods produced locally were not inevitably supplanted by bought-in factory products from specialized manufacturers.[103] The visible sign of Chester's revival was the new fashion to rebuild city centre premises in mock Tudor half-timbered style, a movement whose first phase ran from 1850 to 1865. The character of central Chester today owes much to this phase of mid 19th century prosperity.[104]

The railways brought tourists and racegoers in substantial numbers, and their ability to transport large numbers of city dwellers to the races was scarcely welcomed by everybody in Chester. J. S. Howson, Dean of Chester, attacked the meeting in 1870 because 'each season seems to indicate an increasing tendency to fraud, obscenity, profanity and debauchery'. There was a faction within the city which wanted to stop the races altogether, but horse racing's role in the traditional social round of the area's elite ensured its survival.[105]

In summary, then, Chester found new prosperity in the mid 19th century through the railways, the expanding service economy and some growth in manufacturing. The manufactures exploited both local and wider markets, and their growth helped cushion the continuing impact of structural decline in Chester's traditional activities during this period. The city may have benefited, therefore, from an intermediate phase of integration within the industrial economy in which better linkages stimulated viable local economic activities. Saltney's locational attractions were, furthermore, sufficiently good to promote real industrial development. There is evidence, however, that the threat of substantial growth in industry was unwelcome to some interests in the city, and this attitude may have exercized a repellent effect.[106] It is, of course, the case that Chester was disadvantaged by not being on a coalfield, and many other towns in north-east Wales and north-west England had strong locational attractions. Despite this, there were no *inherent* geographical reasons why the growth of manufacturing was stunted in Chester, and the likelihood remains that the social environment was the repressive factor. The limitations of this situation were to be revealed after 1871.

Chester's new dynamism was not sustained fully into the last quarter of the 19th century. This suggests that the factors which helped its transition in the previous period were outweighed by stronger forces after 1870. The picture is, however, mixed, and the evidence somewhat contradictory. The importance of manufacturing diminished because growth industries did not offset a steep decline in craft production. The fairs effectively disappeared, and the markets dwindled in regional significance. Shopping, on the other hand, continued to grow and many businesses, though not all, did well. There was, however, very little physical expansion of the shopping area. Chester's significance for transport, administration, health and other services was enhanced. The overall trend was even more towards a modernized service-based economy integrated closely with national structures of production and distribution, but the strengths and weaknesses of this trend became more apparent.

Population evidence is most suggestive of the adverse trend. The growth rate of Chester's population fell away sharply after 1871, and out-migration occurred in the late 19th century which exceeded the inflow which had occurred during the mid-century boom (Table 1.1). Although the final decade of the Victorian era saw some slowing of the exodus, thing were to worsen again in Edwardian times. Some of these out-migrants were undoubtedly leaving Britain altogether, joining the national tide of emigration in the late 19th century, but, whatever the reasons, Chester had ceased to be an attractive place to live for many of its inhabitants.[107] A decline in the rate of new house building after 1871 reflected these problems, and it remained low until the 1890s.[108]

By 1900 the division between manufacturing and retailing was more ingrained in the economy, and a much higher proportion of goods was produced in large factories and workshops, distributed by the railways, and sold in specialist retailers.[109] This undermined Chester's handicraft producers and the number of manufacturing workers in Chester actually *decreased* between 1871 and 1911. It was women who suffered particularly, with many jobs in the clothing trade disappearing, whilst few new opportunities emerged in other manufacturing industries.[110] Men's work also changed as the handicrafts were killed off. The most dramatic decline was in shoe-making. As the shoe-trade became more concentrated in specialist towns like Stafford, Northampton and Leicester, and as mechanized factory production progressively eliminated hand-work,[111] so shoe-making as a domestic outwork activity was destroyed in towns like Chester. Attempts were made to move to factory production, but the two main shoe factories had both closed by the 1900s.[112]

Milling, on the other hand, reached its zenith in the late 19th century.[113] The seeds of catastrophic decline were already present, however, and by 1914 milling in Chester was almost dead, though its final demise took place after the Great War. Two structural changes eroded the industry's base: increasing imports of hard foreign wheat from around 1860 and the development of roller milling from the 1870s.[114] Chester's mills were ill-fitted for these challenges. They were in the wrong place and not big enough. The largest concern, Frosts, ultimately moved in 1910 to extensive new mills on the Manchester Ship Canal at Ellesmere Port. The Dee Mills were completely outmoded by the 1890s, closing finally in 1908, and the other mills were also at the point of terminal decline.[115]

During the mid-century the city had become a centre for market gardening, plant nurseries and seed merchants, and this industry did continue to grow in the late-Victorian period. There were a number of market gardening firms, but Dicksons were pre-eminent by the 1880s, with nurseries covering over 400 acres at Upton and Newton. In 1883 James Hunter established a farm seed business in Chester, again attracted by its central location, and by 1900 it was becoming one of the leading farm seed suppliers in the country.[116] Brewing, on the other hand, almost disappeared from the city in the late 19th century. The decline was due to the elimination of home-brew public houses and a process of takeover and concentrated ownership amongst the commercial brewery companies. All the pub breweries had ceased operation by 1892, and two of the three commercial breweries closed in 1889 and 1902 respectively. Only the Chester Northgate Brewery survived. It was ultimately taken over, in 1949, by Greenall Whitley, and was closed in 1969.[117]

The history of brewing in Chester between 1871 and 1914 illustrates the transition from small-scale production to industrialized methods and concentrated ownership which was happening more widely in the economy. It was a change which weakened the city's manufacturing base, and only a few industrial concerns contradicted the trend. The main exception was the leadworks, which reached its peak of importance in the late 19th century, partly through the introduction of new processes and partly through processes relocated in Chester from North Wales.[118]

Chester's engineering industry was very volatile during this period. During the national economic boom of the early 1870s the number of engineering firms in Chester increased from 11 in 1870 to 16 in 1876, but thereafter the industry contracted until the 1890s.[119] The real success story was the Hydraulic Engineering Co. at the old Flookersbrook Foundry. The firm moved into manufacturing hydraulic machinery for dock installations, railway yards and similar purposes, and it opened offices in London, Paris and Brussels, developing a substantial export trade. By the 1890s around 400 workers were employed. Hydraulic Engineering illustrates how, given entrepreneurial dynamism, there was no inherent reason why manufacturing businesses could not prosper in Chester. Nevertheless, the works remained on a cramped inner city site, and the failure to move to a better location suggests a certain lack of enterprise during the firm's most successful period.[120]

Hughes and Lancaster illustrates an engineering firm which found Chester an unsuitable place for expansion and did something about it. Founded in 1865, it established a works in City Road near the railway station to exploit the growing market for water and sewerage machinery, but the premises were too small and impossible to expand. In 1892 it moved to Acrefair near Ruabon.[121] Its disappearance was ultimately counterbalanced in 1900 by the founding of Brookhirst, a firm which exploited the new market for electrical switchgear. It was located in Chester purely because one of the owners thought the city a more 'reasonable place to live' than his native Manchester, and would provide 'gentle and pleasing conditions' for his workers.[122]

Saltney, by contrast, was far from 'gentle and pleasing' in late Victorian times. In 1884 the local newspaper reported that:

> Saltney presents the appearance of a miniature 'Black Country'; unusually high chimneys soar into the sky and the atmosphere is impregnated with thick heavy smoke. Large works abound on all sides [and] the place is alive with all the signs of industrial activity.[123]

The fact was, however, that Saltney had little extra potential for development. Some of the existing plants continued to grow, notably Wood's chain and anchor works and Proctor and Ryland's bone manure plant. This was taken over around 1894 by Edward Webb and Sons, the Stourbridge seed merchants.[124] The railways were also taking on more workers, notably with the opening of Mold Junction engine sheds in 1890; they had 200 workers by 1899.[125] Saltney wharf, on the other hand, was almost moribund, whilst the oil industry was dying, only the Dee Oil Co's refinery surviving beyond 1890 by using imported oil rather than the oil from local cannel coal.[126]

It seems clear that, in the thirty years before 1900, the limited expansion of modern manufacturing industry in Chester depended on the exploitation by local firms of markets in the national and international economy. We have seen how the city had two engineering companies, Hydraulic Engineering and Henry Wood's, which were leaders in their fields and these, together with the leadworks, gave the city a more significant national presence in manufacturing than is commonly thought. Growth in such firms barely offset, however, the decline of other manufactures and the local craft sector resulting from better communications and factory production elsewhere. The opening of John Summers' Shotton steelworks on Deeside in 1896 proved to be the most important industrial development in the sub-region in the late 19th century.[127] That event, together with the rapid growth of industry in Ellesmere Port, confirmed that other localities in the area were more attractive than Chester to major industrial investors.

The faltering of industrial development in late 19th century Chester weakened its trend to diversification and increased its reliance on shops and services. Evidence on shopping is elusive and somewhat contradictory, but it suggests that, although the pattern of shops changed and their quality improved, absolute growth in the sector was relatively modest. Overall, the number of Cestrians working in services increased at a lower rate than in the country as a whole, and competitors were emerging, notably Wrexham, Birkenhead, and, to a much lesser extent, Ellesmere Port, Northwich and Crewe. These towns may have diverted some trade from Chester.[128]

The general rise in the standard of living in the late 19th century was probably the main factor behind the growth of Chester's shops and services. Despite wide disparities in wealth and income, there was more money around in the economy overall which could be spent on goods and services, something reflected both in a greater diversity of shops and services and the clear prosperity of many city centre businesses.[129] This trend was weakened, however, by recessions in the national economy which were reflected locally, for example, in the engineering industry, farming and banking.[130] Chester's hinterland also had problems in the late 19th century which may have limited the growth of the city's service sector. Most of industrial Flintshire was in decline,[131] whilst Chester's importance for the Denbighshire coalfield seems to have lessened after 1871.[132] Wrexham was becoming a substantial service centre in its own right, with markets and a wide range of shops, and the town even began to poach trade from industrial Flintshire.[133] The growth of the North Wales coastal resorts did help Chester, but the city's drawing power in the Wirral and Ellesmere Port area tended to decline. Birkenhead emerged as a clear rival, Liverpool's hold on the area was strengthened by the opening of the Mersey railway tunnel in 1886, and even Ellesmere Port had developed a distinct shopping centre by 1890.[134]

The areas to the east and south east of Chester also saw some decline in fortunes as the traditional cheese trade went into a depression caused partly by foreign imports.[135] There were also limits to the amount of trade such a rural district could offer. Access to the market of the mid-Cheshire saltfield was improved in 1874 with the opening of the railway from Northwich to Chester Northgate, but this unfortunately coincided with the start of a long depression in the salt industry. Thus although the general rise in the standard of living in the late 19th century helped Chester's trade, unfavourable trends in its hinterland may have limited its growth in comparison with other, more prosperous, areas.

It is important to remember that Chester's shops and services depended to a large extent on demand from the city itself. Demand from outside enabled it to support a larger range of shops and services than its own population would have justified, but about 60–65 per cent of Chester's trade probably came from residents of the city and its suburbs.[136] The social character of the city was therefore economically significant. Its limited manufacturing base must have been a weakness here—it was deficient in both an industrial middle class and a skilled working class with jobs in modern manufactures, two groups with increasing purchasing power in the late Victorian economy.[137] Conversely, the presence of declining handicrafts, together with transport and service employment, meant that low paid and vulnerable workers were probably over-represented in the city. The railways continued to be important, and the later 19th century saw substantial expansion of the railway yards, stations and sheds, as well as the widening of the tunnels, Roodee Viaduct and Dee Bridge.[138] Railway construction projects thus provided building work, whilst operating jobs on the railways continued to increase. The problem with railway work was that much was unskilled, dangerous and fairly low paid, though it did offer relative security.[139] It would appear overall that, despite some improvement in the standard of living in late Victorian Britain, Chester's working class population was marginal to the city's economy, just as it was to its elite social and political life. Though there was some development of trade unionism in the late 19th century, Chester's skewed employment structure and its social conservatism were infertile ground for the growth of a strong labour movement.[140]

Chester did benefit from those in the commercial classes of Liverpool, Manchester and other industrial towns who increasingly chose the city as an attractive place to live within easy travel of their businesses.[141] The city was also home to a growing *rentier* class living off inherited wealth, property and investment income. By the Edwardian period this group may have formed about 5 per cent of the population, and its members spent well, particularly in the more elegant shops.[142] It was the presence of these classes, both in the city and the hinterland, which enabled Chester to support such a diverse and high quality range of shops and services. In many ways its economic profile was more akin to south-eastern England than it was to the industrial north-west or Wales, and it lends support to the view that a viable service economy could develop on the back of a limited, but wealthy, clientele.[143] Tourists and long-distance visitors probably provided the icing on the cake—perhaps 5 per cent of the total trade of the better quality shops.[144] Their spending was an important bonus which was largely independent of any weaknesses in the local and regional economy.

In the late-Victorian period Chester's shops made the transition to modern retail businesses. Goods purchased locally from individual craft producers or fairs were superseded by direct supplies from industrial firms or commercial wholesalers, a sign of the retail sector's closer integration within the industrial economy.[145] The relationship depended on efficient distribution brought by the railways and the GPO, one example being T. G. Burrell's drapery and clothing business, which purchased goods from 124 different suppliers in the 1880s, none of them seemingly from Chester.[146] Department and chain stores also started to populate the city centre, and Browns' monopoly was broken by the growth of three firms, Richard Jones, the Chester Co-op and T.G.Burrell, which tapped the increased spending power of the middle and, to a lesser extent, the working classes.[147] The growth of the large stores seems to have undermined the position of older specialist businesses, particularly those in clothing and furniture, whilst chain grocery firms—Lipton's, Maypole and Home and Colonial—started to supplant the older, often more exclusive, food retailers. By 1900 all the banks were owned by national or regional concerns, Chester's last independent bank suffering an enforced take-over by Lloyd's in 1897.[148] This period marked, nevertheless, only the beginning of corporate domination of retailing, and Chester remained a shopping centre heavily populated by local businesses.

Even more of the city centre was rebuilt in half-timbered style between 1888 to 1902, something partly explicable by the service economy's relatively better performance in the 1890s. The rebuilding was concentrated mostly in the better central streets, however, and it accentuated the contrast between the prosperous parts of the urban core and other areas of more limited growth or even of decline.[149] Eastgate Street retained its place as the prestigious heart of commercial Chester, whilst the ends of Bridge Street, Foregate Street and Northgate Street closest to Eastgate Street were also desirable locations. Small businesses tended to be squeezed out of the best sites in these streets by the expansion of the bigger and better shops. The situation was quite otherwise in Lower Bridge Street and Watergate Street. Property there became increasingly subdivided and decrepit, a process reflecting colonization by small, often marginal, businesses needing cheap premises. Overall, however, Chester's central area saw little absolute expansion in the late 19th century. Landowners and developers preferred to invest in the old-established core.[150]

Behind the attractive Georgian and half-timbered facades of the main streets conditions for the court dwellers continued to be appalling. By the late 1870s the 'core of rottenness' of the courts was becoming the subject of debate in the city. The poverty of court dwellers was exposed, but, for most middle class observers, the real fear was that these 'foul and filthy dens' were 'the resorts of thieves, prostitutes and drunkards'.[151] About 25 courts out of 177 had gone by 1894, but this meant that over 1,000 people had been pushed into the remaining slums by their clearance. There was no council rehousing for the luckless people displaced.[152] The most potent force in the elimination of courts was not Town Council action but the fact that some of them occupied sites ripe for redevelopment in the more dynamic parts of the urban core.[153]

Changing patterns of distribution in the late 19th century meant the end for Chester's traditional fairs, and adaptation for its markets. The city's importance as a livestock market declined with the growth of railway-connected marts, notably those at Crewe, Tattenhall Road and Beeston Castle. The corn market dwindled with the decline of grain production in Cheshire after 1879, whilst the cheese trade was chronically depressed and Chester's position in the regional trade was under challenge from the Whitchurch market, established in the 1860s. The general market was also transformed into a permanent outlet for goods sold to the public rather than a periodic one whose main customers were other traders.[154]

Chester's role in the region had historically always been more than that of mere market town, and there was some consolidation of its wider service function in late Victorian times. The placing of the seat of the county council in Chester in 1889, despite its marginal location, was important for maintaining the city's stature and drawing power. The effect overall must have been to sustain links with the hinterland, particularly with those parts of Cheshire which were otherwise more orientated to Manchester, Liverpool, Wrexham or the Potteries. The presence of the law courts, the bishopric and various central government offices also helped maintain the city's nodal role, whilst that of the military became more significant.[155] Chester's continuing role as an administrative, ecclesiastical and military centre may have helped offset its economic weaknesses. The city's social and political sphere of influence was wider than its purely economic one, but the two were interrelated in that elite groups brought to the city because of its social role spent money there, and therefore helped support its service economy.

In summary, therefore, it seems that, despite Chester's continued importance as the regional centre for west Cheshire and north-east Wales, at the close of Victoria's reign the city had experienced thirty difficult years. The problems were to continue into the new century. The superficial gloss of city centre rebuilding tended to obscure the fact that the forces of national integration in markets for goods, services and finance had reduced Chester's potential for a diversified and secure economy, and hence its potential prosperity. Though some modern firms were present, manufacturing in the city had deteriorated from an already narrow base, and it is doubtful whether a larger role providing services, in a region with its own problems, fully compensated. What is clear is that the last decades of Queen Victoria's reign saw an acceleration in Chester's long-established decline relative to other major centres in north-west England.

Victorian Britain was an era of great cities and growing industrial conurbations, and the simplest way to assess Chester's history in this period would be by its overall growth performance. From this perspective the city's record was fairly mediocre. It failed to develop a strong industrial base, its population growth was modest by the standards of the time and, despite the importance of its railways, for the most part it retained the atmosphere of a pre-industrial market town. From this perspective it would be easy to conclude that Chester demonstrated the fundamental inability of such towns to compete with the growing industrial cities of Victorian Britain. Its relative decline was therefore inevitable. There were, however, historic cities in a broadly similar position—York, Lincoln, Coventry and Derby for example—which did better than Chester, so one must beware of deterministic explanations. Despite industrial growth both in the old city and at Saltney, the record shows that successful industrial entrepreneurs, either home-grown or in-migrant, were thin on the ground, and this must be linked to an oppressive social, political and landownership environment. The moment of opportunity for Chester's elite came in the 1840s, but its response to the challenge was ambiguous. Seduced later by the revived prosperity of shops and services, the elite then seems to have accepted, with increasing complacency, the limited horizons which such an economy could offer in late-Victorian Britain. As one councillor put it in 1880:

> I am afraid there is a spirit in [the] council that would really push Chester into a corner and make it little better than a village. . . . Chester had a status for hundreds of years in the kingdom.[156]

Growth and industrial development may not, however, be the only, or most appropriate, criteria by which to judge Chester. Perhaps the notion of adaptation is preferable. To what extent did the city adapt successfully to the challenges posed by the changing regional and national environment around it? The answer to this question would be more positive. It became a successful railway node, its service function was enhanced, and its shopping was of a quality and diversity superior to the city's superficial size. Chester could be seen to have adopted a role complementary to the industrial and port towns of the region and, in doing so, to have enhanced its historic character through pioneering conservation to become an attractive place to visit and to live. The elite of Chester could, therefore, be seen to have fostered an appropriate response to changing circumstances.

There were, nevertheless, weaknesses in this approach. The city's service functions were increasingly overshadowed by the regional metropolises of Liverpool and Manchester, and local rivals emerged to poach some trade away. As an increasingly service-based economy, the city was vulnerable to national economic fluctuations and to structural changes in the region. It had, too, the social defect of a service economy—a polarization between, on the one side, a prosperous bourgeoisie and *rentier* class and, on the other, an impoverished working class whose members were often trapped in decaying manufactures or in poorly-paid and casual service jobs.

Chester in the Victorian era exhibits, therefore, the symptoms of a difficult structural adjustment to the demands of a changing, but increasingly integrated, regional and national economy. These problems proved to be long-term. The search for a viable economic role during the Industrial Revolution continued to be a difficult quest even in later, more interventionist, times, and for much of the 20th century Chester remained a rather down-at-heel place outside its prosperous shopping streets. By the 1980s almost all vestiges of the city's Victorian industries had disappeared, and many newer manufacturing firms in the sub-region had also closed or shed jobs. The result was high unemployment. In the past 20 years Chester has, on the other hand, continued to gain tertiary employment and new residents for whom its historic environment, much of it a legacy of Victorian times, is the main attraction. The conclusion must be, therefore, that Chester's history in the past two hundred years suggests the potential, but also the problems, of basing an economy on shopping, services and tourism.

Notes

1 F. White, *History of Cheshire* (Sheffield, 1860), 106.

2 The main sources on the economy of Victorian Chester are mentioned in the succeeding notes. They are supplemented by A. T. Thacker and C. Lewis (eds), *The Victoria History of the County of Cheshire [VCH]: Vol. V, The City of Chester* (Oxford, in press, 1996), from which aspects of this essay are derived.

3 Perhaps best expressed by Eric Hobsbawm: 'whoever says the Industrial Revolution says cotton . . . The new world of industrialism in its most obvious form was . . . [to be seen] . . . in and around Manchester', E. J. Hobsbawm, *Industry and Empire* (Harmondsworth, 1986), 57–58. The work of T. S. Ashton reflected such a view in, for example, T. S. Ashton, *The Industrial Revolution, 1760–1830* (Oxford, 1948). See P. Hudson, *The Industrial Revolution* (London, 1992) for a modern review emphasizing the regional perspective.

4 The main sources are noted below in discussion of the significance of North Wales for Chester's trade in Victorian times.

5 There is a voluminous literature on Liverpool; for a recent perspective see essays in J. Belchem (ed.), *Popular Politics, Riot and Labour: Essays in Liverpool History, 1790–1940* (Liverpool, 1992). For Cheshire agriculture, see R. E. Porter, 'Agricultural Change in Cheshire during the 19th Century' (unpublished PhD Thesis, University of Liverpool, 1974). For seaside towns the standard work is J. K. Walton, *The English Seaside Resort: A Social History, 1750–1914* (Leicester, 1983), and related writings.

6 For example, B. M. Short, 'The De-industrialisation Process: A Case Study of the Weald, 1600–1850' on P. Hudson (ed.), *Regions and Industries: a Perspective on the Industrial Revolution in Britain* (Cambridge, 1989).

7 J. Langton, 'The industrial revolution and the regional geography of England', *Transactions of the Institute of British Geographers*, NS 9 (1984), 145–67.

8 J. D. Herson, 'Chester 1762–1914: Economic History', in *VCH V: Chester*.

9 C. Armour, 'The Trade of Chester and the State of the Dee Navigation, 1600–1800' (unpublished PhD Thesis, University of London, 1956), *passim*;

A. M. Kennett (ed.), *Georgian Chester: Aspects of Chester's History from 1660 to 1837* (Chester, 1987), 15–19, 9, 19, 31–32, 36.

10 J. Hemingway, *History of the City of Chester* (Chester, 1831), ii, 331–32; G. C. Spence, 'Notes on Clay Tobacco Pipes and Clay Pipe Makers in Cheshire', *Transactions of the Lancashire and Cheshire Antiquarian Society*, lvi, 45; N. Moore, *Chester Clocks and Clockmakers* (Chester, 1975), 4.

11 R. Craig, 'Shipping and Shipbuilding in the Port of Chester in the 18th and early 19th Centuries', *Trans. Hist. Soc. Lancs. and Ches.* cxvi, 59; M. J. Kingman, 'Chester, 1801–1861' (unpublished MA Thesis, University of Leicester, 1969), 12. Hemingway, *Hist. Chester*, ii, 332; A. M. Kennett (ed.), *Chester and the River Dee: An Illustrated History of Chester and its Port* (Chester, 1982), 14–15.

12 Wardle and Bentham, *The Commercial Guide* (Manchester, 1814–1815).

13 L. and M. Hillis, 'The Chester Whiteware Manufactory', *Northern Ceramic Society Journal*, 4 (1980/1), 43.

14 G. L. Fenwick, *A History of the Ancient City of Chester* (Chester, 1896), 477; Hemingway, *Hist. Chester*, map, frontispiece, vol. ii; *Chester Courant*, 14 July 1847.

15 B. Bracegirdle, *Engineering in Chester—200 Years of Progress* (Chester, n.d., c.1966), 36.

16 CRO, CR 586/37, M. H. O. Hoddinott, A Site Development History of the Chester Leadworks of Messrs. Walkers, Parker and Co., . . . 1800–1990; Associated Lead Manufacturers Ltd., *Chester Works* (typescript, Chester Library, P67.1, 1957); A. H. John (ed.), *Minutes Relating to Messrs. Samuel Walker and Co., Rotherham, Iron Founders and Steel Refiners, 1741–1829 and Messrs. Walker, Parker and Co., Lead Manufacturers, 1788–1893* (1951), 35–54.

17 Armour, 'Trade Chester'. 307, 31; Kennett, *Chester and R. Dee*, 11–12; R. Craig, 'Shipping and Shipbldg.', 45

18 J. D. Herson, 'Canals', in *VCH V: Chester*; J. D. Herson, 'Canals, Railways and the Demise of the Port of Chester' in P. Carrington (ed.), *"Where Deva Spreads her Wizard Stream": Trade and the Port of Chester* (Chester, 1996), 75–89.

19 E. M. Willshaw, 'The Inns of Chester, 1775–1832' (unpublished MA Thesis, University of Leicester, 1979), 7, 59–60; W. Harrison, 'Development of the Turnpike System in Lancashire and Cheshire', *Trans. Lancs. and Ches. Antiq. Soc.*, IV (1886), 80–92; W. Albert, *The Turnpike Road System in England, 1663–1840* (Cambridge, 1972), 145.

20 Willshaw, 'Inns Chester', 60.

44 JOHN HERSON

21 Armour, 'Trade Chester', 221, 276.

22 S. I. Mitchell, 'Urban Markets and Retail Distribution, 1730–1815, with particular reference to Macclesfield, Stockport and Chester' (unpublished DPhil Thesis, University of Oxford, 1974), 45–48.

23 G. O'Tuathaigh, *Ireland before the Famine, 1798–1848* (Dublin, 1972), 125.

24 Hemingway, *Hist. Chester*, ii, 9.

25 *Ibid.*, ii, 32–33.

26 J. D. Herson, A. T. Thacker and A. Baggs, 'Physical Development and Social Character, 1762–1914' in *VCH V: Chester*.

27 Hemingway, *Hist. Chester*, ii, 341.

28 Hemingway, *op. cit.*, ii, 341, 346; Herson, Thacker and Baggs, *op. cit.*

29 Hemingway, *op. cit.*, i, 388.

30 Herson, *op. cit.*, table of businesses, Chester, 1781–1834.

31 G. Shaw, 'Recent research on the commercial structure of 19th century British cities', in D. Denecke and G. Shaw (eds.), *Urban Historical Geography: Recent Progress in Britain and Germany* (Cambridge, 1988), 237.

32 Chester, Wrexham and N.Wales Trustee Savings Bank, *150th Annual Report, 1817–1967* (1967), Chester City Library fp33.22; Fenwick, *Hist. Chester*, 511/514; CRO, CR/4,Williams and Co.; D. Nuttall, 'A History of Printing in Chester', *Journal of the Chester Archaeological Society*, liv, 67–74; H. Hughes, *Chronicle of Chester: the 200 Years 1775–1975* (London, 1975), Chaps. 1–4; Willshaw, 'Inns Chester', 7, 23–44; I. Callister, *The Chester Grosvenor: A History* (Chester, 1983), 4–9; Blossoms Hotel, Chester (Brochure, CRO, 942.714/728.5), 1949, 18.

33 Fenwick, *op. cit.*, 249.

34 Cllr Turner, Town Council meeting, July 1847, *Chester Chronicle*, 16 July 1847.

35 *Chester Chronicle*, 20 Jan. 1837.

36 P. E. Baughan, *Regional History of the Railways of Great Britain, Vol. XI, North and Mid Wales* (Newton Abbot, 1980), *passim.*, D. Sylvester and G. Nulty (eds.), *The Historical Atlas of Cheshire* (Chester, 1958), 54–55.

37 Cllr Gamon, *Chester Chronicle*, 17 Jan. 1845.

38 *Census*, 1861, Occupations, Div. V, Table 15; G. R. Hawke, *Railways and Economic Growth in England and Wales, 1840–1870* (Oxford, 1970), 262/3

39 Herson, *op. cit.*, migration estimates; G. Davies. 'The Impact of the Railways on Chester, 1837–1870', (Chester College BEd project, 1981), 11–12.

40 *Chester Chronicle*, leader, 11 May 1838.

41 A ship canal from the Dee at Dawpool (between West Kirby and Heswall) via Frodsham to Manchester was proposed in two abortive schemes of the 1820s, but this would have done nothing to help Chester itself; see C. Hadfield and G. Biddle, *The Canals of North West England, Vol. 1* (Newton Abbot, 1970), 104–06.

42 A. M. Kennett (ed.), *Chester and the River Dee* (Chester, 1982), 10–11.

43 *Chester Chronicle*, 4 Oct. 1839.

44 *Chester Chronicle*, 25 Jan. 1839.

45 *Chester Chronicle*, 15 Feb. 1839.

46 *Chester Chronicle*, 13/20/27 Sept., 4/11 Oct. 1839, 20 Nov. 1840, 5 Feb., 14 Mar. 1841.

47 A. M. Kennett (ed.), *Chester and the River Dee*, 11.

48 *Chester Chronicle*, Sept.–Dec. 1849 *passim.*

49 The Dee Standard Restoration Act, 1851.

50 Kennett, *op. cit.*, 11.

51 *Ibid.*

52 *Chester Chronicle*, 18 June 1847.

53 *Ibid.*

54 *Chester Chronicle*, 16 July 1847.

55 *Ibid.*

56 *Ibid.*, 17 Sept. 1847.

57 *Ibid.*, 19 Oct. 1849.

58 *Ibid.*, *passim.*, 1848–53.

59 R. M. Bevan, *The Roodee: 450 Years of Racing in Chester* (Northwich, 1982), 15–81, *passim.*

60 *Chester Chronicle*, 1848/9 *passim.*

61 *Ibid.*, 5 Mar. 1859.

62 Herson, *op. cit.*, table: employment structure, Chester, 1841–1911; table: manufacturing employment, Chester, 1851, 1871 and 1911.

63 *Ibid.*, table: employment in shoemaking and tailoring, 1860/1.

64 CRO, CR56/1–2, Documents relating to Bridge Street Brewery; CRO, CR122, Documents relating to the Chester Northgate Brewery Co.

65 A. M. Kennett (ed.), *Chester and the River Dee*, 14–15.

66 R. Perren, 'Structural change and market growth in the food industry; flour milling in Britain, Europe and America, 1850–1914', *EcHR*, 2nd ser. xliii(3), 422–23.

67 Bagshaw's *Directory*, 1850; White, *Hist. Ches.*, 1860; Fenwick, *Hist. Chester*, 478.

68 *Cheshire Sheaf*, 1st ser. ii, 242 (item 1503).

69 CRO, CR586/37, M. H. O. Hoddinott, 15, 82, 1, 37.

70 Herson, *op. cit.*, table: manufacturing employment, Chester, 1851, 1871 and 1911; Bagshaw's *Directory*, 1850. Bracegirdle, *200 Years of Engineering in Chester*, 34–36; Hydraulic Eng.Co., *Short History*, 1.

71 Ordnance Survey 1:2,500 Plan, Ches. xxxviii:11, 1875; J. Simmons, *The Railway in Town and Country, 1830–1914* (Newton Abbot, 1986), 126.

72 Saltney and Saltney Ferry History Group, *Saltney and Saltney Ferry: A Third Illustrated History* (Chester, 1992), 12.

73 Clwyd RO, Hawarden, NT/1(a), Rev E.L. Roberts, 'Y Goror', *Cymru*, xxix, (1905); B. D. Clark (ed.), *Saltney and Saltney Ferry: A Short Illustrated History* (Chester, 1988); Clwyd RO, NT/903, Notes and Advertisement relating to Henry Wood and Co.; G. Lloyd, *Notes on Henry Wood and Co. Ltd.* (1964); B. D. Clark (ed.), *Saltney and Saltney Ferry: A Second Illustrated History* (Chester, 1989), 11.

74 H. G. Gregory, 'The Distillation of Oil from Cannel Coal and Shales', *J. Flints. Hist. Soc.*, xxv, 166–69; Clwyd RO, NT/1(a); Clwyd RO, Hawarden, D/BC/3419, Deeds etc. relating to the Flintshire Oil and Cannel Co, Saltney, 1877–87; K. Davies, 'The Growth and Development of Settlement and Population in Flintshire, 1851–1891', *J. Flints. Hist. Soc.*, XXVI, 151.

75 Davies, 'Popn. Growth Flints., 1851–91', 148; Clwyd RO, NT/1(a).

76 Cheshire County Record Office (hereafter CCRO), EDT96/1–2, Chester St Mary-on-the-Hill Tithe Map and Apportionment, 1839.

77 R. Christiansen, *Regional History of the Railways of Great Britain, Vol. 7: The West Midlands* (Newton Abbot, 1973), 98; C. Hamilton Ellis, *British Railway History, 1830–1876* (London, 1954), 198–207.

78 Henry Mackay, *The Stranger's Handbook to Chester* (Chester, 1867), 40

79 *Chester Chronicle*, 17 April 1869.

80 P. J. W. Higson, 'Landlord control and motivation in the parliamentary enclosure of St Mary's-on-the-Hill Parish, Chester', *Trans. Hist. Soc. Lancs. and Ches.*, 136 (1986), 110.

81 Herson, Thacker and Baggs, *op. cit.*

82 CCRO, DBD/116, Land of William and Martha Hamilton, 1804–1891, indenture 27 May 1826 and conveyance 10 Nov. 1891.

83 CCRO, DBD/116, Copy deeds relating to Flookersbrook etc., 1839–67.

84 CCRO, EDT172/1–2, Chester St Oswald's Parish, Great Boughton Township Tithe Apportionment and Map, 1844.

85 J. Garrard, *Leadership and Power in Victorian Industrial Towns, 1830–1880* (Manchester, 1983), 3–4, 41.

86 Their influence on Chester's politics in the early 19th century was legendary although it was contested fiercely by the so-called Independents. Members of the Grosvenor family represented Chester in Parliament almost continuously until 1874. For a brief discussion see A. M. Kennett (ed.), *Georgian Chester* (1987), 20–25. Significantly, Robert Littler, the Marquis of Westminster's property agent in the Chester area, was on the council in the 1850s.

87 This has yet to be demonstrated, however. The Grosvenors identified with the Whigs/Liberals from the 1830s and at general elections Liberal/Reform councillors were active in the Grosvenor cause. Some of these men, for example William Wardell and E. R. Seller were, however, to be found on opposite sides in the Gray Locomotive works vote. Seller was a brewery owner and Wardell a banker, occupations which suggest why the former favoured an influx of thirsty working men and the latter did not. Tory councillors, for example Capt. French and Charles Potts, were also to be found on opposite sides, and the affair was not a simply party political issue. *Chester Chronicle*, 16 July 1847; 19 June 1852.

88 For example, the Browns, silk mercers, the Huxleys, brewers, and the Frosts, corn millers.

89 In the 1850s a wood-turner, a glove manufacturer and an upholsterer were on the council.

90 D. Cannadine, *Patricians, Power and Politics in 19th Century Towns* (Leicester, 1982), 8.

91 *Chester Chronicle*, 16 June 1847.

92 CCRO, DPB1186/1, Potts and Ball, deeds and papers relating to Upton-by-Chester and Saltney.

93 Herson, *op. cit.*, Tables showing the distribution of account customers at 3 Chester shops, 1844–1910. A. H. Dodd, *The Industrial Revolution in North Wales* (Cardiff, 3rd ed., 1971), esp. Chaps V, VI, VII and VIII; K. Davies, 'The Growth and Develpment of Settlement and Population in Flintshire, 1801–1851', *J. Flints. Hist. Soc.*, xxv, 62–97; K. Davies, 'The Growth and Development of Settlement and Population in Flintshire, 1851–1891', *J. Flints. Hist. Soc.*, xxvi, 144–69. D. A. Halsall, 'The Chester and Holyhead Railway and its Branches: a Geographical Perspective' (unpublished PhD Thesis, University of Liverpool, 1976), 83. G. C. Lerry, 'The Industries of Denbighshire: Part I', *Transactions of the Denbighshire Historical Society*, vi, 78.

94 R. E. Porter, 'Agricultural Change in Cheshire during the Nineteenth

Century' (unpublished PhD Thesis, University of Liverpool, 1974), 135 and Fig.4, 18–21, 314, 27, 202–05, 207, 227, 41, 42, 258, 262, 135 and Fig. 14.

95 P. J. Waller, *Town, City and Nation, 1850–1914* (Oxford, 1983), 231. Four markets, Neston, Malpas, Over and Frodsham, disappeared from west Cheshire between 1834 and 1860 and Tarporley followed later. R. E. Porter, 'The Marketing of Agricultural Produce in Cheshire in the Nineteenth Century', *Trans. Hist. Soc. Lancs. and Ches.*, cxxvi, 149.

96 Herson, *op. cit.*, account customers tables.

97 Herson, *op. cit.*, Chester region migration trends.

98 Although many of them were unskilled, it should not be assumed all were—in 1861 only half the Irish living within the Walls were labourers. The rest had other occupations, including skilled and professional jobs. C. Hargreaves, 'Social Areas within the Walls of Chester, 1861', *J. Ches. Arch. Soc.*, 65 (1982), 69.

99 Herson, *op. cit.*

100 Herson, Thacker and Baggs, *op. cit.*, court housing and within-Walls housing; CRO, DH/2/4, Annual Reports of the Medical Officer of Health 1908, 1910, 1911; *Ibid.*, DH/2/5, Reports 1912 and 1919; D. A. Savage, 'Working Class Standards of Living in the City of Chester, 1870–1914' (BA Dissertation, University of Durham, 1990), 40–42; *Chester Chronicle*, 29 Nov. 1879–27 Dec. 1879; 10 Feb. 1894.

101 Herson, Thacker and Baggs, *op. cit.*, Table: number of houses, Chester and suburbs, 1911.

102 Herson, *op. cit.*, Table of number of businesses, Chester, 1840, 1878 and 1906.

103 Mass Observation, *Browns and Chester: Portrait of a Shop* (London, 1947), chap.10.

104 Herson, Thacker and Baggs, *op. cit.*

105 R. M. Bevan, *The Roodee*, 30.

106 This has been argued by M. J. Kingman, 'Chester 1801–1861' (unpublished MA Thesis, University of Leicester, 1969), CRO, 59.

107 Herson, *op. cit.*, tables and figures relating to migration, and appendix in which estimates are given for the emigration component of Chester's net loss of migrants in the late 19th century. Discounting emigration, negative balances still remain for the decades 1871–91 and 1901–11 whereas the decade 1891–1901 shows a small inflow; D. E. Baines, 'Labour Supply and the Labour market 1860–1914', in R. C. Floud and D. C. McCloskey (eds.), *The Economic History of Britain since 1700, Vol. 2: 1860 to the 1970s* (Cambridge, 1981), 159–60; D. E. Baines, *Emigration from Europe, 1815–1930* (Basingstoke, 1991), 21–30.

108 Herson, Thacker and Baggs, *op. cit.*, table: number of houses, Chester, 1811–1911.

109 J. B. Jefferys, *Retail Trading in Britain, 1850–1950* (Cambridge, 1954), Chap I and case study chapters; J. Benson and G. Shaw, *The Evolution of Retail Systems, 1800–1914* (Leicester, 1992); D. Davis, *A History of Shopping* (London, 1966), Chap xii *passim.*; D. Alexander, *Retailing in Britain during the Industrial Revolution* (London, 1970), 12–18; G. Crossick and H-G. Haupt, 'Shopkeepers, master artisans and the historian: the petite bourgeoisie in comparative focus', in Crossick and Haupt (eds.), *Shopkeepers and Master Artisans in Nineteenth Century Europe* (London, 1984), 12–13.

110 Herson, *op. cit.*, table: manufacturing employment, Chester, 1851, 1871, 1911.

111 M. Harrison, 'The Development of Boot and Shoe Manufacturing in Stafford, 1850–1880', *Journal of the Staffordshire Industrial Archaeology Society*, x, 37 and *passim.*; A. Fox, *A History of the National Union of Boot and Shoe Operatives, 1874–1958* (Oxford, 1958), 12–13, 137, 260; K. Brooker, 'The Northampton Shoemakers' Reaction to Industrialization: Some Thoughts', *Northants. Past and Present*, vi (3), 151–59.

112 Herson, *op. cit.*

113 *Ibid.*, and Herson, Thacker and Baggs, *op. cit.*

114 R. Perren, 'Structural change and market growth in the food industry: flour milling in Britain, Europe and America, 1850–1914', *EcHR*, 2nd ser. xliii(3), 423–25.

115 Herson, *op. cit.*

116 *Ibid.*

117 *Ibid.*

118 *Ibid.*

119 *Ibid.*

120 *Ibid.*

121 Robinson, Son and Pike (pub), *Chester in 1892* (Brighton, 1892; copy in CCRO), 27–29; G. G. Lerry, 'The Industries of Denbighshire from Tudor Times to the Present Day: Part II: More Recent Developments (a)', *Trans. Denbighs. Hist. Soc.*, Vol. 8 (1959), 112/3. C. J. Williams, *Industry in Clwyd: An Illustrated History* (Hawarden, 1986), 749.

122 CRO, CR420/2, 'Perfect Control: an Outline History of Brookhirst Switchgear of Chester', *Scope*, Jan. 1948.

123 *Chester Chronicle*, 5 July 1884.

124 Herson, *op. cit.*

125 Clwyd RO, D/DM/1064/1, Register of Railway Employees at Mold

Junction, 1864–1927; B. D. Clark (ed.), *Saltney and Saltney Ferry: A Short Illustrated History*.

126 Herson, *op. cit.*

127 P. S. Richards, 'The Hawarden Bridge, Shotton, Chester, Iron and Steelworks of Messrs. John Summers and Co.', *J. Flints. Hist. Soc.*, 25 (1972/ 3), 102.

128 Herson, *op. cit.*, table: service, administrative and professional employment, Chester, 1871 and 1911; another indicator can be found by using data contained in C. H. Lee, 'The service sector, regional speciali- sation and economic growth in the Victorian economy', *Journal of Historical Geography*, 10, 2 (1984), Tables 6,7 and 8. Service employment in Chester per 10,000 of the population rose by 21.9% between 1861 and 1911 compared with 26.2% for north-west England and 23.7% nationally, though it is still the case that service employment in Chester in 1911 at 2636 per 10,000 was considerably greater than the national proportion of 1760 per 10,000.

129 B. E. Supple, 'Income and Demand, 1860–1914: a Survey', in R. Floud and D. McCloskey (eds.), *The Economic History of Britain since 1700*, Vol. II, (1981), 121–43; Herson, *op. cit.*

130 Herson, *op. cit.*

131 K. Davies, 'The Growth and Development of Settlement and Popu- lation in Flintshire', Part II 1851–1891, and Part III 1891–1931, *Flints. Hist. Soc. Publications*, 26 (1973–74) and 27 (1975–76).

132 Herson, *op. cit.*, table: account customers, 3 Chester businesses.

133 W. T. R. Pryce, 'The Social and Economic Structure of North East Wales, 1750–1890', (unpublished PhD Thesis, Manchester Polytechnic, 1971), 102–11.

134 P. J. Aspinall and D. M. Hudson (ed. R. Lawton), *Ellesmere Port: the Making of an Industrial Borough* (Ellesmere Port, 1982), 18.

135 R. E. Porter, 'Agricultural change in Cheshire during the 19th Century (unpublished PhD Thesis, University of Liverpool, 1974), 136.

136 Herson, *op. cit.*

137 B. E. Supple, *op. cit.*, 123–43.

138 R. Christiansen, *A Regional History of the Railways of Great Britain: Vol. 7: the West Midlands* (Newton Abbot, 1973), 168–86. G. O. Holt, *A Regional History of the Railways of Great Britain, Vol. 10: the North West* (Newton Abbot, 1978), 44–50, 84–85.

139 P. S. Bagwell, *The Railwaymen: the History of the National Union of Railwaymen* (London, 1963), 262; F. McKenna, *The Railway Workers, 1840–1970* (Oxford, 1970), Chap. 2.

140 Herson, Thacker and Baggs, *op. cit.*

141 Herson, *op. cit.*

142 *Ibid.*, table: employment structure, Chester, 1841–1911.

143 C. H. Lee, *op. cit.*, 153.

144 Herson, *op. cit.*, table: account customers, Chester businesses

145 J. B. Jefferys, *Retail Trading in Britain, 1850–1950* (Cambridge, 1954), 9–13; D. Davies, *A History of Shopping*, 276–302; D. Alexander, *Retailing in England during the Industrial Revolution*, 12–18; A. Adburgham, *Shops and Shopping, 1800–1914* (2nd ed., London, 1981), 137–48, 215–26 and *passim.*; P. Mathias, *Retailing Revolution* (London, 1967), Part 1.

146Herson, *op. cit.*, table: T. G. Burrell and Co., location of suppliers; CRO, CR529/16, T. G. Burrell Ltd., Ledger 1883–1890.

147 Herson, *op. cit.*

148 Williams and Co., Chester Old Bank, was subject to a qualified auditors' report in 1894 which criticized the bank's owners severely for imprudent and suspect banking practices. The enforced takeover illustrates dramatically the general trend towards economic integration which is the theme of the period. CRO, CR4/6, Williams and Co.

149 *Ibid.*; *Chester Chronicle*, 9 May 1874, 18 Nov. 1911, 16 Dec. 1911; K. Goulborn and G. Jackson, *Chester: a Portrait in Old Picture Postcards, Vol. 1* (Chester, 1987), and *Vol. 2* (Chester, 1988).

150 Herson, Thacker and Baggs, *op. cit.*, tables on rateable value of property in city centre streets, 1886 and 1908.

151 *Chester Chronicle*, 29 Nov. 1879.

152 *Chester Chronicle*, 10 Feb. 1894.

153 Herson, Thacker and Baggs, *op. cit.*

154 Herson, *op. cit.*

155 *Ibid.*

156 *Chester Chronicle*, 14 Aug. 1880.

2

Common Lodging Houses in Chester, 1841–71

Mary Glazier

During the early-Victorian period, the social problems associated with urban working-class housing, notably in terms of overcrowding, poor living conditions, lack of sanitation and fresh water, and the consequent ill-health of the inhabitants, were exacerbated by both natural population growth and by increased migration to urban areas. Many urban dwellers were transitory either by nature of their occupation or because they were in search of employment, and the growth of common lodging houses was largely a response to a need for temporary accommodation for this increasingly migratory and predominantly working-class population. As Raphael Samuel has observed, common lodging houses became the night-time haven of the wandering tribes, or at least of the better-off portion among them, including hawkers and travelling labourers. and there were few towns without a street or two largely given over to them. They offered cheap overnight accommodation for prices which ranged, at mid-century, from a penny to threepence, although even this was expensive for the very poor, who normally resorted to accommodation in the Casual Wards, which offered warmth and a sometimes cheerful shelter.[1]

By 1851 lodging houses had become a familiar feature of the urban landscape and W. A. Armstrong has suggested that twenty-one per cent of the contemporary population could be defined as 'lodgers' in one form or another.[2] Lodgers may have formed a significant component of eighteenth-century society, but taking into account both increased inter-urban trends and increased immigration, as well as changes in employment brought about by the shift from an agricultural to an industrial economy during the early nineteenth century, one cannot state with any confidence that either the lodgers or the lodging houses of the eighteenth century have any parallel with those of the nineteenth. Moreover, precise definition of the term 'lodger' is somewhat problematic: lodgers could and did encompass friends, relatives, and both short and long-term residents with a variety of occupations, professions or means of subsistence. The term 'lodging house' is also difficult to define, for lodging houses came in various shapes and sizes, both registered and unregistered, catering for a clientele which was far from exclusively working-class. Indeed, only a small proportion of lodgers were accommodated in common lodging houses, for there were also lodging houses situated in recognizably middle class areas which catered for fewer numbers of a more professional class, and although it would appear unlikely that such lodgings would come within the remit of legislation enacted for the control and supervision of common lodging houses, their role being significantly different and their clientele less 'common', these premises also merit inclusion in any study of lodging houses during the period.

The chief motive for taking in lodgers was primarily financial, for some families responded to depressions or troughs in the poverty cycle by economising on space, taking in relatives or lodgers to make the rents go further.[3] However, the most vulnerable groups were single women, widows with children, and deserted wives with families. As Ursula Henriques has observed, these were 'the most defenceless, the most burdensome people' upon parish funds, hence such women, particularly those born outside the borough, continued to feature strongly as lodging house keepers throughout the nineteenth century, perhaps preferring to open their homes to lodgers rather than risk an application for parish relief.[4] The difficulty of identifying, let alone enumerating lodging-houses, is further complicated by the reluctance of some residents to complete census returns with complete veracity, with the result that many houses not designated by the householder as lodging houses actually contained large numbers of lodgers—in many cases, larger than the lodging houses themselves. Indeed, even after 1851, designation as a lodging house depended greatly upon the financial circumstances of the

awful conditions.
Often no beds but straw.

householder, and in some cases, the need to assume an occupation which would relieve any suspicion of potential pauperism. Moreover, many lodging-houses were temporary premises, designed to meet temporary needs, and as such escape identification in the decennial census returns.

The growth of common lodging houses, particularly in high density working-class areas, added considerably to early-Victorian concerns over public health and led ultimately to the passing of the Common Lodging Houses Act in 1851. Lodging houses were condemned by sanitary reformers for chronic overcrowding and the mixing of the sexes, married and unmarried, together with children, in small unventilated rooms, often two or more to a bed (if indeed beds were provided, for in many instances straw, rags or bare boards sufficed). The vast majority of lodging houses also lacked basic sanitary provisions and supplies of clean water and were widely regarded as breeding grounds for epidemic and endemic disease. They were also perceived to be dens of immorality, and many lodging houses acquired the reputation of being harbours for the criminal classes and of housing immigrants of uncertain character and dubious morals. Indeed, as John Burnett has observed, although lodging-houses were intended primarily as a very temporary shelter of a minimal kind, they all too often became permanent homes for the near-destitute and near-criminal classes.[5] In 1845 *The Second Report of the Commissioners of Inquiry into the State of Large Towns and Populous Districts* presented a damning indictment of conditions in lodging houses in contemporary towns and cities, including Chester, where the lodging-houses were reported to be:

> Very miserable and wretched; many have no bedsteads, some not even beds; the people lie down upon straw and huddle together to keep themselves warm. It is in the lodging houses of the worst class, and where the occupants are numerous with no ventilation, that fever first presents itself. There are no police or other regulations regarding them.[6]

The existence of such lodging-houses in early-Victorian Chester was in part the reflection of the steady growth of the population of the city during the first three decades of the nineteenth century. During this period Chester developed as a commercial and tourist centre, whilst its proximity to ports such as Holyhead and Liverpool, to the industrial districts of South Lancashire, and to Cheshire's rich agricultural hinterland promoted it as a stopping place for migratory workers such as tramping artisans and seasonal harvesters, and for the immigrant Irish. Chester's population grew by 43.6 per cent between 1801 and 1831, from 14,860 to 21,344, and by 1861 the population had reached 31,110, an increase of 15.2 per cent per decade between 1831 and 1861. During the eighteenth century the majority of the city's population had lived within the city walls, but by 1801 the central parishes were expanding to take in the extra-mural areas which were developing around the dock and shipbuilding area to the west, and along the main access and exit routes to the north and north-east, notably in the parishes of St John and St Oswald which, by 1831, contained over half of the total population of the city.[7] Working-class dwellings were erected rapidly in these districts: Joseph Hemingway observed in 1831 that there had been 'an extraordinary accumulation of buildings erected in the last ten years' in Boughton, and of 'small cottages lately built in two or three narrow streets [Steven Street, Seaville Street and Russell Street] parallel with Steam Mill Street', a neighbourhood which, he felt, was 'not of the most reputable description'.[8] During the 1840s the growth of extra-mural middle-class areas such as Curzon Park, the gradual evacuation of the middle classes from the city centre, and the continued development and enlargement of working-class districts compounded the problem of urban congestion. In 1846 the *Chester Chronicle* observed that within the city centre, in the courts behind the facade of shops and in streets and passages adjacent to the main commercial thoroughfares of Northgate Street and Foregate Street, lay 'a perfect labyrinth' of working-class dwellings which 'run in all directions without order or regularity, and without due regard to width or means of ventilation'.[9]

The 1841 Census indicates that a substantial proportion of Chester's inhabitants were newcomers to the city. Many came from Chester's largely rural hinterland, but some came from further afield, including Ireland. In 1841 there were 1,013 Irish men and women in the city, many of whom congregated in Boughton, which was perceived as a largely Irish district; in Steven Street alone, 238 out of a total of 454 inhabitants were Irish-born. As Kristina Jeffes shows elsewhere in this volume of essays, this small Irish community expanded during the 1840s, in part in consequence of emigration during the Great Famine,[10] and in January 1847 the *Chester Courant* claimed that there were 756 Irish people living in Steven Street, Canal Side, Boughton and Steam Mill Street.[11] By 1851, 7.3 per cent of the city's population were Irish, although they were not wholly confined to the Boughton area. Indeed, in August 1851 the *Chester Chronicle* referred to the existence of an 'Irish colony' in Bridge Street Row, and census evidence reveals the presence of Irish in most parishes of the city.[12]

The Irish presence compounded the problem of lodging-houses in Chester. In the first place, and as a notoriously transient minority, the Irish were associated in the public mind with both the growth of common lodging houses and the poor conditions which they often exhibited.[13] Michael Anderson has suggested that almost one-third of Irish-born males aged between twenty and forty-four lived as lodgers, and it appears that the Irish comprised a substantial proportion of both lodging-house keepers and lodgers, many of whom lived in extended family or kinship groups, particularly upon their arrival from Ireland. Moreover, the apparent tolerance by the Irish of poor living conditions and their perceived influence in the lowering of standards among the working class served to influence, in turn, the kind of accommodation with which they were provided as well as the attitudes of local authorities towards that accommodation. Indeed, Irish lodging-houses were widely regarded as dens of drunkenness and disorder during the Early Victorian period and were closely monitored by borough police forces.[14]

Nevertheless, Chester's lodging houses were not the sole preserve of the Irish. Lodgers were a common feature in many households not necessarily designated as lodging houses and, as both population and immigration rose, and immigrants included not only single men and women but whole family groups, excessive overcrowding in many smaller households, including Irish households, was to become relatively widespread. With the development of working-class courts during the early 1840s, the consequent increase in the number of working-class men and women who obtained accommodation as lodgers undoubtedly exacerbated urban congestion and insanitary conditions. Moreover, as the middle classes gradually moved out of the city centre so some large centrally-situated dwellings—including the Victoria Building in Bridge Street, which sheltered 12 families and 46 people in 1851—were taken over as lodging houses.[15] The housing of both family groups and single men and women led to increased concerns over health. John Burnett has suggested that the problem was that while a single man 'on tramp' might not take too much harm from one or two night's residence in common lodging houses, they also sometimes accommodated whole families who could not find anything better for a week, a month, or even a quarter.[16] Indeed, there is evidence of some families living as lodgers in Chester for considerably longer than even a quarter, and of Chester-born children of Irish parents who were living, at ten years of age, as lodgers in common lodging houses run by Irish immigrants to whom no relation is stated. Although their length of stay in a particular lodging house is not given, and there is therefore no way of assessing whether this was as a result of recent unemployment or temporary economic need, it is possible that some common lodging houses had a significantly different function in housing more long-stay residents.

The 1841 Census reveals a relatively low number of lodging houses in the city. As far as one can tell from these returns alone, the great majority of lodging house keepers were women, and although marital status is not given, the majority were aged between 40 and 65 years, and many had children, either dependent or engaged in a variety of occupations. These lodging houses were scattered throughout the city, in streets as various as Abbey Street, which contained the lodging house of Mary Rogers, aged 60, with one lodger, a piano tuner, aged 40; White House Yard, containing the lodging house of Mary Evans, aged 45, with two dependent children aged nine and four years (both born in Chester), and three lodgers—a dressmaker of 15, a shoemaker of 20, and an independent lady of 65 years; and Bold Place, containing the house of Elizabeth Spencer, aged 55, with two sons of 20 and 15 years (both born in Chester).[17] Most of these lodging house keepers were immigrants, but were not of Irish origin,

and the variety of streets in which lodging houses were situated
suggests that there were a range of establishments catering for
different clientele. These included Bold Place, which was described
by Hemingway as a pleasant area, and Newgate Street, which
contained the lodging house of Elizabeth Hughes, aged 35, (and two
female lodgers), but which also accommodated residents with occupations as diverse as surgeon, accountant, dancing master, solicitor
and ostler.

Very few of the lodgers in the city centre areas were Irish, and even
those houses named as lodging houses in Steam Mill Street were, at
this point, being run by and accommodating non-Irish. However, if
one examines the residents of Steven Street in 1841, there are several
houses not registered as lodging houses in which large numbers of
Irish were living, with a high proportion of mixed family groups and
single lodgers. These included Hugh Mitchell, aged 30, who lived
with his wife and six children, (the eldest two of whom had been born
in Ireland, the others in Chester), who shared their home with
Michael Gallagher, his wife, and their three children, aged between
six months and 10 years, who had all been born in Chester. Similarly,
Patrick McCardy, aged 35, shared his house with his wife and four
children, and four adult males, two females and three children.[18]
Moreover, whereas in city-centre lodging houses the lodgers had a
variety of occupations such as bricklayers, tailors, dressmakers, and
labourers, these Irish tenants and their lodgers gave their occupation
almost uniformly as 'agricultural labourer'. Of course, this does not
necessarily mean that they were actually employed as agricultural
labourers: as Kingman has observed, it is also possible, particularly in
the post-Famine period, that the Irish may have given a previous
occupation rather than be registered as paupers, given the particular
implications of removal and settlement for those with less than five
years' residence in the parish.[19]

Throughout the 1830s and 1840s there were legislative efforts in
Chester to deal with the problems brought about by increased
population and urban growth. The Poor Law Amendment Act of
1834 had established a more centralized administrative machinery to
deal with the growing numbers of working-class poor, and as Derek
Fraser has observed, much authority in urban areas rested on the

powers of removal and settlement because such districts, as magnets for migrating workers, faced acute difficulties in relieving paupers or potential paupers (who included Irish immigrants) without settlement.[20] Indeed, between 1831 and 1834 the Chester Local Acts Incorporation spent £82.19s.6d. on uncontested removals of persons who had applied to the parish for relief.[21] The establishment of Poor Law Guardians under the 1834 Act provided a level of authority whose duties extended beyond the supervision of paupers and the workhouse, and their role—primarily financial—in overseeing improvements in all aspects of social conditions operated in tandem with individual committees later established by the local authority. Unfortunately, no records exist of the work of the Poor Law Guardians in Chester, although Michael Rose cites an example which demonstrates the extent to which financial considerations became of primary importance, when in 1852 the Chester Poor Law Board ordered an enquiry into the case of a John Ince, a blind pauper, who 'had been harried from one parish to another in the Great Boughton Union of Cheshire', a case which revealed the appalling lengths to which parochial officers were prepared to go in order to prevent the cost of a pauper's relief falling upon the parish.[22] This concern with potential pauper demands is pertinent to the consideration of Chester's common lodging houses because these dwellings accommodated itinerants and vagrants who posed a potential threat in terms of an increased demand upon parish relief.

This said, the immediate responsibility for dealing with problems related to public health and sanitation, including lodging houses, rested initially with the Chester City Assembly and then, after the passing of the Municipal Corporations Act in 1835, the Council of the Borough of Chester. Whereas in October 1830, the old Corporation had been prepared to institute proceedings against the parish of St Mary for the repair of highways,[23] by January 1836 the Council were admitting their liability 'to pave and repair the street Rows, steps and thoroughfares within this Borough', and had formed a Paving Committee.[24] Other Committees followed: although Chester did not establish a local Board of Health under the Public Health Act of 1848, it did establish a Sanitary Committee in 1848 and an Improvement Act Committee in 1846 which, together with the Poor Law

Guardians, were responsible for improvements in all aspects of social conditions throughout the city. In September 1847 the Improvement Committee served notice on owners of premises in Steam Mill Street and Boughton to construct drains from their premises;[25] in September, the same to owners of premises in Foregate Street, Northgate Street and Princess Street, and in March 1849, even the Bishop, Dean and Chapter were ordered to remove the nuisance arising from stagnant water in the Quarry behind Abbey Green.[26] However, as well as establishing an infrastructure of drains, and of supervising the condition of cesspools, middens and privies, which were regarded as being hazardous to health, the City Council had also to deal with the mounting problems of high immigration. In January 1847 it was reported that there were 304 Irish people living in Boughton who were in 'great distress',[27] and in July 1847 the *Chester Courant* reported that the City Council had appointed constables to turn back 'Irish casuals' at the gates of the city.[28] Indeed, Irish casuals comprised almost fifty per cent of all casuals relieved at the Chester Police Office between March and June 1847, when there were 1,329 English casuals, 1,264 Irish, 78 Scots and 96 Welsh.[29]

Concern about the sanitary condition of the common lodging houses in Chester was indicated in the Council Minutes of 12 March 1849, which reveal that these houses were already being inspected under the terms of the Nuisance Removal and Diseases Prevention Act of 1848. Indeed, in noting that 'great advantage having been derived from the inspection of Common Lodging Houses in the city by the police, and there being reason to believe that many of them have been suffered to relapse into their former state of irregularity', the Committee resolved that the Mayor and Magistrates 'be respectfully requested to direct the police to visit them again and report thereon'.[30] Accordingly, on 19 March, the Inspector of Police, Mr Hill, reported:

> There has been of late a considerable influx of vagrants into the Common Lodging Houses in the city which have consequently become so over-crowded that there is reason to apprehend various consequences unless immediate and thorough measures

are taken to establish rules and regulations affecting Common Lodging Houses.[31]

In the same month, Alderman Jones advocated the tighter regulation of lodging houses and called for the City Council to enact a new Bye-Law:

> Whereas the keepers of the Lodging Houses of an inferior description for the accommodation of Mendicant Strangers and other persons for the night or other short periods allow the same to be crowded by receiving more lodgers than such Lodging Houses are adapted to contain with a due regard to health, and allow persons affected with fever and other diseases of a contagious nature to remain in them until infection has been communicated to other lodgers; and receive other lodgers into the appartments [sic] and beds from which diseased persons have been removed without any purifying or other disinfecting process—that no keeper of any such Lodging House within the said Borough shall accommodate or receive such lodgers unless such house shall have been registered in a book kept by the Council or Sanitary Committee for that purpose.[32]

In April 1849 a Committee was appointed to draw up bye-laws for the regulation of Common Lodging Houses,[33] although in the event no bye-laws were passed because at a further meeting on 10 May 1849 the Council decided to refrain from such action as they were by this point anticipating 'a General Enactment for the regulation of Common Lodging Houses'.[34] Accordingly, on 21 May the Chairman of the Council was requested 'to draw up a report of the evils arising from the overcrowding of Lodging Houses and to forward the same to the Secretary of the Board of Health', thereby exerting pressure on central government to respond to a more widespread problem.[35] The Council was also active in inspecting properties in the city: on 10 August 1849 there was an order for certain premises to be 'whitewashed, cleansed and purified',[36] and although the list is obviously partial, including properties in the vicinity of Handbridge, Lower Bridge Street, and Foregate Street, and there is no direct evidence that any of these premises were lodging houses, the streets on this list are also ones in which lodging houses were recorded on the 1851 Census.

Although these initial attempts by the Council to respond to the problems associated with common lodging houses had only a limited impact, they were supported by an editorial in the *Chester Chronicle* on 17 May 1851, which observed:

> Sufficient has appeared in our columns from time to time to justify the interference of the Town Council for the better regulation of Common Lodging Houses. In addition to the great bulk of them being in the most closely built parts of the city, and also being filthy, ill-furnished, imperfectly ventilated and often overcrowded, they exhibit nightly a promiscuous intermixture of the sexes repugnant to common decency. There will always be to a considerable extent, wayfaring poor, such as persons removing from one locality to another in search of employment, and others whose means of obtaining a livelihood may be by perambulating the country. These classes are not indifferent to comfortable and decent lodgings if they could be obtained. But what is the fact? That the Common Lodging Houses are in general not so . . . At present the Common Lodging Houses in this city are under no governance or superintendance, and the keepers of them appear to be utterly indifferent to those ordinary sanatory [sic] arrangements which the most indigent of the well-conducted poor generally observe. They have been over and over again, through the public press and by the magisterial authorities, but all to no purpose . . . We hope (for the sake of the classes who have to frequent these sort of houses) that the Town Council will be stringent.[37]

On 7 August 1851 a permanent Committee was appointed by the Chester City Council to carry into effect the provisions of the recently-enacted Common Lodging House Act. The main restrictions imposed under the 1851 Act were the separation of the sexes into separate quarters (with the exception of family groups) and a limitation upon numbers, which were to be agreed by the Committee upon registration and the issue of a certificate. The Act also stipulated the provision of adequate washing and sanitary facilities for lodgers, and a thorough weekly cleansing of the premises, as well as a twice-yearly limewashing. Most importantly, all common lodging house keepers were required to report to the Council any cases of disease or infection in the house. On 11 November 1851 it was ordered that a list of common lodging houses be made, and that the Houses were to be served with notice of the new regulations and the need for registration.[38] Although the terms of the Act allowed for the appointment of Inspectors from both the Police and the Relieving Officers of the Poor, in practice it was the duty of the Police to arrange for inspection and to report back to the Common Lodging House Committee. Unfortunately, no record exists of either the numbers of lodging houses or the names of their proprietors at this time; the first figures recorded are from 1854, when on 23 November, Inspector Hill gave the number as 261.[39] The 1851 Census Returns also show a marked increase in the number of lodging houses in comparison with the 1841 figures. However, as in 1841, the majority of lodging house keepers nominated on these returns were women, predominantly widows, and there was also the same variety of lodging houses throughout the city. These ranged from the more prestigious dwellings in Nicholas Street, which contained the lodging house of Sarah Rodgers, aged 43, a widow from Denbigh, with three servants, two female 'visitors', and one male 'visitor' (one Edward Bevan, Barrister, from St James, London) to areas such as Hand-bridge and the lodging house of Edward Williams and his wife, whose inhabitants comprised four married couples, two unmarried men, two married men, two widows and one child, and whose occupations were given as schoolmaster, sailor, musician, laundress, striking weaver and shoemaker, from places of origin as diverse as Bath, Cornwall, Warwick and Birmingham. However, and with few exceptions, the largest numbers of lodgers recorded in 1851 lived in the predomi-nantly Irish areas of the city. For example, in Steven Street, the lodging house of John McGough contained 18 residents, as Table 2.1 illustrates.[40]

Indeed, many of the households on Steven Street contained large numbers of Irish lodgers. The Hutchinson household contained 14, the McAndrew household 18, and the Henaghan household 13, but none of these was officially designated a lodging house, possibly

Table 2.1: Occupants of John McGough's Lodging House in Steven Street, 1851.

John McGough	Head of H/hold	M	30	L H Keeper	b. Ireland
Mary McGough	Wife	M	25		b. Ireland
Owen McGough	Son		6 m		b. Chester
Peter Moran	Brother in law	U	25	Agric. Lab	b. Ireland
Patrick Moran	Brother in law	U	23	Agric. Lab	b. Ireland
Bridget Moran	Sister in law	U	17	Gen. Servant	b. Ireland
Thomas Moran	Brother in law	U	16	Agric. Lab	b. Ireland
Anne Moran	Sister	U	18		b. Ireland
Mary Moran	Sister	U	15		b. Ireland
Alice Moran	Sister	U	11		b. Ireland
Thomas Browne	Lodger	U	22	Agric. Lab	b. Ireland
Catherine Browne	Sister	U	18		b. Ireland
John Tracey	Lodger	M	50	Shoemaker	b. Ireland
Mary Tracey	Wife	M	40		b. Ireland
Catherine Burns	Lodger's wife	M	35		b. Ireland
Mathias Burns	Son		4		b. Chester
Honour Burns	Daughter		2		b. Chester
John Burns	Son		1 wk		b. Chester
James Sullivan	Lodger	U	40		b. Ireland

Source: Census Returns, St John's Parish, 1851.

because the Census of April 1851 preceded the enactment of the Common Lodging Houses Act. A rare example of continuity between Census Returns reveals that the overcrowded premises of the McAndrew family had by 1861 become a registered Lodging House, and the marked increase in the number of Lodging Houses in Steven Street by 1861 may well illustrate the effect of the 1851 Act being applied rigorously to areas where dense overcrowding was a perceived health hazard, as well as a degree of suspicion more particularly afforded to the Irish themselves.

It is clear that the late 1840s witnessed increased mobility among Chester's working-class populace, including Irish Famine refugees, and the actions of the City Council during this period reflected a local response to population pressures in an urban environment. Indeed,

Table 2.2: Population Growth in Chester Parishes, 1841–61

Parish	1841			1851			1861		
	Pop.	Houses	Av.	Pop.	Houses	Av.	Pop.	Houses	Av.
St John	6752	1521	4.4	8487	1651	5.1	9835	1993	4.9
St Oswald	5959	1288	4.6	6673	1357	4.9	7534	1536	5.1
Holy Trinity	3340	637	5.2	3374	647	5.2	3606	663	5.4
St Mary	2975	734	4.1	3308	722	4.6	4499	984	4.6
St Michael	649	146	4.4	775	145	5.3	922	172	5.4
St Martin	532	110	4.8	536	112	4.8	694	116	6.0
St Peter	847	190	4.4	948	177	5.4	798	159	5.0
St Olave	430	124	3.5	518	108	4.8	480	103	4.7
St Bridget	675	163	4.1	861	166	5.2	1040	211	4.9
Cathedral/									
Little St John	329	81	4.1	389	79	4.9	431	76	5.7
Spital									
Boughton	191	57	3.3	158	35	4.5	163	35	4.6

Source: Census Returns, City of Chester, 1841–61.

Table 2.2 demonstrates that all areas of Chester except Spital Boughton experienced population growth between 1841 and 1851, and although the greater numbers congregated in the parishes of St John and St Oswald, the average population per household was in fact greater in some of the parishes nearer the city centre, notably in St Michael, St Peter and St Bridget.

The extent of the overcrowding which must have existed is indicated by the population increase of 3,345 for the period 1841–1851, with an increase in the construction of only 148 new houses during the same period. The more central parishes continued to attract a greater variety of lodgers: whereas in Boughton, house-holders and lodgers were predominantly Irish labourers, with occupations such as hawkers, drapers and shoemakers, lodging houses nearer the city centre accommodated lodgers from many parts of the United Kingdom with a similar variety of occupations. For example, in Hamilton Court, Northgate Street, the common lodging house of Susan Eaton, a pauper widow of 70 years of age, originally from

Table 2.3: The Howley family of White House Yard

John Howley	45	Head	Coal Merchant's Lab.	b. Ireland
Maria Howley	35	Wife		b. Cheshire
Edward Howley	20	Son	General Servant	b. Plymouth
Margaret Howley	16	Dtr	General Servant	b. Portsmouth
Emma Howley	12	Dtr	Scholar	b. Carlisle
Peter Howley	10	Son	Scholar	b. Scotland
Elizabeth Howley	7	Dtr	Scholar	b. Chester
Caroline Howley	9m	Dtr		b. Chester

Norfolk, contained a son of 38, three railway labourers from Ireland, and two married couples, described as musicians, whose places of birth are listed as Birmingham, Yorkshire, Yarmouth and London. Moreover, the extent to which families moved in search of employment is demonstrated by the places of birth of the children of some residents, as in the case of the Howley family of White House Yard, as shown in Table 2.3.

Although the Howley dwelling was not registered as a lodging house, its residents also included five unmarried or widowed male lodgers from Hawarden, Flintshire and Cheshire, four of whom were agricultural labourers, and one of whom was a cordwainer. It would appear that due to the high demand for accommodation at this time, some families may have appreciated the opportunity to bolster their income by taking in lodgers, but perhaps had no intention of becoming registered lodging houses under the new regulations. That financial circumstances could alter appreciably is indicated by the example of Margaret Kent of Parry's Court, a widow, who in 1841 was a lodging house keeper, but who was by 1851 supported by her married daughter and son-in-law, both bootmakers, and was no longer registered.[41]

Under the Common Lodging House Act of 1853, powers were given to the Police to enter lodging houses in order to inspect sanitary provisions and to ascertain the number of lodgers resident therein. On 23 November 1854 Mr Hill reported to the Common Lodging House Committee that all 261 Lodging Houses were 'now in a satisfactory state', adding that 88 Lodging House Keepers had been summoned for infringements of the Act and Bye-Laws, of whom 42 had been convicted. At this meeting the Committee resolved that Mr Hill should inquire into both the living accommodation and the water and sanitary provision of lodging houses, on the grounds that 'no fresh licences should be granted until it has been ascertained that the houses are provided with privies and with water'.[42]

There is no definition of what at this point constituted 'a satisfactory state'; all lodging houses had to be cleansed and whitewashed twice yearly, with the main consideration being the prevention of the spread of infectious diseases, and there are no indications to show that the requirements for sanitary provision resulted from an increase of illness or fever. Indeed, Mr Hill reported that in the past year only one licence had been revoked 'owing to fever being in the house', and this had since been re-granted.[43] It would appear that in this respect Chester had escaped some of the worst excesses experienced in other towns, including neighbouring Macclesfield, where it was reported that:

> The first enquiry by the local Board of Health in 1852 'uncovered' 244 lodging houses, many of them dens of filthiness and disease: one house had three bedrooms, the first containing 16 people sleeping on the floor, the second 12, and the third used as a privy 'the boarded floor being literally covered with human ordure.[44]

Enid Gauldie has observed that overcrowding in lodging houses only became technically a 'nuisance' for the first time under the Sanitary Act of 1866.[45] However, both in terms of trying to impose stricter measures on overcrowding and in enforcing improvements in sanitary provision, Chester appears to have been in advance of such legislation. Unfortunately there are no records of the work of the Sanitary Committee between 1856 and 1866, but the Common Lodging House Committee Minutes indicate that by 1859 (if not earlier) the Council was actively pursuing legal measures against those dwellings found to be housing more than their allotted number, and in March 1859 licences were granted to houses in Steven Street and Parry's Entry, and these two-bedroom premises were allowed a maximum of four lodgers.[46] However, in October 1866 the Committee noted:

> Until the passing of the Public Health Act 1866, a doubt was entertained whether persons permitting 'overcrowding' could be proceeded against under the provisions of the Common Lodging House Act, but taking advantage of the doubt, several persons have from time to time been summoned and ordered to comply with its requirements. Now however, that duty is transferred to the Nuisance Authority by the Nineteenth Section of the recent Act.[47]

Such uncertainty about their powers under the 1851 Act may explain some of the apparent overcrowding which still persisted until 1866. The 1861 Census shows that many houses, particularly in Steven Street, contained as many as 16 inhabitants, and 10 would appear to be fairly average. In the household of Patrick Derrick of Canal Side, there were eleven residents, but all were related, what Gauldie terms 'the endless permutations of consanguinity,'[48] whereas in the Brannagan household at 49 Steven Street, there were 13 inhabitants, comprising six children of the tenants and five lodgers—a married couple with one child, and one male and one female lodger.[49] The McAndrew household, also of Steven Street, which in 1851 had 18 residents, was by 1861 a Registered Lodging House, containing the householder, his wife and his father, and 10 lodgers who included a married couple with four children and a childless married couple.[50] Thus it would appear that at this point a degree of overcrowding was either permitted or overlooked by the authorities in these larger Irish households and, relative to evidence from lodging houses in other towns, such households, if administered properly, were not deemed to be excessively overcrowded at this time. The vigilance of the Poor Law Guardians may have been influential in this context: in February 1855 the Common Lodging House Committee received a letter from the Board of Guardians suggesting that lodgers were being received into houses in Parry's Entry, Foregate Street, 'without such houses being registered', and recommending that the Relieving Officers and the Overseer of the Poor in the city be appointed Inspectors under the Act.[51] The allegation was investigated and found to be untrue, and inspection remained the preserve of those policemen appointed by the Committee until November 1860, when the Sanitary Committee was authorized to carry out 'all and every of the powers of the Common Lodging Houses Act'.[52] As later evidence demonstrates, both Parry's Entry and Glegg's Court were of particular concern to the Poor Law Guardians, whose Minutes of February 1864 again referred to the lodging houses and poor sanitary condition of these courts and entries.[53] Such vigilance and concern by the Poor Law Guardians must also have been linked to fears that lodging houses would also provide an easy escape from the poor house, for the 1851 Act forbade the entry into lodging houses by persons in receipt of poor relief.[54] The Act also allowed local authorities to erect their own lodging houses, and some authorities—notably Huddersfield, Birmingham and Dundee—who took advantage of this provision, found that the need for such houses remained constant throughout the later Victorian period. However in Chester, it would appear that the imposition of restrictions upon numbers acted as an effective measure in dissuading potentially undesirable persons from taking up residence in the city, and the increased housebuilding in the years 1851 to 1861 eased some of the problems of overcrowding.

By the time of the 1861 Census, the number of lodging houses in the city had declined from 261 in 1854, to 179 in July 1859, 145 in November 1859, and 143 in 1860.[55] However, the Census returns show that lodging house keepers were by this date increasingly male, particularly in Steven Street, where an increased number of Irish married men with large households now gave their occupation as lodging house keepers.[56] The Common Lodging House Committee Minutes also record a series of inspections of sanitary provision in February 1861 when, of 39 houses inspected in Steven Street, including the aforementioned Brannagan and McAndrew households, only six were recorded as 'dirty'.[57]

The sanitary condition of lodging houses assumed precedence over all other considerations. The Inspector's report of 2 July 1859 recorded 179 lodging houses registered, 103 discontinued, and nine lodging-house keepers summoned for infringements of the Act, of whom eight were dismissed on payment of costs and only one was convicted and ordered to pay £5 (or three months imprisonment). It is reasonable to assume that such offences were in contravention of rules governing sanitary conditions, for the same report recorded that 'the lodging houses are in a clean and healthy state and at present free from any diseases, and the whole have been cleansed and whitewashed'.[58] A list of those lodging houses inspected on February 1861 reveals that although the largest numbers were in the Boughton area, with 39 in Steven Street, 21 in Boughton and five each in Steam Mill Street and Davies Court, there were still lodging houses in many parts of the city, and the same variety continued in both types of houses and their residents.[59] Women, unmarried or widowed, and predominantly middle-aged or older, continued to run lodging houses. These included Sarah Rodgers of Nicholas Street, who in 1861 had a more 'select' household, with two lodgers, a Rector of 68 years, and a bank accountant, and Jane Done of Eastgate Street, who had seven male unmarried lodgers from North Wales, Lancashire and Manchester, of whom six were either chemist's assistants or clerks. There were also larger houses near the city centre housing greater numbers, including that of Samuel Ducker of Princess Street, who had a household of 21, including lodgers from Scotland, Ireland, Lancashire and Shropshire.[60] Regular inspections continued to be made throughout 1861 and 1862, and the Committee Minutes record the twice-yearly cleansing and whitewashing of these premises. Of all those inspected, the areas which were of greatest concern continued to be Parry's Entry and Glegg's Court, where it was observed:

> *Parry's Entry*—the Privies and Ashpits are full and in a disgraceful condition and if not cleaned out are going to cause fever in that neighbourhood.
> *Glegg's Court*—the Privies and Ashpits are full and in a most filthy state.[61]

Indeed, of the 115 lodging houses inspected in the Chester in November 1861, only eight required cleansing, and six of these were in Parry's Entry and two in Steam Mill Street.[62] The attention of the Poor Law Guardians to these areas has already been noted, and in the absence of evidence of the work of both the Guardians and the Sanitary Committee for this period, it is not possible to conclude that these areas alone constituted 'black spots' within the city. However, their repeated nomination must indicate that they received greater attention due to an apparently lower standard of sanitation and cleanliness, which although greater in the court developments, was not revealed in inspections of similar properties throughout the city. In April 1862, of 116 lodging houses inspected in the city, 27 were ordered to be cleansed and whitewashed, but this would appear to be as part of the twice-yearly programme in operation,[63] and in July 1862 all were declared to be 'clean and in a healthy state'.[64] The number of lodging houses gradually decreased in the early 1860s, and by May 1864, numbered 103.[65] Although it is tempting to attribute this decline to increased vigilance and supervision, the Poor Law Guardians argued in January 1864 that:

> the Common Lodging Houses are not efficiently inspected, and that there are many unlicensed houses in which lodgers are taken in and that are unfit to accommodate them.[66]

and a Sanitary Committee Minute of October 1866 reinforced these observations, suggesting that such problems were omnipresent:

> Representations having been made to the Committee that many of the lodging houses which do not come within the provision of the Common Lodging Houses Act and over which the Council has no control, were in a very filthy condition and frequently so overcrowded as to be dangerous to health, and the Committee consider it desirable that such houses be placed under supervision and made subject to regulations for the keeping of the same in a cleanly state, and for limiting the numbers of occupants thereof, ordered that it be recommended to the Council to make application to the Secretary of State for the Home Department, and declare the enactment of the Sanitary Act 1866 with reference to the Regulation of Lodging Houses to be in force in this city and Borough.[67]

    While it is possible that the need for lodging houses diminished due to increased housebuilding—for 849 new homes were constructed in the decade 1851 to 1861—the population growth for this decade of 3,975 was greater than that of the previous decade, 3,348. Furthermore, although population growth may be attributed to the 'natural'

growth of the resident population, rather than the same level of immigration, and whilst the need for lodging houses diminished in tandem with greater economic stability (and consequently less financial need to take in lodgers as a temporary financial measure), the existence of two different types of lodging houses in the city, and the evidence of the Sanitary Committee, may well indicate a far greater number of lodgers than those recorded by the Common Lodging House Committee alone.

By October 1866 there were only 89 lodging houses registered with the Common Lodging House Committee, houses which presumably offered accommodation on a nightly basis, for a Committee Minute of October 1866 noted that

> By the 35th. Section of the same Act [i.e. the Public Health Act] provision is made for the registration of Houses (not being Common Lodging Houses) of taking in weekly or other lodgers.[68]

From 1867 therefore, when Bye-Laws were drawn up by the Sanitary Committee and passed by the Secretary of State, the supervision of lodging houses became split under separate classifications and separate authorities. Accordingly, the Common Lodging House Committee decided to revise the regulations governing registration on the grounds that:

> Ten to twelve years have elapsed since the Chester Lodging Houses were registered, and the families and keepers have in most instances so increased and the lodging houses have in so many cases changed hands.[69]

At this meeting, the Committee adopted new regulations regarding the provision of space in lodging houses, and it was ordered that each adult lodger was to be accorded 350 cubic feet of living space, with half that for each child under 12 years of age. The Committee further resolved that 'in no case be a bed allowed in the living room or kitchen downstairs', concluding:

> Calculating from this basis, 39 of the present houses, viz. 26 in Steven Street, 7 in Parry's Entry, 4 in Boughton, 2 elsewhere, are

altogether unfit for Common Lodging Houses either from want of space or from not being provided with a yard and privy accommodation. If these licences be cancelled, the number of houses will be reduced to 50, with accommodation for 247 lodgers.[70]

On 24 October 1866, these licences were indeed withdrawn, and a new register drawn up of lodging houses which now numbered 51. The Public Health Act of 1866 had defined the powers of local authorities to take action against overcrowding and as early as January 1864 19 lodging houses had been inspected in Chester during the night, and four had been reported for having a greater number of lodgers than that for which they were registered.[71] After 1866, such supervision became even more stringent: in December 1867 it was reported that 'many lodging houses inspected almost nightly for the last 6 weeks—no irregularity reported, very few lodgers accommodated at present.'[72]

Clearly, the existence of two types of lodging houses and two separate registers complicates the study of lodging houses in Chester after 1866. In July 1869, the Committee reported

The Common Lodging Houses in the city would accommodate 228 people. Yet at this busy season when overcrowding might have been suspected, they are not more than half full.[73]

However, their suspicions tended to fall upon those houses registered with the Committee, with apparently little regard for either those lodging houses registered with the Sanitary Committee, or indeed, premises taking in lodgers without a licence from either authority. The confusion which must have resulted from a lack of co-ordination between these dual yet separate controls is indicated by the case of Johanna Collins of Boughton, a widow aged 80, who in 1870 was reported for having eight lodgers instead of three, but was found to have a certificate from the Sanitary Committee allowing seven lodgers. Accordingly—some three years after the legislation had been passed—it was resolved that the inspectors appointed by the rival bodies should meet 'and arrange as to registering both descriptions of Lodging Houses in future', and in March 1871, the said

Johanna Collins was removed from the common lodging house register as she held a licence under the Lodging House bye laws.[74] Further examples of discrepancies are evident in the Sanitary Committee Minutes of June and December 1868, which record the inspection of houses in Steven Street and Parry's Entry previously registered as common lodging houses,[75] and in the Common Lodging House Committee Minutes of 3 June 1868 which recorded that three houses in Steven Street (nos. 53, 20 and 41) had applied for and been refused a licence for want of space, yet two weeks later, on 17 June, the Sanitary Committee Minutes reported the inspection of no. 53, with eight lodgers, and no. 41 with six.[76] As both Committees employed the same rulings on space, it is difficult to understand the rationale behind these conflicting decisions, and one must suspect that perhaps the new restrictions, which resulted in a loss of earnings for lodging house keepers, may have prompted some keepers to be either less than honest in their applications, or to adjust their details in a re-application to the Sanitary authority, having failed to achieve registration with the Common Lodging House Committee.

Throughout the nineteenth century, contemporary concern over the state of common lodging houses focused largely on issues related to public health, particularly during periods of epidemic disease, such as 1848–49, 1866 and 1871–72. However, there were also fears that lodging houses both housed and encouraged criminal activities, and the extension of controls over such houses may have been used, and may have been effective in, rooting out criminals in order to allow more room for more decent migrant labourers.[77] Moreover, it was widely held that common lodging houses often served as brothels,[78] although there is little evidence in Chester to support this view, despite a report of December 1866 that:

> A House in Handbridge kept by Edward Clancey was recorded to be badly conducted and to be a harbour for prostitutes. Steps were taken which resulted in Clancey leaving the house—the new tenant will not be allowed to take nightly lodgers without having first obtained a lodging house licence.[79]

Certainly, increased inspection, often at night by plain-clothed policemen, appears to have ensured the relative respectability of the city's lodging houses. Even the dearth of such 'undesirable' characters as vagrants in nightly lodging houses was recorded on 6 January 1869, when a general fall in lodgers was attributed by some lodging house keepers to 'the facility with which an order for the Vagrant Ward can be obtained'.[80] Indeed, the report continued,

> There is no doubt here. Where the vagrants are hoarded together in twenties, such as at the Chester Workhouse, old 'pals' meet, civilities such as tobacco and pipes are exchanged, and when discharged in the morning, the relieved are better 'tramps', i.e. they know more of the amenities of tramp life than when they entered on the previous night.[81]

However, although the Census returns of 1871 reveal the continued decline in the number of registered lodging houses—the last recorded figure in the Committee Minutes is 40 in July 1869—anomalies exist due largely to the absence of information regarding the separate categorization of lodging houses in the city. Many houses in Steven Street were no longer nominated on the Census as lodgings, but the majority appear to have continued to take lodgers, albeit in smaller numbers, with two or three being the average. However, some households with larger numbers of lodgers do appear on a list of those inspected by the Sanitary Committee in 1868, including those of Patrick Kivell, a gardener's labourer, who lived with his wife, five children, his mother, and seven lodgers; Patrick Flanagan, pugilist and stone mason, with his wife, son and six lodgers; and Michael Walsh, agricultural labourer, with his wife, six children and five lodgers.[82] Cases such as these may well indicate a change of status and registration under the new bye-laws. The 1871 Census also reveals that in Steven Street, only two householders were now registered as lodging house keepers. Both were widows: Margaret Moran, aged 43, (at No. 20) and Catherine McAndrew, aged 50 (at No. 46). Both had two single male Irish lodgers, as well as three sons or daughters, some of whom were adults, and all of whom were Chester-born, indicating that these families were by this time established residents of the city, and that registration of their homes as lodging houses was in response to financial need. Many of the lodging house keepers continued to be widows in many different parts of the city; from

Nicholas Street, and the house of Elizabeth Ainsworth, who resided with two daughters, and five lodgers (including Frederick Barker, Minor Canon of Chester Cathedral and Curate of St Michael's Church), to Brittam's Entry (Watergate Row) and the residence of Irish-born Mary Egain, with eight sons and daughters aged between 26 and 49, and four lodgers from Chester, Ireland and Wales. Continuity between Census Returns is rare, although one example of a change in circumstances is that of Mary Tilston, who on the 1861 Census was recorded as a Lodging House Keeper, living at 4 New Crane Street, but who by 1871 had become a lodger in the household of Edward and Mary Rowland of 2 Crane Street, an address which in 1861 had been a Boarding House run by Ann Turner, a widow of 75 years, but which was no longer registered as such in 1871.[83]

Under the Public Health Act of 1872 the Council became an Urban Sanitary Authority, and on the recommendation of the Sanitary Committee, the functions of the Common Lodging House Committee were transferred to the Public Health Committee. Clearly, by this date, changes in status and registration of lodging houses, together with greater stability of both population and employment, had made the Common Lodging House Committee redundant, and improvements in sanitary conditions, together with increased housing, had lessened problems of overcrowding and the concomitant concerns over health in the lodging houses themselves.

It is not easy to assess the effectiveness of the Common Lodging House Committee in controlling and supervising lodging houses in the city, in part due to the limitations of the evidence. Apart from reports in the local newspapers, and early comments in the Minutes regarding sanitation and overcrowding, there are no actual descriptions or eye-witness accounts of the conditions which prevailed, and judging by the number of larger households in areas such as Steven Street, the definition of what constituted overcrowding must be seen as relative to the period itself. Certainly, the Council pre-empted government legislation in its attempts to regulate lodging houses in Chester before 1851, and the frequency of inspection recorded suggests a high degree of assiduousness. However, comments made by the Poor Law Guardians also suggest that problems such as overcrowding, insanitary conditions and the presence of lodgers in unregistered and dirty houses, continued throughout the period, demonstrating the difficulties of maintaining vigilance at a time of continued immigration and fluctuations in the movement of population. The decline in the number of lodging houses after 1854, and more particularly after 1866, cannot however be attributed solely to the work of the Committee, for it is possible that higher numbers of immigrants initially gave their occupation as 'Lodging House Keeper' in order to escape possible repercussions under the council's powers of removal and settlement, or opened their homes to lodgers because of temporary financial need. Similarly, the high numbers of lodgers in the 1840s and 1850s is attributable to the increased mobility of the populace, the influx of Irish immigrants, and also to the shortage of housing in the city, with many houses taking in lodgers in response to a growing demand for accommodation. Certainly after 1866 the work of the Committee was complicated by the promotion of bye-laws by the Sanitary Committee. Nevertheless, anomalies continued throughout the period, with many lodging houses accommodating persons who, judging by their professions or occupations, fell outside those categories who usually sought temporary shelter on a nightly basis, and who seem to have lodged for longer periods, albeit possibly as a temporary measure until permanent accommodation could be found, or because the nature of their profession involved fixed or short-term employment.

The examination of lodgers in Chester reveals a mixture of both family groups and married and unmarried men and women. During this period, both the presence of some married men as lodgers without their wives, and married women nominated as heads of households but without their husbands present, suggests that the search for employment took married men away from home. However, in the case of Irish lodgers one finds entire families who had come to escape the worst of the Famine, and these constituted the greatest number of lodgers in family groups living in the households of family groups, themselves Irish immigrants who had settled in the city during the pre-Famine period. It would however be an error to attribute all the ills of Chester's lodging houses to the Irish alone; at a time of greater demand for accommodation, many households throughout the city who took advantage of the opportunity to increase their income may not have been scrupulous about the type of accommodation offered, whilst insanitary and overcrowded conditions were not the peculiar preserve of lodging houses alone but pervaded the whole city.

Throughout the period the control and supervision of common lodging houses formed part of a broader local concern, if not fear, over large numbers of working-class poor taking up residence in the city, with consequent repercussions in terms of possible immorality, crime, and financial demands upon the poor-rate. Unfortunately, the absence of records of the work of the Poor Law Guardians hinders any attempt to assess the extent to which the high immigration added to the financial burdens of the city. However, incidents such as the closing of the gates to migrant workers in 1847 are perhaps indicative of the degree of concern which prevailed, for as Michael Rose has observed, a particular fear of parish union authorities in years of distress such as the late 1840s was the invasion of their area of responsibility by hordes of pauper vagrants attracted by tales of easy relief, and the 'terror of the tramp' aroused considerable fears in towns which were experiencing a large influx of ragged Irish refugees from the Great Famine.[84] By 1869, with some stability in the population, and the reduction in numbers of Irish immigrants—by 1871 the percentage of Irish in the city was down to 5.9 of the total population[85]—attention was still being given to the same concerns, and a Minute of 1869, which recorded the 'facility' with which vagrants could seek relief, noted 'some improvement is I believe, contemplated by the Board of Guardians which will have the effect, I hope, of lessening very materially the number of tramps who make the city a hailing point'.[86]

Clearly, local responses to the problems associated with common lodging houses was bound up with both financial concerns and the desire to dissuade large numbers of working-class poor from taking up residence in the city. The implementation of measures for the regulation of numbers in lodging houses may therefore be seen as particularly pertinent to cities such as Chester, whose low industrial growth and limited employment opportunities did not allow for sustainable large-scale growth in its working-class population. The concerns over health which came about as a natural consequence of increasing concentrations of working-class people, and at a time when the links between disease and poor sanitation were becoming more publicized, as Jacqueline Perry has shown in her study of public health reform in Victorian Chester,[87] was also of primary importance, and the powers of supervision and inspection afforded by the Common Lodging Houses Act of 1851 enabled the council to institute a measure of control over those sections of society who were deemed to constitute the greatest threat in social and financial terms. The willingness to implement social measures, coupled with the relatively small size of the city, enabled Chester to escape the worst of the social ills associated with common lodging houses in larger towns, some of whom lacked the administrative machinery of a chartered borough, and where the 'contagion of numbers' was less easy to control. However, just as a city such as Chester possessed its own particular and individual character, so its common lodging houses appear to have catered for a wider variety of lodgers than has hitherto been recognized, and the evidence suggests that their functions and conditions varied significantly according to residential area and economic need.

Notes

1 Raphael Samuel, 'Comers and Goers', in H. J.Dyos and M. Wolff (eds.), *The Victorian City: Images and Realities* (London, 1973), Vol.1, 127–28.

2 W. A. Armstrong, 'Mid-nineteenth century York', in P. Laslett and R. Wall (eds.), *Household and Family in Past Time* (Cambridge, 1977), 207, 214.

3 J. K. Walton, 'The North-West', in F. M. L. Thompson (ed.), *The Cambridge Social History of Britain 1750–1950, Vol.1* (Cambridge, 1990), 369.

4 Ursula R. Q. Henriques, *Before the Welfare State:Social Administration in Early Industrial Britain* (London, 1979), 14.

5 J. Burnett, *A Social History of Housing 1815–1985* (London, 1986), 62; for further details, see also J. Burnett, *A Social History of Housing 1815–*

1885 (London, 1986); John Rule, *The Labouring Classes in Early Industrial England 1750–1850* (London, 1991).

6 *The Second Report of the Commissioners of Inquiry into the State of Large Towns and Populous Districts, Parliamentary Papers* (1845).

7 M. J. Kingman, 'Chester 1801–1861' (unpublished MA Thesis, University of Leicester, 1969), 4, 21.

8 Joseph Hemingway, *History of the City of Chester, Vol.1* (1831), 421, 428.

9 M. J. Kingman, *op. cit.*, 35.

10 Kristina Jeffes, 'The Irish in Early Victorian Chester: An Outcast Community?', Chapter 3 below; see also, Colin Pooley, 'Separation or Integration?: the residential experience of the Irish in mid-Victorian Britain', in Roger Swift and Sheridan Gilley (eds.), *The Irish in Britain, 1815–1939* (London, 1989), 66.

11 *Chester Courant*, 6 Jan. 1847.

12 *Chester Chronicle*, Aug. 1851.

13 Michael Anderson, 'The social implications of demographic change', in F. M. L. Thompson (ed.), *The Cambridge Social History of Britain 1750–1950* (Cambridge, 1990), Vol. 2, 64.

14 Roger Swift, 'Crime and the Irish in nineteenth-century Britain', in Swift and Gilley, *op. cit.*, 168.

15 M. J. Kingman, *op. cit.*, 83.

16 J. Burnett, *op. cit.*, 62–63.

17 Chester City Record Office [thereafter CRO], *Census*, 1841, City of Chester.

18 *Ibid.*

19 M. J. Kingman, *op. cit.*, 87.

20 D. Fraser (ed.), *The New Poor Law in the Nineteenth Century* (London, 1976), 2.

21 M. D. Handley, *Local Administration of the Poor Law in Great Boughton and Wirral Union, and the Chester Local Act Incorporation 1834–71*, (unpublished MA Thesis, University of Wales, 1969), quoted in Michael E. Rose, 'Settlement, Removal and the New Poor Law', in D. Fraser (ed.), *op. cit.*

22 *Ibid.*

23 CRO, Assembly Book, AB/6, 20 Oct. 1830.

24 *Ibid.*, 12 Jan. 1836.

25 CRO, Improvement Committee Minutes 1846–51, CCB/47, 6 Sept.1847.

26 CRO, Special Committee Minute Book, CCB/34, 19 March 1849.

27 *Chester Courant*, 6 Jan. 1847.

28 *Ibid.*, 14 July 1847.

29 *Ibid.*

30 Special Committee Minute Book, CCB/34, 12 March 1849.

31 CRO, Assembly Book, AB/6, 19 March 1849.

32 *Ibid.*, 9 March 1849.

33 CCB/34 13 April 1849.

34 CCB/34 10 May 1849.

35 CCB/34, 21 May 1849.

36 AB/6, 10 Aug. 1849.

37 *Chester Chronicle*, 17 May 1851.

38 CRO, Common Lodging Houses Committee Book, CCB/35, 11 Nov. 1851.

39 *Ibid.*, 23 Nov. 1854.

40 *Census* 1851, City of Chester.

41 *Ibid.*

42 CCB/35, 23 Nov. 1854.

43 *Ibid.*

44 Gail Malmgreen, *Silk Town: Industrialization and Culture in Macclesfield 1750–1835* (Hull, 1985), cited in J. Belchem, *Industrialization and the Working Class: The English Experience 1750–1900* (London, 1991), 39.

45 Enid Gauldie, *Cruel Habitations: A History of Working-Class Housing 1780–1918* (London, 1974), 84.

46 CCB/35, 7 March 1859.

47 *Ibid.*, 3 Oct. 1866.

48 Enid Gauldie, *op. cit.*, 246.

49 *Census* 1851, City of Chester.

50 *Ibid.*, 1861, City of Chester.

51 CCB/35, 26 Feb. 1855.

52 *Ibid.*, 9 Nov. 1860.

53 *Ibid.*, 3 Feb. 1864.

54 Enid Gauldie, *op. cit.*, 242.

55 CCB/35.

56 *Census*, 1861, City of Chester.

57 CCB/35, 6, 20 and 27 Feb. 1861.

58 *Ibid.*, 8 July 1859.

59 *Ibid.*, 6 Feb.1861.

60 *Census* 1861, City of Chester.

61 CCB/35, 20 Nov. 1861.

62 *Ibid.*

63 *Ibid.*, 2 April 1862.

64 *Ibid.*, 2 July 1862.

65 *Ibid.*, 3 May 1864.

66 *Ibid.*, Letter from Clerk to the Board of Guardians of 28 Jan.1864, in minute of 3 Feb. 1864.

67 Minutes of Sanitary Committee 3 Oct. 1866, in *The Chester Record*, 13 Oct. 1866.

68 CCB/35, 3 Oct. 1866.

69 *Ibid.*

70 *Ibid.*

71 *Ibid.*, 24 Oct. 1866.

72 *Ibid.*, 4 Dec. 1867.

73 *Ibid.*, 7 July 1869.

74 *Ibid*, 7 Sept. 1870.

75 Sanitary Committee Minutes, CCB/76, 17 June 1868 and 2 Dec. 1868.

76 CCB/35, 3 June 1868; CCB/76, 17 June 1868.

77 Enid Gauldie, *op. cit.*, 245.

78 Ursula Henriques, *op. cit.*, 120.

80 CCB/35, 6 Jan. 1869.

81 *Ibid.*; according to the 1871 Census, the numbers of paupers recorded at Chester Workhouse in April 1871 were 323, of whom 200 were men and 123 women. These figures are largely inconclusive in attempting to determine the number of vagrants or nightly residents.

82 CCB/76, 17 June 1868.

83 *Census* 1871, City of Chester.

84 Michael Rose, *op. cit.*, 31.

85 Colin Pooley, *op. cit.*, 67.

86 CCB/35, 6 Jan 1869.

87 Jacqueline Perry, 'Cholera and Public Health Reform in Early Victorian Chester', Chapter 4 below.

3

The Irish in
Early Victorian Chester:
An Outcast Community?

Kristina Jeffes

The past decade has witnessed the emergence of a considerable body
of research devoted to the study of the experiences of Irish immigrants in nineteenth-century Britain, and many of these studies have
focused on Irish settlement in large industrial towns and cities.[1]
Although Chester differed greatly from the types of city commonly
associated with Irish settlement during the period, there had long
been an Irish presence in the city and its immediate environs. Due to
the county's strategic position, some of the well-defined migrant
routes ran through Cheshire and it is likely that these circuits, which
went through Lancashire to North Wales, passed through the city of
Chester. The men and women who traversed the country, often
following the trail of hay and corn harvests, traditionally included
many migrant Irish workers.[2] They also included Irish vagrants: in
1785, a local magistrate's report on vagrancy showed that 4,686 Irish
vagrants had been conveyed through the county of Chester during the
previous three years.[3] The *Report on the State of the Irish Poor* of 1836
confirms that Irish migrant labour was used in the surrounding
neighbourhood and in less populous districts of the county.[4] There is
also evidence to suggest that immigration from Ireland into Chester
increased significantly in the early part of the nineteenth century.
Catholic baptism registers indicate that there was a steady growth in
the numbers of Catholics within the city in the period from 1794 to
1883, with the years between 1814 and 1823 showing the biggest

percentage increase.[5] In 1841 there were over 1,013 Irish-born recorded on the census returns for the city of Chester, which represented 4.4% of the total population. By 1851 this figure had doubled to 2,032, or 7.3% of the whole population.[6] Therefore, although the impact of the Great Famine of 1845–52 brought considerable numbers of Irish to Chester, Irish migration to the city was a continuous process during the early nineteenth century, involving both push and pull factors and not simply the push factor of the Famine.[7]

Central to the debate over the extent to which the Irish in Victorian Britain were outcast and alienated from the host population, is the question of ghettoization. Studies of the Irish presence in Bradford, Leeds, Manchester and Stockport, have suggested that during the early and mid-Victorian periods the Irish were located in socially immobile and unintegrated ghettos in which they were isolated in particular streets and courts from the surrounding hostile population.[8] The traditional Irish ghetto, of which Manchester's Little Ireland was the most notorious, also displayed the worst living conditions which the Victorian slum could offer.[9] This essay explores the extent to which the concept of Irish ghettoization may be applied to the Irish-born population of Chester, with particular reference to the themes of residential segregation, occupational and social mobility, poverty and communal violence.

A study of the census returns for Chester in the pre-Famine year of 1841, when the census schedules first recorded the birthplace of the inhabitants, and in 1851, when the Famine had almost abated, provide a useful means for examining the extent to which the Irish in Chester conformed to the traditional picture of the ghettoized, socially immobile, unintegrated and alienated immigrant community. Roy Wilding has shown that the Irish-born were distributed in relatively small numbers in most Chester parishes in 1841 and 1851, but with an inordinate concentration in both census years in the parish of St John the Baptist.[10] In this context, a closer study of this parish is particularly valuable, for St John's was noted during the period for its growing population, the development of working-class housing, the presence of a few industrial concerns and the desertion of the area by the gentry. Moreover, the parish contained the district

Table 3.1: The location of the Irish population in St John's Parish in 1841

Street	No.of Irish born	Irish born (of total no. of Irish born in St John's)	Irish born (of total no. of Irish born in Chester)	No. in Irish community
Steven Street	240	50.9	23.7	327
Boughton	84	17.8	8.3	121
Foregate Street	20	4.2	2.0	39
Steam Mill Street	16	3.4	1.6	25
Seaville Street	15	3.1	1.5	16
Parry's Court	10	2.1	1.0	16
Others with less than 10 Irish-born	86	18.3	8.5	171
Total	471	100	46.6	715

Source: Census Enumerators' Book, Parish of St John the Baptist, 1841.

of Boughton, where an 'Irish Quarter' had been established prior to the 1840s.

The 1841 census confirms that there was a high concentration of Irish people living in Boughton,[11] for out of the 1,013 Irish-born recorded as living in the Chester, 471 lived in St John's parish (46.5% of the total Irish-born population).[12] Much more significant is the concentration of Irish-born living within one particular street, as Table 3.1 illustrates: in 1841, 240 Irish were found to be residing in Steven Street, 56.9% of the parish's Irish-born population and almost a quarter of the city's Irish population. Moreover, if the definition of an 'Irish community' is extended to include not only the Irish-born but also the non-Irish-born spouses and children of those born in Ireland, then Steven Street appears to be even more 'Irish', as this then raises the figure to 327. It could be argued, therefore, that out of the 422 inhabitants in Steven Street, 77.5% belonged to what might be defined as 'the Irish community'. There were also 84 Irish-born residing on the main road of Boughton, although all other streets within the parish housed less than 20 Irish-born. In short, these two

Table 3.2: The location of the Irish population in St John's Parish in 1851

Street	No. of Irish born	Irish born (of total no. of Irish born in St John's)	Irish born (of total no. of Irish born in Chester)	No. in Irish community
Steven Street	546	50.6	26.9	687
Boughton	162	15.0	8.0	238
Canal Side	84	7.8	4.1	98
Parry's Court	60	5.6	2.9	80
Kay's Court	39	3.6	1.9	52
Steam Mill Street	33	3.1	1.6	40
Union Walk	17	1.6	0.8	21
Brook Street	16	1.5	0.7	23
Thomas Buildings	14	1.3	0.7	26
Seaville Street	13	1.2	0.6	12
Machine Bank	12	1.1	0.6	12
Others	81	7.5	4.0	144
Total	1077	100	52.8	1445

Source: Census, Parish of St John the Baptist, 1851.

streets alone were inhabited by 68.7% of the Irish-born in St John's, which represented almost a third of Chester's Irish population. By 1851, a similar census 'snapshot' reveals that not only had the number of Irish located within the parish increased, but also that there was a greater concentration in the street where the Irish had been found a decade earlier, as Table 3.2 illustrates.

In 1851, 1,077 (or 53%) of Chester's 2,032 Irish lived in the parish of St John. Of these, 546 lived in Steven Street (50.6% of the Irish-born population of the parish or 26.9% of the total number of Irish-born in the city). This street now had 740 inhabitants, an increase of 43% from 1841, which was accompanied by a rise in the level of overcrowding. Moreover, the composition of Steven Street became even more 'Irish' with the Irish making up 73.8% of the street's inhabitants, and all but ten of the 110 households were Irish.[13] If the broader definition of an 'Irish community' is again employed, then

Table 3.3: Top 10 Occupations of Irishmen in St John's Parish : 1841

	No.	*%*
Labourer	110	60.4*
Agricultural Labourer	10	5.5*
Shoemaker Journeyman	7	3.8
Hawker (various)	7	3.8
Gardener	6	3.3
Tailor	5	2.7
Pensioner (Army)	4	2.2
Basket Maker	2	1.1
Policeman	2	1.1
Teacher	2	1.1
Miller	2	1.1
Painter Journeyman	2	1.1
Other occupations	23	12.6
Total	182	100

*NB: The distinction between 1 and 2 was not systematically applied.

92.8% of the inhabitants of Steven Street were Irish. The census also shows that there was an increase in the number of Irish in other streets in this locality. In Steven Street, Boughton and Canal Side, there were almost three-quarters of the parish's total Irish-born population, which represented 39% of the city's Irish population. Therefore, in 1851, St John's Parish was 12.7% Irish (or 17% if the term 'Irish community' is used) in a city where the Irish-born were only 7.3% of the total population.

In occupational terms, both the 1841 and 1851 censuses suggest that the Irish within St John's parish were predominantly unskilled and overwhelmingly employed as labourers, although there is some difficulty in comparing census data from these two years, as in 1841 the type of labourer is rarely specified, whereas in 1851 distinctions are made.[14] Nevertheless, as Table 3.3 illustrates, the Irish-born males living in St John's Parish in 1841 were employed in 31 different occupations, although of 182 employed men, no fewer than 120 were

Table 3.4: Top 10 Occupations of Irishmen in St John's Parish : 1851

	No.	%
Agricultural Labourer	141	29.9 ⎫ 57.5
Farm Labourer	130	27.6 ⎭
Hawker (various)	27	5.7
Bricklayers Labourer	16	3.4
Shoemaker/Master	14	3.0
Railway Labourer	12	2.5
Labourer	10	2.1
Leadworks Labourer	9	1.9
Gardener's Labourer	7	1.5
Lodging House Keeper	5	1.1
General Labourer	5	1.1
Chelsea Pensioner	5	1.1
Other Occupations	90	19.1
Total	471	100

Sources : Census, Parish of St John the Baptist, 1841 and 1851.

entered as labourers (65.9% of the whole), and of these, 74 lived in Steven Street and represented 83.1% of those all male occupations specified for the Irish in this street. By 1851 the number of Irish labourers in St John's had increased in relation to the 1841 figure, as Table 3.4 shows. In this year, 348 out of the 471 Irishmen who specified an occupation were labourers (73%), of whom 216 lived in Steven Street. Therefore out of all the Irish males in this street, 85.4% were employed as labourers. Moreover, by using Armstrong's social status classification,[15] as Table 3.5 illustrates, 92.2% of the male occupations given for Steven Street in 1841 fell into Classes IV and V, whilst in 1851, as Table 3.6 indicates, 92.9% of all males living in Steven Street were found in classes IV and V .

The differentiation made between different types of labourers in the census year of 1851 provides a better indication of the type of work the Irish found in a city such as Chester. The census returns reveal that 278 of the labourers in the parish were agricultural, farm

Table 3.5: Occupational Status of the Irish-born males in St John's Parish

Class	1841		1851	
	No.	%	No.	%
I	2	1.1	4	0.8
II	13	7.1	35	7.3
III	30	16.5	45	9.4
IV	19*	10.4*	285	59.8
V	118*	64.8*	108	22.6

*N.B.—problems in classifying labouring Irish, as type not specified in 1841. In this case, labourers have been placed in class V cf. 1851 where agricultural labourers etc. are in IV
Source: Census, Parish of St John the Baptist, 1841 and 1851.

or gardener's labourers, that is 58.3% of all those males employed in St John's parish. It is therefore quite probable that a majority of the Irish labourers in 1841 also worked on the land. It is of course possible that a number of those listed in the census may not have been currently employed in the occupation they specified and that the large numbers of agricultural labourers is an indication of the occupation which Irish immigrants had held in Ireland. This would account for some proportion of the 'agricultural labourers', especially as a large number of lodgers, who may have been recent arrivals, specified this as their occupation. Yet taking into consideration the absence of employment opportunities in the industrial sector in Chester, and the predominance of skilled crafts and trade opportunities within the city, it would not be surprising if significant numbers of Irish did in fact find employment in agriculture, most notably in the considerable market gardening industries in Sealand, Saltney and Handbridge. It is also likely that there would have been agricultural work available in the countryside around the city, for despite urban expansion beyond the city walls, at the outer limits of which Steven Street was located, Chester's hinterland was still essentially rural. Moreover, it was not unusual for the Irish to tramp out of the cities in which they resided to find work, the settlement laws encouraging landlords to allow workers to reside on their land: this was certainly the case in York,

Table 3.6: Occupational Status of the Irish-born population in St John's Parish, contrasting Steven Street with the remainder of the parish

1841	Steven Street		St John's Parish	
Class	No. of Irish	%	No. of Irish	%
I	0	0	2	2.2
II	1	1.1	12	12.9
III	6	6.7	24	25.8
IV	2	2.3	17	18.9
V	80	89.9	38	40.9
	89	100	93	100
1851				
Class	No. of Irish	%	No. of Irish	%
I	0	0	4	1.8
II	6	2.4	29	13.0
III	12	4.7	33	14.7
IV	188	74.3	97	43.3
V	47	18.6	61	27.2
	253		224	

(Based on Armstrong's Occupational Status classification)
Source : Census, Parish of St John the Baptist, 1841 and 1851

where gangs of Irish agricultural labourers tramped out the city for up to ten miles to work in the outlying chicory fields.[16] This may well have been the case in Chester, for the northern counties, especially those near the rapidly-expanding industrial conurbations, offered a high level of wages for agricultural labouring.[17] The small numbers employed in industrial occupations, indicates that there were few opportunities available for large numbers of Irish in this sector, despite the fact that the Leadworks, the Steam Mill, the Iron Foundry and the railway terminal were found within the parish. Some

Irish did find employment in these areas, and in 1851 there were 12 railway labourers and nine leadworkers listed among the Irish-born: indeed, the Irish made up 11.4% of the labourers employed at the leadworks. Nevertheless, the opportunities in Chester for this kind of work were so limited that it is likely that a majority of the Irish of St John's parish, who were overwhelmingly unskilled, found employment on the land.

A further aspect of the traditional 'Irish ghetto' stereotype concerns the poverty and slum conditions experienced by its inhabitants. Contemporary reports in the *Chester Chronicle* suggest that there was a great deal of suffering among the Chester Irish, and particularly those in Steven Street, during the Famine period, revealing widespread concern about the effect of the immigrants on the physical and moral condition of the host population and the effect on the poor rates.[18] In January 1847, at the height of the famine influx, the *Chronicle* expressed concern at the level of immigration into the city, observing that a 'great deal of distress' prevailed, with 'more suffering amongst the lower orders than is generally imagined'.[19] This article specifically drew attention to the neighbourhood of Boughton, 'chiefly inhabited by the Irish', where a statistical enquiry carried out by Father Carbery, the local Catholic priest, had revealed that many of the Irish were in great distress, including 129 out of 469 in Steven Street, 67 out of 151 in Boughton, 49 out of 71 in Steam Mill Street, and 65 on Canal Side.[20] In February it was reported that over 300 destitute Irish had been relieved with soup, coal and money at the hands of Father Carbery and his Charity,[21] the *Chronicle* noting that these 'unfortunate and starving creatures were huddled up in large numbers in very confined and filthy dwellings'.[22] Indeed, the overcrowded and insanitary conditions of the so-called 'miserable Irish quarter' were frequently brought to public attention by the *Chronicle* during a period when, as Jacqueline Perry has shown, the city authorities were becoming increasingly concerned with public health issues.[23] The increased overcrowding in the two-bedroomed back-to-back houses in Steven Street is confirmed by the fact that the number of inhabitants rose from 422 to 740 between 1841 and 1851.[24] However, as Mary Glazier has illustrated, it was in some of the lodging houses of Boughton, those 'hot beds of fever, pestilence and poverty', where conditions were perceived to be most desperate,[25] and in April 1851 the *Chronicle* described these dwellings as 'filthy, ill-furnished, imperfectly ventilated and often overcrowded'.[26] The newspaper also claimed that these lodging houses 'exhibit almost nightly a promiscuous intermixture of the sexes, repugnant to common decency', and described the lodging house keepers as 'utterly indifferent to those ordinary, domestic arrangements which the most indigent of the well-conducted poor generally observe'.[27] Moreover, the insanitary conditions in this neighbourhood were attributed to the 'carelessness, ignorance and superstition' of the local Irish population and were perceived as an unnecessary burden for the city's 'industrious classes', so much so that in March 1851 the *Chronicle* called for the Irish 'nuisance' to be promptly dealt with:

> We believe that the parochial authorities are willing to enforce the law and are prepared to put the Irish Removal Act into force . . . A very little rigour will have a good effect, and when this class finds that Chester will not be suffered to be subject to their maraudings, they will remove themselves.[28]

The *Chronicle* also condemned the habit of killing dying and diseased calves and preparing them for food in the 'filthy hovels of Steven Street', a practice which was 'highly dangerous to the health of its inhabitants',[29] whilst reported cases of smallpox and cholera gave the impression that disease was rife in the area and there were demands that:

> the state of Boughton and its purlieus should be rigidly investigated in a sanitary point of view and that if existing measures prove insufficient, the Corporation should pass by-laws to invest the officers with sufficient powers to mitigate the nuisance which is increasing in its intensity . . . filling our gaols with criminals, our hospitals with disease, our poor houses with destitution and in addition permeating the public health by a constant importation of squalid misery and infectious distemper.[30]

Not surprisingly, the *Chronicle* welcomed the passing of the Common Lodging- Houses Act in 1851 on the grounds that 'no scrutiny can be too rigid to prevent thoughtless or greedy persons (lodging house keepers) from trafficking with the health and lives of the wretched occupants'.[31]

Thus a preliminary examination of the residential distribution, occupational structure and social condition of the Irish population of St John's parish would appear to suggest that the experience of the Irish in this district conforms to at least three points on which most studies of the Irish in British towns are unanimous : large numbers of Irish were found concentrated in particular courts, streets and districts of Victorian cities, these streets were witness to some of the worst living conditions the city could offer, and the Irish were found predominantly in low-skilled, low-status, employment. Yet looked at from another perspective, the picture does not seem to be quite so clearly drawn. It has been suggested that the levels of residential and occupational segregation within Irish communities are open to subjective influences. Depending on the point of view adopted by the researcher, evidence can be interpreted as revealing either highly differentiated social groups or showing a considerable amount of intermixing between them, leading Colin Pooley to conclude that studies 'which seek to fit Irish migrants into a 'ghetto' model of residential segregation will usually succeed in doing so'.[32] Of course, this does not mean that all, or even a majority of migrants lived in the 'ghettos', and despite the very high concentration of Irish within Steven Street and its surrounding streets and courts, it is important to note the even at the peak of the overcrowding in this 'Irish quarter' in 1851, 73.1% of Chester's Irish-born population did not live in Steven Street and over half the city's Irish population did not live in St John's Parish.[33] Yet it is not surprising that a study of St John's parish (the area with the very high levels of Irish within particular streets) should emphasize segregation and spatial clustering, for this district was one which featured a high density of working-class housing, and was also the largest parish within Chester and thus more likely to contain a significant proportion of the low-skilled Irish population within its boundaries. Although it is impossible, without further research, to draw any conclusions on the spatial distribution of the Irish in the city as a whole, it is possible that there were other streets which contained clusters of Irish people, although not to the extent of Steven Street and its adjacent courts. This said, the value of using the concept of the 'Irish community' beyond St John's parish, where smaller numbers of Irish were located, seems highly dubious. In a street such as Steven Street, the term is perhaps helpful to draw attention to those children or spouses of the Irish-born who were themselves born outside Ireland. Yet it would undoubtedly be unhelpful to label the children of Irish parents living in a street with no other (or even several other) Irish households, as belonging to an 'Irish community', in the same way as those in Steven Street. For example, it would be difficult to regard the family of Bridget Molloy, of Sidney Place, as belonging to an 'Irish community': although she had been born in Ireland, her children (aged between 3 and 10) were born in Chester, and although her household included two Irish-born 'visitors', this was the only household in Sidney Place with any Irish-born inhabitants.[34] If it is assumed that the inhabitants in Steven Street had less contact with the host society, then those living in streets with fewer Irish would have undoubtedly had more occasion to mix with the non-Irish.

Moreover, if the Irish population in St John's Parish, excluding Steven Street, is compared with the Irish population inside Steven Street then differences between the two groups, besides the levels of residential concentration are apparent. The Irish population within the rest of St John's parish was more skilled than in Steven Street. Again, as Table 3.6 illustrates, 40.3% of the Irish-born population in 1841 were in categories I and II and III, whereas in Steven Street in the same year only 7.8% were in these three categories. Yet in 1851, although the contrast was not quite as sharp, 29.5% of the Irish population were classified in the top three categories, whereas for Steven Street, the figure was only 7.1%. Not surprisingly, there seems to be a correlation between those Irish living in streets with low numbers of Irish and those with a higher occupational status and, despite the fact that nearly three-quarters of those Irish outside Steven Street were in the lowest two occupational classes, it is possible that they would not have shared a common sense of identity with those inside this enclave, especially the skilled and professional classes

Local middle-class concern over Irish immigration was perhaps understandable in the context of contemporary issues such as urban squalor, disease, disorder, vagrancy and unemployment, which at the time of the famine influx were arousing growing public concern. Despite the fact that the *Chronicle* gave the impression that the conditions in Steven Street were the worst in the city, which is understandable in terms of the numbers of famine Irish located there, the whole Boughton district, including those areas that were visibly Irish, was viewed with concern. In October 1851 the *Chronicle* was obliged to clear up a controversy over the definition of the term 'Boughtonians'. The paper made it clear that the terms had been used not to describe the gentry of Boughton, but the 'poachers, vagrants and idle persons who infest that neighbourhood and who are a pest to the whole community'.[35] Indeed, the district had a bad reputation and was viewed with suspicion and hostility even before the famine influx, although Irish immigration undoubtedly magnified and exacerbated the social problems, notably in regard to overcrowding. The hostility towards the Irish from the authorities was directed essentially at the poorest Irish, not the 'industrious Irish' who worked and lived alongside the host population. Hence a distinction can be made between the Famine Irish and the longer-established Irish population, indicating a distinction between those living within the area of high concentration of Irish and those living outside these particular streets.

From the census information it is possible to confirm that those Irish who lived outside Steven Street within St John's parish were indeed longer established within the city, another indication that those Irish outside Steven Street did not share a common identity or sense of community with those within it. In 1851, 77% of children born to Irish parents residing in Steven Street were born in Ireland whereas in St John's (excluding Steven Street) 52% of the children of the Irish were born in Chester (Table 3.7). Of the households in Steven Street in 1851 according to the ages of the eldest child born in Chester, 74% of families had been in the city less than 10 years, whereas in the rest of St John's 42% of the families had been there longer than 10 years. (See Table 3.8). It is also the case that few children born to Irish parents residing in St John's parish were born in places other than Chester or Ireland.

These findings indicate the possibility of two different patterns.

Table 3.7: Birthplace of children born to Irish parents residing in the Parish of St John the Baptist in 1851

| | St John's Parish excluding Steven Street | | Steven Street | | St John's Parish | |
	No.	%	No	%	No.	%
Born in Ireland	145	42.0	472	77.1	617	64.5
Born in Chester	180	52.2	131	21.4	311	32.5
Born elsewhere	20	5.8	9	1.5	29	3.0
	345		612		957	

Source: Census Enumerators' Returns, Parish of St John the Baptist, 1851.

Table 3.8: Ages of the eldest child of Irish-born parents born in Chester and living in St John's Parish

| Age | 1841 % of total no. of eldest children born in each age group | | 1851 % of total no. of eldest children born in each age group | |
	Steven St	St John's (excluding Steven St)	Steven St	St John's (excluding Steven St)
0–4	46.5	38.3	48.0	31.6
5–9	28.0	29.8	26.0	26.6
10–14	16.3	12.8	15.0	21.5
15–19	9.3	8.5	5.5	14.0
20–24	0	8.5	2.7	3.8
25–29	0	2.1	1.4	0
30–34	0	0	1.4	2.5

Source: Census, Parish of St John the Baptist, 1841 and 1851.

Firstly, it seems likely that Chester was a first port of call for the Irish, due to the low number of children born elsewhere and the fact that there were so many very new arrivals, e.g. in 1851, 39.5% of the children born to Irish parents in St John's were under 5 years old. In Steven Street, the area of first reception, 48% of the children were under 5. It may be that many of these new arrivals would move on to other place in Britain at a later date. This would perhaps be especially true for the high numbers of single male lodgers in Steven Street (97 in 1851), who would be more likely to leave Chester in search of employment. Secondly, it is also possible that there was a pattern of dispersal of the Irish from Steven Street into other streets within the parish of St John's and perhaps other areas of the city. Thernstrom's study of migration to and from the slums of Boston has suggested that it was the ghetto rather than its inhabitants that was permanent, whilst Frances Finnegan has concluded that there was a large turnover of the inhabitants within the Irish districts of mid-Victorian York.[36] This may well have been the case in Chester, for Ruth McNally's study of Irish settlement in St John's during the mid-Victorian period suggests that by 1871, when there were 1,885 Irish-born living within the parish, the Irish-born population of Steven Street, the area of first reception, had declined to 436 persons, or only 23% of the Irish-born population of St John's.[37] This pattern of dispersal suggests both residential and social mobility, as those outside Steven Street were on the whole more likely to be employed in a better status occupation, were more likely to enjoy better living conditions and were more likely to have neighbours of higher social status. They would also be more likely to mix with members of the host population in comparison with those in Steven Street.

A further indication that those outside Steven Street were more integrated into the host society, is the higher level of marriage between the Irish and the non-Irish in St John's parish, excluding Steven Street (see Table 3.9). Although the total percentage of mixed marriages decreased between 1841 and 1851, it is significant that in 1851, 26.7% of all marriages outside Steven Street were mixed unions, whereas out of the total number of marriages in Steven Street the figure was only 5.1%. Again this can be seen as a reflection of a higher level of association between the Irish and the host population

Table 3.9: Marital status of the Irish in St John's Parish, 1841–51

1841	Steven St		St John's excluding Steven St		Total of St John's Parish	
	No.	%	No.	%	No.	%
*Irish-born married to Irish-born	43	91.5	41	64.0	84	75.7
*Irish-born male married to non-Irish-born female	3	6.4	9	14.1	12	10.8
*Irish-born female married to non-Irish -born male	1	2.1	14	21.9	15	13.5
	47		64		111	

1841	Steven St		St John's excluding Steven St		Total of St John's Parish	
	No.	%	No.	%	No.	%
Irish-born married to Irish-born	93	94.9	88	73.3	181	83.0
Irish-born male married to non-Irish-born female	3	3.1	20	16.6	23	10.6
Irish-born female married to non-Irish-born male	2	2.0	12	10.0	14	6.4
	98		120		218	

*N.B. For 1841 this is an assumed relationship.
Source : Census, Parish of St John the Baptist, 1841 and 1851.

outside of the Steven Street area of large numbers of Irish, and also a reflection of the fact that the St John's Irish population was longer established than in Steven Street.

Thus the analysis of census data indicates a certain fluidity of the residential situation. This was not a static population. This highlights the fundamental problem with the concept of ghettoization. If the inhabitants of the ghetto were largely new arrivals or were frequently on the move, then this questions the extent to which they developed the degree of communal identity associated with the process of ghettoization, for the traditional view suggests that it is the inner cohesion of the 'ghetto' community that enables it to stand apart, hermetically sealed, in face of hostility and alienation from outside.

Yet Steven Street did possess some features of the traditional ghetto. It had an exceptionally high proportion of Irish within its boundaries, which without referring to the ethnicity of its occupants is very difficult to explain fully. It is probable that there would have been well developed patterns of chain migration in operation. The occupants of Steven Street also conformed to the aspect of ghettoization, relating to the predominantly low-skilled nature of the population, although the fact that the Irish in Chester were overwhelmingly agricultural labourers rather than industrial labourers, reflects the economic structure in Chester and in this way differs from the traditional picture (e.g. in contrast to 'Little Ireland' in Manchester). It was also the case that, especially with the famine influx, there was extreme poverty and appalling living conditions amongst the Irish in this area, even if it was not on such a wide scale as in the big cities. Therefore Steven Street was quite distinctive, and was made so visible by the concentration of the Irish within it. It is not so surprising that great attention was paid to the area in the *Chester Chronicle* and by the authorities.

Yet it is questionable whether this area can indeed be called an Irish ghetto, even if it was popularly regarded as such. Despite the high numbers within it, Steven Street was the only street with such a concentration of numbers, and although there were other streets with large numbers of Irish, they were not all adjacent to Steven Street, e.g. Seaville Street which was parallel to it only had 13 Irish born within it in 1851 (see Table 2). Moreover, movement out of Steven Street would have often resulted in a different experience of Irish life within Chester as the Irish in the rest of the parish were more residentially scattered, more skilled, less poor, more established within the city, and more integrated with the host population. Hence the concept of ghettoization is not applicable to describe the Irish experience in Chester as this experience was much wider than just that on the Steven Street area.

Nevertheless, there were other factors which contrived to set the Irish apart from the host society. These included the popular belief that the Irish constituted a threat to law and order: as Thomas Carlyle observed in 1839, the Irishman, 'in his squalor, and unreason, in his falsity and drunken violence' emerged as 'the ready-made nucleus of degradation and disorder'.[38] Indeed, besides the inextricable link in Victorian society between vagrancy and crime which clearly placed the Irish among the numbers of the dangerous classes, the Irish were also perceived to have certain intrinsic characteristics which were consistently highlighted and reinforced by the provincial press.[39] Therefore, the Irish were seen as having a propensity for drunkenness, violence, brutality and criminal behaviour, which to the respectable classes was further evidence to show that the Irishman was, as Engels suggested 'placed little above the savage' and that his emigration to Britain was an example of a 'less-civilized population spreading themselves as a kind of substratum, beneath a more civilized community'.[40]

One way of testing this assertion in a local context is by examining the extent to which the Irish population was presented by the *Chester Chronicle* as a lawless minority during the critical years of the 1840s.[41] Indeed, there is some evidence to suggest that the *Chronicle* portrayed the Irish population as posing a great problem to the municipal authorities, not only through their perceived impact on health and sanitation, but also through their reputation for violent and drunken behaviour, which headings such as the 'Irish Nuisance' and 'Another Irish Row in Steven Street', and comments to the effect that 'the miserable Irish quarter of Boughton is infested with poachers, vagrants and idle persons . . . who are a pest to the whole community' indicate.[42] Moreover, during the famine year of 1847, when British public opinion was becoming increasingly concerned with the influx of Irish immigrants, the *Chronicle* focused greater attention on Irish criminality, notably in regard to begging, theft and drunken and disorderly behaviour, the latter of which on occasions turned into those ubiquitous 'Irish rows' which received great attention from the Victorian press.[43]

Begging was inextricably linked to the image of poverty and degradation associated the famine emigrants. As early as February 1847, there were calls by the *Chronicle* for this mendicancy to be put down strongly by the police in order to clear Irish beggars from the streets. Such reports often clearly labelled the offenders as Irish, and even when they did not, the names and the locations specified, such as 'Steven Street' made readers perfectly aware that these were Irish offenders. For example, under the heading 'The Irish Nuisance', a fourteen year old 'Irish lad' was reported as having been sentenced to ten days hard labour for begging and it was stated that he 'has been a complete worry to the town and had proved utterly regardless of caution or threats since he came over from Ireland'.[44] One week later the *Chronicle* reported that an Irish lodging house keeper from Boughton had received fourteen days' imprisonment for begging at a doctor's house in Abbey Square (a respectable area in the north of the city), adding that his lodging house was the 'filthiest den of the dirty Irish quarter'.[45] The same edition of the newspaper also carried an article entitled 'An Irish Solicitor' which treated another Irish beggar, Patrick McGuire, as a figure for ridicule. McGuire was described as an 'Irish dwarf, humped-backed like Quasimodo in the *Hunchback of Notre Dame*' who, when charged with begging from door to door, interrupted the policeman with, 'You're a liar, I was thinking of begging but I had not begun'. Accordingly, 'amid a torrent of abuse', McGuire was hurried off to imprisonment for fourteen days as a rogue and a vagabond.[46] This kind of reporting is reminiscent of the humour used in the traditional Irish, or rather anti-Irish, joke. A similarly 'amusing' anecdote published in the *Chronicle* under the title 'Sad but True' also reinforced the stereotypical view of the Irish as both dishonest and also rather lacking in intelligence, for it ran as follows : 'Mr Baron Platt, at the Westmoreland Assizes in a colloquy with an Irish priest asked "Why did you not stay in your own country and rob there?". Mr Serjeant Murphy, with ready wit answered for his countrymen "Because my lord, there's nothing to steal there" '.[47] This tale can be seen in a darker light since it highlights ironically the propensity to steal as a common trait amongst Irishmen, and is made no less menacing by the stupidity of the self-confession. Nevertheless, such reports support Sheridan Gilley's claim that there was a more benign and comical side to the Irish stereotype, despite the seriousness of the points being expressed.[48] In contrast, a more violent, menacing and yet somehow more childish side to the Irish character was reflected in a report of an 'Impudent Vagabond' who was refused a loaf of bread by a Baker, due to his 'well-dressed' and 'plump and hearty appearance'. As a result, this vagabond threatened the shop keeper, put his fist through the shop window and lay on the pavement in front of the shop until the police came. For this disturbance the Irishman was fined £5 but as he did not comply, he was sent to gaol for seven days, perhaps indicating that his appearance was deceptive as a measure of his true circumstances.[49]

Apart from instances of begging and petty theft, most of the Irish offences reported in the *Chronicle* comprised assaults and disorderly behaviour. Most of these incidents were reported in such a way as to suggest that they were not infrequent. An assault by an Irish boy on his father was headed 'Morals and Manners of Steven Street'.[50] The 'Disgraceful Assault' by Joseph Kelly on a neighbour in Boughton entailed the inference by Mrs. Kelly that the complainant 'was in the habit of sleeping under a hedge with an old Irishman', whilst Mr Kelly was accused of throwing clods of earth and attempting to assault the complainant.[51] Such reports revealed the petty, squabbling character of the Irish neighbourhood and of those living within it, indicating the lack of social order and ability to peacefully interact at the most basic level. This same petty element was also evident in the reports of 'Irish rows', although in these cases the violent and aggressive nature of the Irish was presented in a more alarming light. Indeed, like other provincial newspapers of the period, the *Chester Chronicle* portrayed the 'Irish row' as a common feature of the Irish way of life in Chester. As early as 1834, it was reported, under the heading of 'Irish Row in Boughton', that 'a turn up took place of the same character as those which frequently occur in the neighbourhood of Boughton'.[52] Similar sentiments were echoed in June 1850 when another 'Irish Row' was introduced in the following way:

The natives of the Sister Isle resident in Boughton—especially the O'Rooke's, O'Donnells's, O'Gormans and O'Briens etc., have for years been the general disturbers of the peace of our city, and in our police reports of days gone by, we have had to record many murderous conflicts disgraceful to any civilized country.[53]

These 'Irish rows' were presented as a threat to the calm and stability of the 'venerable' city of Chester and were regarded as essentially tribal and characterized by indiscriminate violence, as a report of 29 June 1850, entitled quite simply 'An Irish Row in Steven Street', illustrates:

> On Sunday evening last, the whole tribe of Andersons who some four or five years ago were imported from their country of Kilkenny, turned out of their dwelling armed with pokers and tongs, and the first fortunate neighbour they happened to meet was poor Pat Devan, whose pate they laboured most unmercifully with the 'soft end of a poker' until they felled him to the ground.[54]

In reporting the activities of this 'clan of wild Irish', the *Chronicle* recalled the words of Mr Recorder Rider of New York, who had dealt recently with a similar case of Irish disorder and who had stated, in passing sentence on the offenders:

> Wherever you go you bring turbulence and disorder with you and your mode of life is incompatible with the good order and comfort of any society. You are unwelcome visitors and wherever you settle the vicinity is forthwith demoralized; our motto is liberty and public order, but you construe our liberty into licence to annoy every quiet and decent citizen. Such a course cannot be tolerated, but must be put down with the utmost severity of the court.[55]

In endorsing this view, the newspaper portrayed the Chester Irish as a group set apart from society by their uncivilized and tribal behaviour. Moreover, Irish disorders which involved the police were seen in an even more sinister light, and one was even described as 'a riot'. A 'Disgraceful Irish Row' simply started as a fight between two Irish men and accordingly 'upwards of two hundred of the Irish residents, men and women turned out'. The attempt by two police officers and a local bricklayer (a 'young man they called to their assistance') to interfere, raised a general cry by the mob to 'fetch out yer shillelahs, pokers and tongs and kill the devils'. This assault on the police only ended when more officers were sent for and the 'cowardly mob' retreated to their houses.[56] The resulting police action was to enter every house in Steven Street and arrest one Irishman, who they recognized as a ring leader, and an Irish woman who had apparently encouraged the Irishmen to go for weapons. These two were committed to gaol for two months hard labour on failure to pay a fine of £5 each.[57]

Such 'rows' varied in intensity and their extent, and Roger Swift has suggested that disturbances involving the Irish fell into two broad categories: first, intra-communal disorders, which comprised drunken brawls, quarrels between neighbours and domestic disputes, and which were confined to 'Irish districts', and second, inter-communal disorders which reflected hostilities between the Irish and sections of the host society, including clashes with the police.[58] However, despite the impression given in the *Chronicle* that such disorders were a common occurrence in Chester, it was only in 1850 and 1851 that these were widely reported. In a sense, this is not surprising, for the influx of Irish immigrants into British towns and cities during the Great Famine exacerbated contemporary concerns about the social condition of the Irish poor, within which questions pertaining to law and order (given the legendary reputation of the Irish for disorderly behaviour) loomed large. This may have led to the targeting of the Irish in Boughton by the Chester police force, which had been reformed in 1836 in consequence of the Municipal Corporations Act of 1835. Indeed, the enforcement by the police of the Beer Regulation Act of 1848 (there were 35 public houses in the Boughton district[59]) and the Common Lodging Houses Act of 1851 brought them into direct contact with the local Irish population. Moreover, the Chester magistrates expected the police to be vigilant in Boughton and three extra policemen, two in 1846 and one in 1850, were appointed to the district, with a police station located on the main road of Boughton.[60] Thus, by mid-century the Boughton Irish were receiving greater police surveillance and, in turn, wider coverage in the *Chronicle*.[61] In 1850 and 1851, the *Chronicle* reported three Irish 'rows', one Irish 'riot' and three cases of assault, all of the latter being rather petty incidents. The 'row' of 30 November 1850 and the 'riot' of 17 March 1851 were little more than intra-communal disputes, but due to the presence of the police, they escalated into conflicts beyond their original form. Nevertheless, the violence displayed towards the police during these disorders was accidental rather than premeditated, a product of police attempts to arrest disorderly persons rather than of a concerted attempt by the Boughton Irish to attack the police, several of whom were themselves Irish, including Police Constable Summers, who, according to the *Chronicle*, had been 'ferociously' attacked by the mob on 17 March 1851.[62]

Yet the *Chronicle* had not been averse to highlighting instances of Irish disorder even before the Famine exodus. In 1835 there was an affray in the city when a party of Irish road makers was attacked by Chester labourers and 'two of them were much beaten and abused'.[63] Another incident of some notoriety was the pitched battle in 1839 between English and Irish navvies at Childer Thornton, on the Chester to Birkenhead railway, when troops were summoned from Chester to restore order,[64] whilst another clash, between Lancashire, Cheshire and Welsh agricultural labourers and Irish agricultural labourers, occurred in the countryside around Chester in 1834. The cause of this affray was given by Mr Potts, Clerk of the Peace, as being 'the English party who look upon the Irish with much jealousy' in the belief that the Irish are undercutting their wages.[65] Economic rivalry underpinned much English working-classes hostility towards the Irish immigrant during the nineteenth century, and although this view has been challenged recently by Jeffrey Williamson[66] it was generally thought in Chester during the 1830s that the Irish had the effect of lowering wages, particularly in the occupations of road-making, harvesting hay, corn and potatoes.[67] Yet beneath the colourful reporting of the disorders of 1850 and 1851 in the *Chronicle*, there is little evidence to suggest that there was serious inter-communal hostility between the local Irish and the host society in Chester during the 1840s. Conflicts were confined essentially to the Irish 'quarter' and consisted of intra-communal disputes. Moreover, such disorders, possibly the result of rivalries between Irish men and women from different counties in Ireland, question the application of the concept of Irish outcastness to early Victorian Chester. The Irish in Chester were not a homogeneous group, as these intra-communal disputes reveal, and it is also important to remember that over half the Irish born population in Chester were not located in the Boughton area, despite the very high concentration in Steven Street. Thus, despite the impressions given in the *Chronicle* of an Irish population set apart by its uncivilized, violent and criminal nature, and thereby presenting a threat to Cestrian society, it seems that this was not the case and that the *Chronicle* overstated its case at a time when Irish immigration and its consequences were receiving considerable attention in the national press.

Moreover, there is little evidence of sectarian violence in Chester during the period. This is significant in the context of any assessment of the extent to which the Irish in Chester constituted an outcast element in local society, for the terms 'Irish' and 'Catholic' were regarded as synonymous by contemporaries and provided further grounds for Irish alienation in face of deep-rooted anti-Catholic prejudices in English society. The growth of the Roman Catholic Church in Chester was a direct consequence of immigration from Ireland during the late-eighteenth and early-nineteenth centuries, and by the 1850s the Catholic Chapel in Queen Street, which had been built in 1799, was far too small for the expanding congregation.[68] Unlike their compatriots in Liverpool, the Irish Catholics of Chester did not mark St Patrick's Day with great celebrations or parades and the *Chester Chronicle* rarely highlighted the link between the Chester Irish and the Roman Catholic Church except for an article on 5 April 1851 which reported that on St Patrick's Day 'a short stick loaded at one end with about half a pound of lead was picked up near one of the Cheshire ferries'. The *Chronicle* could not resist from concluding that it had 'doubtless been dropped by some enthusiastic 'paddy' whose idea of 'keeping' the day of his patron saint consisted in knocking down all who differed from him'.[69] However, the Restoration of the Catholic hierarchy in England and Wales in 1850, presented 'an occasion for venting resentment at Catholicism generally and assuaging injured national pride',[70] and unleashed a wave of journalistic fervour throughout the country. The *Chester Chronicle* was no exception to this, paying great attention to the anti-popery theme and to public meetings held in Chester and in other towns. In Chester, the Reverend John Brindley, at the request of the clergy of various denominations in the city, gave a public address attacking the Restoration which when published went through two editions.[71] Yet this address was not aimed specifically at the local Irish population and there is no evidence to suggest that it exacerbated anti-Irish feeling among the working classes. Indeed, Chester escaped the violent manifestations of anti-Catholicism witnessed in Birkenhead on 30 November 1850, when police reinforcements from Liverpool were required to assist the local authorities in suppressing a riot which involved 2,000 Irish navigators.[72]

Nevertheless, the whole 'Papal Aggression' controversy drew attention not only to the increased numbers of Catholics within the city of Chester, which was largely a result of Irish immigration, but also publicized the issue of the education of the Catholic poor, an issue which had obvious implications for the Irish within the city. In an open letter to the *Chronicle*, Mr George Wilbraham, formerly MP for South Cheshire, in responding to an appeal for aid from the Catholic Poor Schools Committee, declined to help, although he stressed that under ordinary circumstances he would have

> been ready to promote the great cause of education for the poor and destitute Catholics of this city . . . without adverting to the religious tenets of its promoters or to the peculiar forms of Christianity which it was their intention to establish in their Romanish Schools.[73]

Wilbraham explained his refusal on the grounds of the 'insolence' of the Catholic Church in restoring its hierarchy in Britain, which he felt had created disgust in the great mass of the people of England and threatened the peace and tranquillity of the country. His reference to the 'poor and destitute Catholics of this city' no doubt referred to the local Catholic Irish, and the education issue was one of direct relevance to the Irish-born and those of Irish parentage. Despite the presence of Protestant demonstrations, petitions and no-Popery sermons in Chester, this animosity towards the Catholics, brought to the surface by the Papal Aggression issue, did not seem to manifest itself, as far as the sources reveal, in any form of inter-communal violence before the end of 1851, although the ramifications of this controversy extended beyond 1851 elsewhere, including serious disturbances in Stockport in 1852.[74]

In general the *Chester Chronicle* took a tolerant line towards the Roman Catholic Church and if this reflected the views of the population as a whole then it may go some way in explaining the lack of religious violence in this period, despite the heightened tensions associated with the tractarian controversy and the re-establishment of the Roman Catholic hierarchy. It is possible that this general tolerance was in part the product of the esteem with which Father Carbery, the Catholic priest of the Queen Street Chapel near Boughton from 1838 to 1861, was held in the city.[75] Father Carbery's work within the Irish community in Chester helped the immigrants in two different ways. His efforts on behalf of the famine Irish, especially in the most desperate days of 1847, by encouraging a charitable response from the host population, and by running a soup kitchen and general refuge in the Catholic Chapel, eased the immediate problems of the immigrants and lessened, if only slightly, the severity of their effect on the city. For this and other duties amongst the Irish, Father Carbery was well-respected, although he was himself Irish, and he was congratulated on many occasions by the *Chester Chronicle* for his pastoral efforts on behalf of his Irish flock. In this way that the Catholic Church in Chester eased the immigrants' transition from rural Ireland to their new setting in Britain, rather than automatically making them outcasts from British society as has been traditionally thought. The Catholic Church developed a relatively low profile in Chester during a period when Catholic Emancipation, granted in 1829, was relatively novel and Father Carbery helped to soothe tensions and minimize anti-Catholic feeling in an overwhelmingly Protestant city. Even Mr Wilbraham in his letter to the *Chronicle* in 1850 conceded that 'the Catholics of Chester are in no way connected with, or responsible for the insolent usurptions',[76] and it appears that Chester's Catholic population, including its Irish Catholic population, was not held in such low esteem by the *Chronicle* as were their compatriots by the Tory press of Liverpool.

Therefore, although the period 1841–51 witnessed increased religious tensions within Chester, there were no serious manifestations of anti-Irish Catholic feeling, and the explosive combination of Irish immigration and anti-Catholicism which fuelled the disorders in Birkenhead did not result in similar troubles in Chester. One reflection of the lack of inter-communal and sectarian hostility in Chester was the laying out of the body of Daniel O'Connell, 'the Catholic Emancipator', in the Queen Street Chapel in July 1847. Apparently, Chester was chosen due to its 'quietness . . . in order to avoid that excitement which necessarily would have arisen had they passed through Liverpool'.[77]

Thus the apparent threat to the city from the lawlessness and violent behaviour of the Irish population in Chester was more imaginary than real. The so-called 'Irish Quarter' of the Boughton area was undoubtedly a bad area, having been described in 1852 as 'the Saint Giles of Chester' by the *Visitors Guide in Chester*.[78] Yet it was not a completely Irish district, and it must also be remembered that over half the Irish-born population in Chester did not live in the Boughton area. In a city the size of Chester, the Irish could not have avoided mostly living and working alongside the native working classes, and inter-communal strife was conspicuous by its absence. Nevertheless, the popular perception of the poor Irish Catholic population of Boughton as a lawless minority persisted, as Julian Reed Purvis shows in his study of the reactions of the local populace to the activities of the Salvation Army in the district in 1882.[79]

This study suggests that it is difficult to strike a proper balance between the lighter and darker shades of the Irish urban experience in early Victorian Chester. On the surface there is some evidence to suggest that the Boughton Irish were segregated, alienated and despised. Yet there is also evidence which presents a rather different picture. An examination of St John's Parish—a district where there was known to be a high concentration of Irish—was likely to reveal a pattern of segregation rather than spatial scattering and a more accurate picture of the Irish experience in Chester can only be obtained by a demographic analysis of the whole Irish-born population of the city in the census years of 1841 and 1851, for three-quarters of the Chester Irish did not live in the Steven Street 'ghetto', and there remains approximately half of the Irish-born population about whom little is known. In this sense, the way of life experienced by the Irish in the Steven Street district—and denounced by the *Chester Chronicle*—was untypical of 'Irish life' in Chester and the diversity of the Irish experience places doubt on the extent to which the Chester Irish formed an outcast community. Indeed, the presence of the Irish-born in the skilled and middle-class populations of St John's parish beyond Steven Street suggests that ethnicity was not necessarily a barrier to social mobility. Moreover, the fact that Steven Street was the area of first reception for the immigrants highlights the unstable, fluid nature of the population within this street, a fact which must have hindered the development of a community or common sense of identity, (issues which are vital to the concept of the 'ghetto'), there is no evidence of a cohesive Irish 'community'. It could also be argued that the conservative and non-industrial nature of the city enabled the Irish to escape the extreme levels of social deprivation and the inter-communal antagonism faced by the Irish in larger industrial cities. Chester's occupational structure was broadly based, the strength of the local economy lay in the lack of a dominant industry or company, and the city was relatively free from major fluctuations in trade, all of which may have enabled Chester to absorb more easily—and with fewer inter-communal conflicts—its Irish immigrant population.[80] This case study has wider implications for the general debate in regard to Irish immigration and settlement in Victorian Britain and, as such, it illustrates the value of examining the urban experiences of the Irish in a 'small-town' context, for which John Herson has pleaded.[81]

Notes

1 For further details, see especially J. A. Jackson, *The Irish in Britain* (London, 1963); Roger Swift and Sheridan Gilley (eds.), *The Irish in the Victorian City* (London, 1985); Roger Swift and Sheridan Gilley (eds.), *The Irish in Britain, 1815–1914* (London, 1989); Graham Davis, *The Irish in Britain, 1815–1914* (Dublin, 1991); Roger Swift, 'The Historiography of the Irish in Nineteenth Century Britain', in Patrick O'Sullivan (ed.), *The Irish World Wide, Vol.2, The Irish in the New Communities* (Leicester, 1992), 52–81.

2 A. Redford, *Labour Migration in England, 1800–1850* (1926; revised edition, Manchester, 1964), 144

3 CRO, Petition of the JPs, 1785.

4 *Report on the State of the Irish Poor, Parliamentary Papers*, 40 (1836) XXXIV, 41.

5 M. E. Sturman, *Catholicism in Chester, A Double Centenary* (Chester,1975), 50; Sister Sturman directly attributes this increase in the number of Catholics to the rising level of Irish immigration into the city.

6 CRO, Census abstracts 1841 and 1851.

7 This contrasts well with F. Finnegan's findings in York, another medium size town and in many ways similar to Chester. Here, the pre-famine 1841 Irish born population was only 430, out of a population of 28,842, 1.52%. But by 1851 the Irish born population was 1963, out of a population of 36,303, 5.4% of the total. This was a percentage increase of 357% in comparison with Chester's 100% increase between the same years. See F. Finnegan, *Poverty and Prejudice, A Study of Irish Immigrants in York, 1840–1875* (Cork, 1982), 6.

8 See for example, C. Richardson, 'The Irish in Victorian Bradford', *Bradford Antiquary*, ix (1976), 294–316; J. M. Werly, 'The Irish in Manchester 1932–49', *Irish Historical Studies*, xviii, no. 71 March 1973, 345–58; unpublished MPhil Thesis, University of Manchester, 1982).

9 M. A. G. O'Tuathaigh, 'The Irish in Nineteenth Century Britain: Problems of Integration', in Swift and Gilley (eds), *The Irish in the Victorian City* (1985), 16.

10 D. R. Wilding, 'A Statistical Study of the Irish Community in Chester's Inner Parishes, 1841–51', unpublished Diploma in Victorian Studies Dissertation, Chester College of Higher Education, 1994), 40., Table 1. Wilding enumerates the numbers and percentages of Irish-born in Chester parishes in 1841 and 1851 as follows:

Parish	Population 1841			Population 1851		
	Total	Irish	Irish % of Total	Total	Irish	Irish % of Total
Chester Castle						
St John	6752	474	7.02	8493	1087	12.80
St Mary	2975	36	1.21	3415	173	5.07
St Olave	430	2	0.47	518	31	5.97
St Michael	649	16	2.47	775	30	3.87
Spital Boughton	191	0	0.00	158	0	0.00

Chester Castle Gaol	178	17	9.55	215	34	15.81
Chester Barracks						
Civilians	54	32	59.26	60	33	55.00
Military	204	75	36.76	316	164	51.90
Cathedral						
St Oswald	5959	138	2.32	6702	231	3.45
Little St John	0	0	0.00	51	1	1.96
Cathedral Precincts	329	1	0.30	377	3	0.80
St Peter	847	16	1.89	948	21	2.22
St Bridget	675	20	2.96	861	20	2.32
St Martin	532	22	4.14	536	9	1.68
Holy Trinity	3340	92	2.75	3375	74	2.19
Total	23 115	935	4.07	26 800	1911	7.13

11 CRO, Census Enumerators' Books, 1841 and 1851, for the parish of St John the Baptist, Chester.

12 For the purposes of this study, the term 'Irish' will be used to apply to those born in Ireland.

13 Here, an Irish household is taken to be one which for census purposes the head is Irish-born, and includes in it all the individuals who are named on the census schedule, underneath the head, whether born in Ireland or not.

14 Even so it must be taken into consideration that individual enumerators were likely to have made differing assumptions about what constituted a particular occupation. See E. Higgs, *Making Sense of the Census* (London, 1989), 78.

15 Armstrong's Classification of occupational status: I Professional; II Intermediate; or Commercial; III Skilled Occupations; IV Agricultural Labourers and other semi-skilled workers; V General Labourers and other unskilled occupations; W. A. Armstrong, 'The Use of Information about Occupation' in E. A. Wrigley (ed.), *Nineteenth Century Society—Essays in the Use of Quantitative Methods for the Study of Social Data* (Cambridge, 1972), Chapter 6. When analysing the results of this classification, it is important to bear in mind the distinction which is made between agricultural labourers (IV) and other labourers (V). John Herson, while finding that the scheme proved to be robust and useful in general, finds the distinction rather questionable: see John Herson, *Why the Irish went to Stafford. A Case Study of Irish Settlement in England, 1830–1871* (Liverpool Papers in Social Studies No. 1, 1988), 7.

16 F. Finnegan, *Poverty and Prejudice: Irish Immigrants in York 1840–75* (Cork, 1982), 100.

17 James Caird, *English Agriculture (1850–51)*, Letter 55. Caird notes that the average wage for agricultural work in 1850 was 11s 9d per week in the north whereas the national average was only 9s 6d.

18 It should be noted that the *Chester Chronicle* was the city's liberal newspaper. The paper considered itself to be 'always independent of the establishment of the day' and at its conception it was stated by the editorial (2 May 1775) that the aims of the paper were 'to accelerate the commercial and domestic intelligence of the ancient and respectable city, and the neighbouring counties, upon a more liberal and extensive plan . . .'

19 *Chester Chronicle*, 15 Jan. 1847.

20 *Ibid.*

21 *Chester Chronicle*, 14 Feb. 1847.

22 *Chester Chronicle*, 15 Jan. 1847.

23 Jacqueline Perry, 'Cholera and Public Health Reform in Early Victorian Chester', Chapter 4 below.

24 Census Enumerator's Returns, 1841 and 1851, St John's Parish.

25 Mary Glazier, 'Common Lodging Houses in Chester, 1841–1871', Chapter 2 above.

26 *Chester Chronicle*, 26 April 1851.

27 *Ibid.*

28 *Chester Chronicle*, 22 March 1851; in the following week, 40 Irish paupers were removed from the city and returned to Ireland: *Chronicle*, 29 March 1851.

29 *Chester Chronicle*, 17 May 1851.

30 *Chester Chronicle*, 12 April 1851.

31 *Chester Chronicle*, 9 Aug. 1851.

32 Colin Pooley, 'Segregation or integration? The residential experience of the Irish in mid-Victorian Britain', in Swift and Gilley (eds.), *The Irish in Britain, 1815–1939* (1989), 72.

33 Census Enumerator's Returns, 1851, St John's Parish.

34 *Ibid.*

35 *Chester Chronicle*, 18 Oct. 1850.

36 S. Thernstrom, *Poverty and Progress; Social Mobility in a Nineteenth Century City* (Harvard, 1964), in F. Finnegan, *op. cit.*, 120.

37 R. McNally, 'The Irish Community in Chester' (unpublished BA dissertation, Chester College of Higher Education, 1985), 28., Table 4.

38 Thomas Carlyle, *Chartism* (1839), Everyman ed. (London, 1972), 183.

39 For the link between crime and vagrancy see D. Jones, *Crime, Protest, Community and Police in Nineteenth Century Britain* (London, 1982), 178.

40 F. Engels, *The Condition of the Working Classes in England* (1844, reprinted with introduction by E.Hobsbawm, St Albans, 1969), 123; *Report of the Select Committee in the State of the Irish Poor in Great Britain, P.P.,* (1836), 40, XXXIV, iv.

41 As previously mentioned, the *Chester Chronicle* was the city's liberal newspaper and therefore would not have reflected the views of all the educated class within the city.

42 *Chester Chronicle*, 18 Oct. 1851.

43 See, for example, F. Neal, 'The Birkenhead Garibaldi Riots 1862', *The Transactions of the Historic Society of Lancashire and Cheshire*, 134 (1982), 87.

44 *Chester Chronicle*, 29 March 1851.

45 *Ibid.*, 5 April 1851.

46 *Ibid.*

47 *Ibid.*, 22 March 1851.

48 S. Gilley, 'English attitudes to the Irish in England 1780–1900', in C.Holmes (ed), *Immigrants and Minorities in British Society* (Where?, 1978), 81–110.

49 *Chester Chronicle*, 26 Jan. 1850.

50 *Ibid.*, 29 March 1851.

51 *Ibid.*, 19 June 1851.

52 *Ibid.*, 25 July 1834. With thanks to Terence Kavanagh for this reference.

53 *Chester Chronicle*, 29 June 1850.

54 *Ibid.*

55 *Ibid.*

56 *Ibid.*, 30 Nov. 1850.

57 *Ibid.*

58 R. Swift, 'Crime and the Irish in Nineteenth Century Britain', in R. Swift and S. Gilley (eds.), *The Irish in Britain 1815–1939* (1989), 168.

59 *Chester Chronicle*, 9 Feb. 1850, for the information concerning the numbers of public houses in Chester.

60 *Chester Chronicle*, 23 Nov. 1850; see also F. Jackson, 'Police and Prisons in Chester, 1830–1850' (unpublished BA Thesis, University of Manchester, 1966).

61 R. Swift, in his study of the Irish in Wolverhampton, finds no evidence to suggest that other unsavoury working class districts were monitored as closely by the police as the Irish quarter. 'Another Stafford Street Row: Law

and Order and the Irish Presence in Mid- Victorian Wolverhampton', in R. Swift and S. Gilley (eds.), *The Irish in the Victorian City* (1985), 186.

62 S. J. Davis has noted that the police force in Manchester in 1845 was 25% Irish. 'Classes and Police in Manchester, 1829–1880', in A. J. Kidd and K. W. Roberts (eds.), *City, Class and Culture : Studies of Cultural Production and Social Policy in Victorian Manchester* (Manchester, 1985), 34.

63 *Report on the State of the Irish Poor*, *P.P.* (1836), 40.

64 R. Swift, 'Crime and the Irish', 171.

65 *Report on the State of the Irish Poor*, *P.P.* (1836), 41.

66 Jeffrey G. Williamson, 'The Impact of the Irish on Britain's labour markets during the Industrial Revolution', *Journal of Economic History*, XIVI (1980), 693–720.

67 *Report on the State of the Irish Poor*, *P.P.* (1836), 41.

68 Sister Mary Winefride Sturman OSU, *Catholicism in Chester. A Double Centenary 1875–1975* (Chester, 1975), 38.

69 *Chester Chronicle,* 5 April 1851.

70 W. J. Lowe, *The Irish in Mid-Victorian Lancashire: The Shaping of a Working Class Community* (New York, 1989), 150.

71 B. E. Harris (ed.), *A History of the County of Chester. The Victoria History of the counties of England* (Oxford, 1980), Vol. III, 95.

72 See especially Neal, *THSL* (1982), 87–111.

73 *Chester Chronicle*, 9 Nov. 1850. An open letter to the Rev. E. Carbery from Mr George Wilbraham of Delamere House.

74 See especially Pauline Milward, 'The Stockport Riots of 1852: a study of anti-Catholic and anti-Irish sentiment', in Swift and Gilley, *The Irish in the Victorian City*, 207–224.

75 M. W. Sturman, *op. cit.*, 38.

76 *Chester Chronicle*, 9 Nov. 1850.

77 *Chester Chronicle*, 23 June 1847. Daniel O'Connell, Irish national leader, campaigned for the repeal of the Act of Union. Founder of the Catholic Association in 1823. MP for Clare 1828. Died in exile in Geneva.

78 D. Thomas, *Visitors Guide in Chester* (Chester, 1852), 47–48.

79 Julian Reed-Purvis and Roger Swift, ' "Black Sunday": Skeleton Army Disturbances in Late Victorian Chester', Chapter 6 below.

80 M. J. Kingman, 'Chester 1801–1861' (unpublished MA thesis, University of Leicester, 1969), Conclusion.

81 J. Herson. 'Irish migration and settlement in Victorian England: A small-town perspective', in Swift and Gilley (eds), *The Irish in Britain, 1815–1939* (1989), 84–103.

4

Cholera and Public Health Reform in Early Victorian Chester

Jacqueline Perry

The early Victorian period witnessed considerable public concern in regard to the health of towns and parliamentary and extra-parliamentary pressures for sanitary reform culminated in the Public Health Act of 1848.[1] In this context, some historians have suggested that the cholera epidemics of 1831–32 and 1848–49 provided the catalyst for public health measures and sanitary reform during the period.[2] Yet the reasons why cholera gained this reputation, and the extent to which it was deserved are worthy of closer scrutiny, for it is difficult to see why one epidemic should provide a major impetus for public health reform in early Victorian Britain at a time when thousands of people died every year from endemic diseases such as typhus, typhoid, measles, scarlet fever, influenza, and tuberculosis.[3] This essay explores these issues with particular reference to the cholera epidemic of 1848–49 and its impact on sanitary reform in early Victorian Chester.

The cholera epidemic of 1848–49 hit the North West in the autumn of 1848, petered out over the winter, and struck again in the latter part of 1849. The large industrial city of Manchester recorded 878 deaths, which equates to 0.45 per cent of the 1841 population,[4] whilst the port of Liverpool, the English city which suffered the worst loss of life, recorded 4173 deaths, or 1.9 per cent of its 1841 population.[5] However in Chester, a comparatively non-industrialized market town, only five recorded fatalities were attributed to cholera in 1848 and only ninety-one deaths ascribed to the disease in 1849, which equates to only 0.19 per cent of the 1841 population of the city[6] Although the 1848/9 epidemic officially lasted for a period of fifteen calendar months, there were two distinct periods in which most of the deaths from cholera occurred. The cholera vibrio requires certain favourable climatic conditions in order to survive for any length of time, notably high temperatures and atmospheric humidity, therefore rapid dissemination of the disease in Britain is most likely to occur in the months of August and September. The majority of deaths in Chester occurred during the second period of the epidemic in the summer and early autumn of 1849. However, although the mortality figures recorded in the Registrar General's Annual Reports look small as a percentage of the yearly totals, they could equate to comparatively large numbers on a daily or weekly basis.[7] Therefore, it is quite possible that cholera could have had a local shock impact. A sudden increase in the numbers of deaths concentrated in a specific locality would have been highly visible at the time even if they were later hidden by the yearly total. However, this is difficult to substantiate by an examination of Chester's parish burial records during the 1840s, when 700 burials a year took place, because the cause of death was not recorded.[8] Indeed, towards the end of the epidemic, the *Chester Chronicle* observed:

> We do not think it needful to make a handle of an epidemic which, after all, has not been more than ordinarily destructive of human life, and which has not materially increased the mortality of our ancient city.[9]

The editorial implied that certain individuals had indeed 'made a handle' of the epidemic, and the Chronicle was clearly at pains to dismiss the notion that cholera had influenced unduly the reconsideration of issues pertaining to health and sanitation in the city. However, the extent to which cholera induced panic in Chester remains problematic.

The early Victorians relied heavily on the use of comparative mortality rates in assessing the health of their cities, and William Farr's statistical analyses of comparative mortality rates between different towns and cities provided valuable ammunition for sanitary reformers during the period. Nevertheless, it should be borne in mind that nineteenth-century cholera statistics should be treated with caution. Although details of cases and deaths from cholera were supposed to have been returned from every district in England and Wales by local Registrars, operating through the Poor Law Union, these did not always represent an accurate return of the number of attacks and deaths. Indeed, the General Board of Health's Report on the 1848/9 cholera epidemic acknowledged that the first cases of cholera were either concealed or recorded under different disease categories on the grounds that it was unwise to excite alarm.[10] It is also possible that the incidence of cholera was understated, especially in seaside resorts and tourists centres, where prosperity depended on visitors. Chester would not have wished to jeopardize its position as the main base for the expanding tourist industry in North Wales and would have wanted to continue to attract visitors to the races. Moreover, cholera cases treated by doctors in private practice were excluded from the returns and post-mortems were only carried out on suspected cholera victims unfortunate enough to have died in public institutions such as the workhouse or prison. The inaccuracy of the Registrar General's returns was exacerbated by the often inaccurate diagnosis of disease during the period. Diseases with similar symptoms such as typhus and typhoid were often classified together under the general heading of 'fever' or 'zymotic' disease, and it was often impossible to make an accurate distinction between dysentery, diarrhoea, the affliction known colloquially as 'English cholera', or 'summer diarrhoea' and Asiatic cholera.

The *Chester Chronicle* charted the progress of the epidemic across India and Russia towards Europe. The newspaper did not seek to sensationalize or exaggerate its reports of the epidemic but fatalistic statements such as 'all the precautions in the world would fail to prevent its raging'[11] may have imparted to readers a sense of inevitability and foreboding. It is interesting to note that the *Chronicle* did not miss the opportunity to moralize to its readers about the evils of intemperance as a precursor to catching cholera, observing that during the cholera epidemic of 1831 'five sixths of all those who fell in England by the disease were from the ranks of the intemperate and dissolute'.[12] This comment may have been merely a ploy to allay the fears of the newspaper's readership: after all, if one was middle class and temperate, then the approaching epidemic was nothing to worry about, for cholera was just another disease which selected its victims from among the poor. Even when cholera reached Liverpool, only twenty miles from Chester, in December 1848, there was little evidence of apprehension or alarm in the columns of the *Chronicle*. Neither did disaffected inhabitants take to the streets in protest against the authorities' complacency in regard to the epidemic.

Asa Briggs has suggested that cholera had the ability to induce a level of panic greater than it might otherwise have warranted. According to Briggs, the first feature which distinguished cholera from other nineteenth-century diseases was its unpredictability.[13] Normally, endemic fevers were an accepted part of slum living. In the novel *Mary Barton*, Elizabeth Gaskell described a harrowing death-bed scene when Ben Davenport came 'down wi' the fever', which was 'brought on by miserable living, filthy neighbourhood, and a great depression of mind and body.'[14] Indeed, typhus, a disease carried by the body louse, attacked dirty people living in filthy conditions. But, according to Briggs, cholera was not confined to one socio-economic class: although it hit the poor, it also occasionally attacked the middle classes. However, the only reported fatal case of cholera during the 1848/9 epidemic which occurred among a social group other than the working class in Chester was that of the Reverend Joseph Akrill, Wesleyan Minister of St John's Parish. Although the disease was widely believed by contemporaries to be non-contagious, the Reverend Akrill could have contracted it during his visits among the poor of his parish, for a major channel for the transmission of cholera is through contact with cholera victims.[15] Thus, in Chester, the cholera epidemic was confined overwhelmingly to the working-class populace, which may well explain why the disease failed to engender widespread public alarm.

Briggs' interpretation differs from that of the General Board of Health, whose analysis of the epidemic was presented to Parliament in 1850. This report observed that cholera had returned to its former haunts—the same towns and cities, and even the same streets, houses and rooms, in which it had appeared in 1831–32. These seats of cholera had already been distinguished by Ashley, Chadwick and

Southwood Smith, the authors of the report, as the 'habitats of fever'.[16] The correlation between dirt and disease had already been identified and in 1847 the Metropolitan Sanitary Commission advised local authorities of the danger of overcrowded and filthy conditions with defective sewerage and sanitation. The Commissioners were confident that cholera would 'present nothing peculiar in its course; [would be] governed by the same laws as other epidemics, and [would] attack in largest numbers with most severity, the same class of persons and same places as typhus, scarlet fever, diarrhoea and zymotic diseases.'[17] The Board of Health substantiated this prediction in 1850, noting—contrary to contemporary popular belief—that the approach of cholera had been slow and gradual rather than sudden and unpredictable, thereby providing local authorities with ample time to institute preventative measures if they wished. Yet Briggs has also observed that local authorities were administratively unequipped in 1848 to cope with a potentially virulent disease such as cholera. Despite the epidemic of 1831–32, cholera was still regarded by contemporaries as a 'foreign' and 'exotic' disease, and although the epidemic of 1831–32 had evoked temporary responses to the emergency in the form of central and local boards of health, these were allowed to lapse once the epidemic had waned.[18] Thus by 1848, when the second cholera epidemic struck, local authorities, including the Chester Corporation, were barely equipped to cope with the disease: corporate memory was short-lived, and it had been sixteen years since the previous visitation.

Nevertheless, to the casual observer, early Victorian Chester may well have appeared to possess the ability to absorb the effects of a cholera epidemic with comparative ease. To outward appearances Chester was a wealthy city, a stable society with a resident population of gentry serviced by retail trades and service industries who were relatively free from trade fluctuations and class-conflict. *The Chester Directory* of 1840 listed over seventy-five shoe makers and forty-five milliners and dressmakers in the city, whilst other crafts and businesses included bookbinders, jewellers, tailors and cabinet makers. Indeed, Kingman has suggested that Chester failed to develop its industrial potential during the period: unlike the industrial towns of the North West, large-scale manufacturing did not evolve in Chester and less than twenty per cent of the population were engaged entirely in industrial manufacturing.[19] It should therefore follow that not only was there less risk of occupational disease in Chester but that there was also a comparatively smaller residue of poor due to cyclical unemployment arising from trade fluctuations. Moreover, Chester was still surrounded by the agricultural areas of Saltney and Sealand, and by pasture land to the east of Handbridge, with occupations such as market gardeners, nurseryman and cowman listed in the trade directories, whilst horticulture and the cheese trade were obviously important to the local economy.

However, as agricultural work was seasonal, unemployment probably existed in Chester especially during a protracted winter such as that of 1845, when an appeal was made in the *Chronicle* for donations of cast-off clothing and soup on behalf of the 'suffering poor'.[20] Poverty was subsequently exacerbated by the influx of Irish immigrants to the city during the Great Famine of 1845–52 and, as Kristina Jeffes has shown, many of these poor people settled in the Boughton district of Chester, in the parish of St John the Baptist, thereby adding to the pool of unskilled labour in the city.[21] Moreover, Chester found considerable difficulty in absorbing its growing population during the 1840s: the city was prevented from expanding in an easterly direction by the Grosvenor Estate and was contained naturally by the city walls,[22] and the increase in the size of its population put pressure on both existing amenities and housing stock and caused overcrowding within the walls. The problem was particularly acute in the poorer parishes of St Oswald and St John, which experienced the greatest population increase. In particular, Steven Street became the focal point for poor Irish immigrants who congregated in an established Irish community within a deprived neighbourhood. Thus although Chester may not have been industrialized, it still had its filthy and overcrowded slum areas characterized by courtyards, lodging houses and beer shops, and the inhabitants of such areas were no doubt particularly susceptible to fever and disease, including cholera.

Moreover, medical practitioners in Chester, as elsewhere, were ill-prepared in the treatment of cholera when an epidemic struck. The treatment of cholera had not advanced significantly since the epidemic of 1832, hence there was still no known cure for cholera and only a limited chance of recovery from an attack. Furthermore, when cholera is left untreated it has a case mortality of between 40–60 per cent.[23] Therefore, the prognosis was not good. The sudden onset of cholera in apparently healthy people, rather than the weak, and from among the twenty to forty year age group, rather than the very young or old, must have alarmed middle-class rate payers. The potential increase in pauperism from widowhood and orphanage and the consequential increase in the poor rates would have been a major concern. The speed with which death followed an attack must also have been particularly alarming. An attack could last anything from six hours to five days, with the average being about forty-eight hours duration. Cholera is also a disease with particularly unpleasant symptoms. It affects the sodium pump mechanism of the body cells causing death by sudden dehydration following cramps, vomiting and severe diarrhoea characterized by an excavation of watery fluid from the bowel. Victims shrivel up 'like raisins' and their extremities turn a bluish black colour.[24] Limited advances in medical knowledge also meant there was a lack of choice available in drug therapy: opium, the drug most frequently employed, acted as both sedative and constipator but had no specific effect on cholera. Yet sensational claims for successful treatments were published in the *Chester Chronicle*. Remedies ranged from inhaling sulphuric ether,[25] drinking fifteen to twenty drops of Naptha (a coal tar product),[26] and inhaling chloroform,[27] to drinking powdered charcoal in wine and taking violent exercise.[28] People were, in effect, defenceless, but these 'remedies' illustrated the desperate measures some members of the public were prepared to try. The remedy advocated by the Board of Health, which was also published in the *Chronicle*, was twenty grains of opiate confection mixed with two tablespoons of peppermint water, or weak brandy and water, repeated every three hours until the patient's diarrhoea had stopped, and the newspaper also published a list of twenty-two recommendations for the prevention of cholera issued by the Board, which included well-meaning advice on clothing and diet and on personal cleanliness and the importance of ventilation.[29]

The constant emphasis by the General Board of Health on the 'premonitory' stage of cholera, comprising the slightest disorder of the bowels, as being the beginning of the disease, may well have contributed to public alarm,[30] although some physicians believed that cholera could be prevented or cured in this first stage of premonitory diarrhoea. These included Chester's own 'esteemed and respected fellow citizen', Dr Richard Phillips Jones, who published a second edition of his work *Cholera Asiatica*, which was based on his observations of the cholera epidemic in Denbigh in 1832. Jones claimed in the *Chronicle* that:

> By judicious and appropriate treatment in the early premonitory stage of the disease, often fatal symptoms are prevented and life preserved. Therefore, no time should be lost in applying remedies.[31]

Moreover, the Chronicle also drew attention to 'Summer diarrhoea' or 'English cholera', which had long been an accepted part of insanitary living conditions and lack of personal hygiene. Gastric upsets were undoubtedly caused by the ingestion of adulterated and tainted food. It must have been alarming to suddenly be told that one's life depended on obtaining prompt medical assistance for symptoms previously considered tolerable. Some people were obviously taking heed of the General Board of Health's advice because a report taken from *The Fife Herald* and reprinted in the *Chronicle*[32] stated that Medical Officers in Aberdeen had been subjected to harassment day and night due to the Board of Health's cautionary statements. It appears that a similar situation existed in Chester, for in July 1849 Mr Boden, a dispensing chemist in Eastgate Row, placed an advertisement in the *Chronicle* newspaper stating that his personal attendance would be immediately available at all times 'during the night' should any urgent cases of cholera require the prompt dispensing of medicine, and that he had attached a special bell to his shop door for the purpose, with the promise that he would answer it immediately.[33] Mr Boden was clearly responding to a need as well as exploiting a commercial opportunity created by public concern. However, the Chester poor could not afford expensive patent 'Cholera Medicine' costing four shillings for twelve doses, let alone doctors' fees, so a system was established whereby they could gain access to help. The Chester Infirmary dispensary had given free medical advice since 1838, and under the terms of the Poor Law Amendment Act of 1834 the Poor Law Guardians were empowered to employ doctors, for a nominal fee, to deal with the local poor. During the cholera epidemic of 1848–49 the Chester Guardians merely modified this system by adopting a uniform approach to the payment of bills for medical attendance on poor cholera patients. The respective parishes settled these with the same sum being paid for each visit.[34] However, the job of Union Medical Officer was neither a prestigious nor a well paid one. At a meeting of the Guardians of Great Boughton Union in March 1849, Mr Moffat, the Medical Officer for the Hawarden district, made an application for additional remuneration to his annual salary of sixty pounds in consideration of the large increase in the number of applicants for medical aid. Although the Reverend Cottingham moved that a gratuity of twenty pounds be given to Mr Moffatt, the board rejected his application by fifty-two votes to thirty-six, thereby preventing an increase in the poor rate.[35]

Clearly, the presence of a strong united church would no doubt have done much to placate any fear and panic among the population of Chester by offering spiritual solace in a time of need. The Church could either promote the fatalistic view that the visitation was a 'Providential Judgement from God' for the sins of the people and was therefore outside human control, or it could use the epidemic to encourage practical measures for the prevention of cholera through its established network of domiciliary visitation among the poor. The latter approach was adopted by the Chester clergy, who were encouraged by the Bishop of Chester to promote ventilation, cleanliness and temperance among their parishioners during their regular house to house visits.[36] After his death in 1856, the Reverend Mr Massie, an active campaigner for sanitary reform and a member of the Sanitary Committee, received glowing obituary praise for his administration to the poor of his parish:

> Wherever in his parish the plague spot appeared, there in the midst was the faithful pastor to be found . . . in the house of sickness he was fearless in the midst of fear.[37]

On a national level, several fast days and services of intercession were organized throughout the country to plead with God to avert the epidemic. Once the main danger had passed in October 1849 a special day was appointed as one of humiliation and prayer when all commercial business was suspended in Chester so that the inhabitants could attend divine worship. The Mayor and other city dignitaries attended a service held in the Cathedral at which the Bishop of Chester preached the sermon. This, and other church services held on the day, were well attended by congregations of all denominations, suggesting that during the epidemic many people felt that they had no alternative but to put their trust in God.

Nevertheless, there is no direct evidence to suggest that the cholera epidemic induced panic amongst the population of Chester. Whilst there was an understandable degree of public concern, as the editorials in the *Chronicle* illustrate, the population at large appears to have taken the epidemic in their stride. But did the epidemic hasten public health reform in the city ? In order to resolve this question it is first necessary to examine the sanitary state of Chester and the provisions for dealing with public health issues prior to the epidemic.

The potential health problems associated with towns and the consequent need for sanitary reform had been recognized during the late 1830s. Edwin Chadwick began his systematic enquiry into the causes of disease among the labouring classes in 1838 and presented his conclusions in the form of a *Report on the Sanitary Condition of the Labouring Population of Great Britain* to Parliament in July 1842. Chadwick stressed the need for a unified system of control of street cleaning, working-class housing and the introduction of an arterial drainage system. This enthusiasm for enquiry was continued by the 1843 Royal Commission on the Health of Towns, and the replies given to this Commission by the Chester authorities implied that although the general health of the town was considered good, the poor suffered severely in the worst parts of the city from fever caused by over-crowding and inadequate ventilation. Moreover, these returns suggest that during the early 1840s the streets of Chester were indifferently drained and paved, with open ditches and stagnant pools existing next to dwelling houses. The public sewers were not trapped to prevent the escape of offensive smells. Local regulations in regard to the systematic drainage of streets and houses and the prevention of public nuisances were either inadequate or not systematically enforced. Liquid refuse was allowed to flow into water courses. The courts and alleys were never cleaned by public scavengers. Domestic refuse was thrown into open spaces behind the privies, thus providing the perfect predisposing conditions for disease.[38]

Yet the city authorities were aware of these health hazards and they embarked upon a programme of sanitary reform in advance of the cholera epidemic of 1848. The Chester Improvement Act of 1845—'an Act for better paving, lighting and improving the borough of Chester and for establishing new Market Places therein'—contained a number of sanitary provisions; indeed, no fewer than 66 of the 351 clauses related to sanitary and public health issues including the paving of streets, responsibility for the construction and maintenance of drains and sewers, cleansing and scavenging, the supply of water, and the prevention of nuisances. The Council was empowered to order property owners to carry out necessary improvements or could carry out the work themselves and recover the expenses from the owners. Magistrates could order filthy houses to be cleaned and whitewashed if they felt that the health of the inhabitants or the public was endangered. The Act also contained the power to construct common sewers, wells and pumps as was thought 'fit or necessary', and various penalties, including fines, were specified for failure to comply with orders to abate nuisances or for neglecting to whitewash premises. However, although the sanitary clauses appeared to be all-embracing, the phraseology was ambiguous: statements such as 'fit and sufficient' or 'as think expedient' were clearly open to interpretation and subsequently frustrated the strict enforcement of the Act.[39]

The Minutes of the Improvement Committee survive for the years between 1846 and 1851 and provide a useful reflection of local attitudes towards sanitary reform. Although the Committee relied initially upon the Chester police for the reporting of nuisances, it could also act on complaints received by letter or in person from inhabitants. The Minutes of 1846 refer to the abatement of smoke nuisances from the Roodee foundry and from Mr Glover's Boiling

House in Northgate Street, but by March 1847 the surveyor's attention had been directed towards ditches in Brook Lane and Steven Street, and the first notices were served on the owners and occupiers of premises in Eastgate and Foregate Street to construct covered drains from their premises to the sewer within twenty-eight days. Various schemes to flush the drains in Steam Mill Street, Brook Street and Steven Street were also recorded, and it is perhaps significant that although improvements focused largely on the main thoroughfares and commercial districts of the city, the Committee also directed its attention towards some of the poorer districts.[40] By 19 November 1847 these improvements had increased the demand for flags and curb stones and the committee recorded the difficulty it found in obtaining bricks in sufficient quantity and quality for the construction of sewers and drains. Moreover, the Committee acknowledged the necessity for a more efficient street cleaning plan in the light of complaints about accumulations of filth in the courts. This concern coincided with the typhus epidemic of 1847, which was particularly virulent in the poor, densely-populated and insanitary parishes of St John and St Oswald, areas which had already been singled out as fever traps.[41]

By the summer of 1849, with the threat of cholera hanging over Chester, the Committee increasingly concentrated on the provision of privies and ashpits, emphasising the implications for public health of failure to comply with their orders. On 11 May 1849, Samuel Jones, owner of premises in Love Street, was ordered to provide ashpits for the use of the occupiers.[42] On 8 June 1849, John Edwards, the owner of premises in Boughton was given one month to provide 'fit and sufficient' ashpits for his dwelling houses and premises.[43] Moreover, in order to prevent the spread of infectious and contagious diseases, 209 householders were ordered to whitewash, cleanse and purify their dwellings in the vicinity of Boughton, Dee Lane and Steam Mill Street.[44] The Minutes of 24 August 1849, in the midst of the cholera epidemic, contained plans and a surveyor's report for the drainage of Handbridge. The Committee had clearly acted in response to the cholera outbreak in the district (although the outbreak was not specifically mentioned in the Minutes), and 46 people were ordered to connect their drains to the sewer.[45] However, in the aftermath of the epidemic, the Committee returned its attentions once more to the abatement of smoke nuisances from Chester's breweries, including Joseph Huxley's brewery in King Street, saw-mills and foundries.[46]

Thus it would appear that the activities of the Improvement Committee in regard to public health reform were prompted by the typhus epidemic, extended during the cholera epidemic and decreased once the danger had passed. Contemporary reactions to the measures carried out by the Improvement Committee were mixed. In November 1848 Mr Mortimer Maurice addressed a letter to the editor of the *Chronicle* on the subject of the city drainage as it affected health. Mr Maurice gave his impression of Steam Mill Street, one of the streets recently drained to the satisfaction of the Improvement Committee. According to Mr Maurice, the pedestrian walking along the street was unaware of any noxious smells, and therefore concluded that the street was excellently drained and the neighbourhood healthy. However, each house had a cess pool connected to a drain, which carried liquid matter from the 'midden' to the barrel drain in the street with the result that the 'most disgusting and noxious effluvia was brought into the very houses of the tenants'. Mr Maurice concluded that these exhalations must have been prejudicial to health. Insights such as these highlight the discrepancy between the self satisfaction of the Committee members and the reality of what was actually achieved.[47] In contrast, at a meeting of the Improvement Committee in August 1849, Dr Jones congratulated the Town Council upon the 'gratifying state' of the health of the city suggesting that the comparatively low number of cholera deaths was directly attributable to measures carried out under the Improvement Act.[48] Yet the Committee was reactive rather than proactive, only acting when complaints drew attention to an existing nuisance, and failed to draw up an effective plan either for the systematic removal of nuisances or for a comprehensive system of drainage for Chester. Instead they relied on a piecemeal approach. The outbreak of cholera in 1848 did not alter substantially the activities of the Improvement Committee, but merely shifted the emphasis away from the abatement of smoke nuisance towards the need for sanitary improvements as a means of reducing the severity of, and ultimately preventing, disease. But this activity was not sustained and was concentrated almost exclusively on the provision of drains.

This said, it is important to recognize that the early Victorians focused their attention almost exclusively on the removal of filth as the main preventative measure against disease. Other causes of ill health such as poor diet and inadequate housing were not recognized as contributory factors nor given the same emphasis. This can be attributed, at least in part, to contemporary acceptance of the miasmatic theory of epidemiology during the early 1840s. In essence, it was widely held that the atmosphere was contaminated by 'emanations' arising from filth (especially human excrement) accumulated in and around dwellings, and that people were poisoned by inhaling the 'noxious matters' suspended in the air. Therefore the first priority of sanitary reformers was to remove the accumulated waste from privies, cesspools, stables and stagnant ditches. Edwin Chadwick demonstrated that decomposing matter could be removed from the towns by an effective system of drainage, and it is hardly surprising, once the relationship between insanitary conditions and excessive sickness and mortality had been established, that the Chester City Council concentrated its improvement legislation on the removal of offensive nuisances and the building of a sewerage system.

Norman Longmate has suggested that cholera exercised a powerful influence on the passing of Lord Morpeth's Public Health Bill in 1848, for the threat of cholera silenced opposition: 'What argument had failed to achieve in 1848, the fear of cholera achieved in 1848.'[49] Morpeth's Bill sought to establish local sanitary authorities in areas where there was not already a municipal body available for the purpose, and the proposed powers essentially comprised a collection of clauses from local Acts which had already been obtained by some local authorities, of which Chester Council was one. The Act established a central authority, the Board of Health, which was based in London, and empowered local authorities to establish local Boards of Health if they so wished, and subject to inspection by the central authority. However, due to the permissive nature of the Act, the responsibility for sanitary affairs remained largely in the hands of local bodies. Cholera may well have been a powerful ally close to the seat of power in London, but it did not automatically follow that fear of the epidemic exerted pressure at a local level. Chester had already adopted many of the obligatory duties under its own Improvement Act of 1845, including the appointment of a surveyor and an inspector of nuisances, the construction of public sewers, and provisions for street cleaning. Moreover, it is clear from comments in the *Chester Chronicle* that the Council objected to the Public Health Act, with its dangerous centralising tendencies, and failed to take advantage of its provisions. Indeed, the city Councillors decided not to adopt the Act which, it was held, would necessitate an increase in local taxation. Expensive and unnecessary improvements were associated with central government intervention, and the *Chronicle* argued that the most important consideration in deciding whether or not to adopt the Act for Chester was cost. The mortality rate of Chester was slightly in excess of twenty-three per thousand, the number above which the government could impose adoption, and the newspaper urged rate-payers to press for more action to reduce the mortality rate through locally-initiated improvement schemes which could be funded from a more efficient administration of the Borough Fund without increasing local rates. Accordingly, the Council decided not to adopt the Public Health Act and local control of sanitary reform was reasserted.[50]

However, the Council did take advantage of the Nuisances Removal and Diseases Prevention Act of 1848 (which was designed to complement the 1848 Public Health Act by making provisions for the protection of the public health on the outbreak of epidemics), and a Sanitary Committee, comprising members of the Council and Poor Law Guardians, was established in accordance with the Act. The Committee received weekly reports from the Poor Law Guardians and the police about existing nuisances, a function that encroached on the responsibilities of the Improvement Committee in regard to nuisance removal. The Poor Law Guardians were also responsible for providing a sufficient number of paupers to remove the accumulations of filth from all the streets, lanes and alleys in the city. The Sanitary Committee's activities included the inspection of all privies, cess pools, manure heaps, pigsties and other nuisances in the Guardian's respective parishes. However, the Guardians were required to inspect only those houses in the parish where the evidence of nuisances was suspected. In August 1849 a deputation from the

Parish of St Mary's stated to the Sanitary Committee that parts of Handbridge were in a very filthy state and that several people had died of cholera in Sty Lane, a low lying area near to the river inhabited mainly by fishermen. Although steps were taken immediately to thoroughly cleanse the area, the Guardians ought to have been aware of the situation and taken action to prevent the cholera deaths.[51] Once again, this incident illustrates not only the reactive rather than proactive policies of the city authorities in regard to sanitary reform but also highlights the administrative overlap which existed among local agencies with responsibilities for health and sanitation in Chester.

The Report of the General Board of Health on the Epidemic Cholera of 1848 and 1849 expressed disappointment at the way in which the Nuisances Removal and Diseases Prevention Act had worked in practice, due largely to the inappropriate and inadequate machinery provided by the Act for its local administration.[52] In Chester the Sanitary Committee only met weekly, which reduced significantly the chance of prompt action. The General Board of Health duly realized its mistake in appointing the Poor Law Boards as administrators of the Act, whilst at the same time expecting other local authorities, in Chester's case the City Council, to take responsibility for the draining, paving and cleansing provisions, which divided responsibility locally and led to neglect and delay. Hence whilst the Guardians continued to act as if administering poor relief to the destitute, and adhered rigidly to the procedure of application, inquiry and adjudication, the cholera epidemic in Chester required quick and decisive action to prevent further deaths.

Between November 1848 and September 1849 seventy-two inspections, reports, summons and notices to clean privies, drains and ditches in all parts of the city were recorded in the Minutes of the Sanitary Committee, which suggests that the Committee was quite active in its efforts to clean the city. Yet the Committee was not always decisive in utilising its powers of prosecution under the Diseases Prevention Act in order to force Cestrians to comply with the legislation, and some property owners persistently ignored the legislation. For example, Mr Hamilton was served with his first notice to clean Hamilton Court in March 1849, but it was reported in April that the nuisance still existed and in June the Committee sent an 'earnest request' to Mr Hamilton that he carry out the suggestions made in the surveyor's report of his property. When a case of cholera occurred in Welsh Yard, next to Mr Hamilton's property, he was required by the Committee to remove the nuisance 'without delay', and Hamilton attended a Committee meeting in July and undertook to use the 'best means' he could to remove the nuisance. Nevertheless, Hamilton was subsequently issued with another notice.[53] The final outcome of this saga was not recorded but it would appear that Mr Hamilton had been given ample opportunity to plead his case in front of the Committee and that the Committee were willing to accept vague assurances of action from him. Of course, many property owners may have regarded themselves as respectable pillars of the community and would have believed that it was an acceptable practice to delay improvement or nuisance removal until compulsorily ordered to do so in order to save on the expense. Prominent citizens were recorded as offenders in the Minutes, including the Bishop and Dean and Chapter, who were given twenty-four hours to remove stagnant water behind Abbey Green,[54] and the Marquis of Westminster's Agent, Mr Hope, who was ordered to drain several Grosvenor properties.[55] Even members of the Committee themselves, such as Mr Littler and Mr Harrison, owned property in area most in need of improvement, including Handbridge. They too were not prepared to act without compulsion, which may explain why such sympathetic consideration was given to persistent offenders such as Mr Hamilton. Moreover, even in the midst of the cholera epidemic, when supported by the authority of the Nuisances Removal and Diseases Prevention Act, the Sanitary Committee did not make effective use of its powers, relying on persuasion to encourage compliance, and this policy proved unsuccessful.

In the context of improvements pertaining to sewerage and drainage, local schemes could not be effective without an adequate supply of water, which was needed not only to flush decomposing waste into the River Dee but also for street cleaning and for domestic purposes such as cooking, drinking and for personal hygiene. Water is the prime medium for the transmission of cholera and inadequate personal cleanliness is an important contributory factor in the spread of the disease. It was undoubtedly difficult for the Chester poor to keep their homes and themselves clean when they relied on access to communal, shared stand pipes for their intermittent and scanty water supply. Indeed, of the 4,800 inhabited houses in Chester in 1843, only 2,000 were connected to the water mains and had either a tank or cistern for water storage. About five hundred houses in courts and entries were supplied by communal pipes, averaging ten houses to each pipe.[56] The Chester Council had contemplated the provision of public baths and washing facilities for the working classes of Chester several years before the outbreak of cholera in 1848. Somewhat coincidentally, their plans for a public bath house finally came to fruition in 1849. The water supplying the public baths and wash-houses in Chester came from the Shropshire Union Canal and the baths proved popular, with over 6,000 visitors on the opening day in June 1849. The baths were intended to improve the health, comfort and habits of cleanliness of the poor and to 'counteract the prevalence of contagious diseases',[57] although the *Chronicle* observed that frequent bathing 'secure[d] vigorous and buoyant existence',[58] thereby emphasising the pleasurable and rejuvenating qualities rather than the hygienic effect of bathing. Nevertheless, it is difficult to evaluate the effect of the new baths on health in Chester. The provision of bathing facilities may have helped to reduce the prevalence of typhus, a disease carried by the body louse, but this may not have been the case with cholera; indeed, it is possible that the public baths may have encouraged the transmission of the disease in Chester, for the cholera vibrio can survive for up to twenty one days in unfiltered water and for up to three days on cloth and cotton clothes.[59] Yet until the 1860s, when John Snow's theory that cholera infection was spread by the ingestion of water contaminated with the excreta of cholera victims was accepted, the need for a pure water supply was not properly understood.[60] But the early Victorians did make a connection between the proximity of dwellings to polluted water and the prevalence of fever, and people relied on vision and taste to assess the quality of their water: if it looked clear it was presumed to be clean. Chester's water was taken principally from the River Dee (into which the contents of the town sewers were flushed) and was supplied by a private profit-making joint stock company incorporated by an Act of Parliament in 1826.[61] Most local complaints about the quality of the water occurred after heavy rain stirred up mud from the bottom of the river bed. Private filters were used in the higher class of house, but these were not used extensively throughout the city. Only one advertisement for a private 'Pure Water Improved Filter' was carried in the *Chester Directory* in 1840. The manufacturer, Mr Harbridge, listed thirty-two of his satisfied customers, but, from the given professions such as solicitor, Dean, wine merchant and Tithe Commissioner and exclusive addresses in Abbey Square, Stanley Place and King Street, it is reasonable to presume that the cost of the filters was well beyond the means of the average working-class citizen. In 1843 the water was supplied to certain districts for only three hours on three to five days a week. The Waterworks Company Clauses Act of 1847 stated that the Water Company was bound to supply Chester with 'pure and wholesome' water but it did not specify for how many hours per day.[62] Nor was the Waterworks Company obliged to filter the water it supplied, which was important in view of the fact that cholera bacteria can only survive for short periods of time in filtered water. Mr Harbridge's privileged customers unwittingly protected themselves against contracting cholera through the use of his water filters, but as the population of Chester increased so the pressure on the water supply intensified and the inhabitants became increasingly dissatisfied with both the quantity and quality of their water.

When the *Chester Chronicle* recorded the appearance of cholera in Handbridge during August 1849, it also commented on the 'lamentable deficiency of wholesome water in the district'.[63] The subject of the drainage of Handbridge had been discussed by the Improvement Committee two weeks previously, when Committee members were concerned that the drinking of contaminated water by the inhabitants predisposed them to disease. Having brought the situation to the attention of the Sanitary Committee, a Sub-Committee of Inquiry was appointed and chaired by the Reverend Mr Massie. The Committee reported that the inhabitants of streets without water, such as Browns Lane and Sty Lane, had to either collect rainwater in tubs or carry water, contaminated with sewage, up a steep ascent from the river, a distance of nearly half a mile from the centre of

Handbridge. According to Mr Massie, who had conducted a door to door survey of the inhabitants, the average cost of water for the smaller class of cottager who bought water from a water seller, was approximately one shilling per week. There were formerly two public pumps in Handbridge but they had been dismantled because they were continuously out of repair and because they were 'subject to civil wars and far from civil language'. The irony was that the scanty supply of water had not been worth fighting about, often being brackish, hard and undrinkable. From a sanitary viewpoint, the cleanliness, health and comfort of the citizens of Chester was materially dependent on an abundant supply of water, and Mr Massie stressed that the Waterworks Company had a duty to relieve the needs of the poor. After canvassing the opinions of property-owners in the district, Massie concluded that the majority were willing to become customers of the Waterworks Company and had agreed provisionally to take the water when the mains were laid, which would also increase the value of their properties. Moreover, the tenants themselves had expressed a desire to pay for the laying of water pipes, when the landlord was unwilling to do so, rather than be without water. The report was unanimously adopted and a copy was forwarded to the directors of the Waterworks Company with an 'earnest request' that they might give the report their immediate attention.[64] Although at least two members of the Water Inquiry Committee, Mr Littler and Mr Harrison, owned property in Handbridge, genuine concern for the inhabitants and a desire to reduce the severity of the cholera outbreak in the district, rather than self interest, was the motivating factor behind the inquiry.

In December 1849 the *Chronicle* reported that the Chester citizens were looking forward to the speedy completion of the water improvement works designed to filter and blend together water from the River Dee with local spring water.[65] However, as the threat from cholera waned so too did the sense of urgency for providing an adequate supply of water to the poor of Handbridge. The water supply saga, chronicled in the Special Sanitary Committee minutes, was one of a series of delays, extensions and excuses on the part of the Waterworks Company, who finally obtained the Chester Waterworks Act in 1857. The terms of this Act required that the Waterworks

Company supplied water at least once a day, with the exception of Sunday, but it was not bound to supply water constantly under pressure. The Council was easily satisfied. Chester had been given the possibility of power over the water supply in the 1848 Public Health Act but the Council chose not to adopt this permissive clause and, despite having expressed a lack of confidence in the Waterworks Company in 1849, they did nothing to remedy the problem. According to the *Chester Courant*, the Council would have had the backing and support of the inhabitants for a take-over of the Waterworks Company[66] but, despite the threat of a major cholera epidemic, the Council's half-hearted attempts to improve the water supply of Chester resulted in an unsatisfactory compromise heavily weighted in favour of the Waterworks Company.

Attention was also focused on the state of the common lodging-houses in the city, particularly in relation to the spread of infection exacerbated by overcrowding. Many of the lodging-houses in Chester were 'very miserable and wretched', and it was not uncommon for the residents to lie on straw and huddle together to keep warm as beds were not always provided.[67] It was widely believed that fever originated in such houses, a belief which stemmed from the idea that most diseases were imported into the towns by migratory populations, including tramps, vagrants, casual labourers and Irish immigrants, for which lodging-houses catered. The Chester Council expressed its concern about the dirty and overcrowded state of the lodging houses in Chester in July 1847, when ninety-three cases of fever were reported,[68] and the first named cholera case in Chester was that of a visiting American sailor, Anthony Badgley, who was found lying unconscious in a ditch in Hoole.[69] In March 1849 the Sanitary Committee reported that 'great advantage' had been derived from the consequent police inspection of the common lodging houses in the city,[70] but during the following week, the Chief Constable, Mr Hill, reported that there had been an influx of vagrants resulting in overcrowding, notably in Steven Street, and Hill recommended that the Committee adopt immediate measures to remedy the problem. Mr Hill was not specifically concerned with the health of the lodgers but was more concerned about the morality of accommodating six lodgers per bed without any attempt to segregate the sexes.[71]

However, health and morality were inextricably linked in lodging-houses. Moreover, overcrowding led to a lack of adequate ventilation, which was also widely regarded as the precursor to disease on the grounds that people were exposed to the dangers of inhaling vitiated air, believed to contain a poisonous gas (carbonic acid gas) and highly putrescent animal matter which was deposited on the walls and clung to clothing and bedding. Thus lodging houses were identified as the source as well as the means of the spread of infection.

Dr Phillips Jones recommended the adoption of bye-laws to regulate the lodging houses. He informed the Council in April 1849 that if cholera were to break out while the lodging houses were in such a deplorable state, he doubted whether any medical men would risk their own lives by visiting such places.[72] Accordingly, the Council formed a Committee to draw up bye-laws for the regulation of the lodging houses in the city. On 19 April this Committee resolved to request the Town Clerk to obtain a copy of Liverpool's bye-laws and regulations relating to lodging houses. However, on 10 May it was decided to continue to rely on the powers of the Chester Improvement Act as it was understood that a 'general enactment [in regard to Common Lodging-Houses] was in contemplation'.[73] Thus, as Mary Glazier has shown, little was actually done by the Council in regard to lodging-houses until the Common Lodging Houses Act was introduced in 1851.[74]

The contemporary fear of inhaling 'noxious gasses' also extended to provisions for the burial of the dead, for the state of graveyards was widely regarded as a public health issue and was diagnosed as a primary cause of ill-health. Chester's graveyards were already overcrowded by 1848, with multiple bodies in many of the graves. In Chester, separate churchyards were attached to all thirteen parish churches and these were usually sited in the middle of crowded residential areas. The 'noxious effluvia' arising from the new burial ground of St Mary's in Nicholas Street was cited as the cause of 'Irish fever' in the town,[75] and in January 1848 a letter from Mr Ford was laid before the Improvement Committee which complained about the bad sewerage in the neighbourhood of Grey Friars. In particular, Ford was concerned about the damaging health consequences of 'putrescent effluvia' from the churchyard which flowed into the sewers and escaped into the atmosphere.[76] Between 1841 and 1847 an annual average of seven hundred burials took place in Chester and the graveyards were so full that by 1848 the need for a new cemetery was self-evident. On 18 February 1848, Mr Whalley, the surveyor, held a public inquiry at the town hall to discuss the necessity for a new cemetery to be sited outside the town limits. Mr Whalley reported that existing cottages which stood at a distance of only ten yards from the proposed new cemetery site would not be 'injuriously affected' by the development, but he also suggested that any house over the annual value of £50 should be sited at least three hundred yards away.[77] The Marquis of Westminster duly agreed to sell a suitably secluded piece of land in Handbridge and on 3 March 1848 the Chester Cemetery Bill was enacted. At the half-yearly meeting of the shareholders in July 1849 a progress report confidently stated that the cemetery would be completed by the end of 1849. The citizens of Chester had acted in time, although the cemetery was owned by a private company rather by the Corporation. Nevertheless, in October 1853 the Sanitary Committee called for the Town Council to become the proprietors of the cemetery and again drew attention to the 'disgraceful state' of the graveyards in Chester, for although the Bishop of Chester was empowered to close overcrowded church-yards, burials in existing grounds had continued.

Finally, it is perhaps significant that whilst some local authorities sought to contain cholera by isolating cholera patients, this was not the case in Chester, where it was accepted practice for victims of the epidemic to be nursed at home. Although Chester Infirmary. built in 1761, was the first in the country to institute wards for the isolation of fever patients suffering from typhus and smallpox, it was not prepared to admit cholera patients. Mr Jones, the House Surgeon to the Infirmary, reported that it was inadvisable to admit cholera cases because the existence of sickness and fever in the infirmary would predispose the patients to attack by cholera; a disease he did not believe to be contagious to healthy people,[78] and it was not until the cholera epidemic of 1866 that separate accommodation was provided for cholera patients in a disused farmhouse in New Park (Grosvenor Park) run by lady district visitors of the city.[79]

Contemporaries assessed the effectiveness of sanitary reform by its ability to reduce mortality rates and, although cholera did not have a dramatic impact on mortality rates in Chester, the *Chester Chronicle* announced triumphantly on 24 August 1849 that:

> for the last few days no fresh cases [of cholera] have appeared in the city. The general health of the city was never better and we believe that no cause for alarm exists on account of cholera. The Sanitary Committee have, however, taken effective measures to grapple with it should it again make its reappearance. As it is, rather more has been made of the visitation than was necessary. The mortality of the city is at present below average.[80]

This statement implies that the measures adopted by the Sanitary Committee in response to the cholera epidemic had been effective and were intended to be permanent. In reality, however, only modest improvements had been made and these were not sustained. It is perhaps unfair to criticize the early Victorians for their misunderstanding of the important role that water played in transmitting cholera but this does not detract from the Council's mismanagement of Chester's water supply. Although the central government had placed responsibility for combating the epidemic upon local authorities, progress towards public health reform was hindered by the absence of a coherent and effective policy. In Chester the various committees appointed to implement sanitary reform possessed overlapping functions and responsibilities that ensured confusion, duplication and inefficiency. The Sanitary Committee encroached on the responsibilities of the Improvement Committee in regard to nuisance removal. Sanitary Committee members were also involved in matters dealing with the state of lodging-houses and water supply, both of which had their own separate committees. Neither Committee made effective use of the powers they possessed under the Chester Improvement Act or the Nuisances Removal and Diseases Prevention Act, and a reluctance to prosecute offenders ensured their ineffectiveness. They also failed to take advantage of the permissive clauses in the Public Health Act of 1848, with the result that the potential for the comprehensive reform of provisions for public health in Chester was never fully realized.

Neither is it clear that the limited sanitary improvements achieved in Chester were stimulated by the fear of cholera. There was little direct evidence of panic among the citizens of Chester although some middle-class inhabitants did express their concerns about the possibility of an increase in the poor rate and improvement rate. By 1845, with the adoption of the Chester Improvement Act, the Council was already moving, albeit somewhat hesitantly, towards sanitary reform. But the city authorities were content to rely on this Act, which was not directed specifically towards combating disease. Although the General Board of Health itself acknowledged that even minor sanitary improvements reduced the severity of epidemic attacks, the Commissioners agreed that 'The simple abatement of a few nuisances, though praiseworthy in itself and useful as far as it went, was by no means sufficient to protect the public health.'[81] Thus although the cholera epidemic of 1848–9 played a part in public health reform in Chester, it was not a major impetus for reform. Instead, cholera occupied a more moderate role alongside the endemic diseases in general, for contemporaries understood that less-dramatic diseases such as typhoid and typhus caused more deaths in the long run than cholera. Moreover, although the epidemic did not last long enough to create a consistent demand for public health reform, it did highlight the lack of long-term planning on the part of the Council. Indeed, by the time of the cholera epidemic of 1866 the Council had once again lapsed into complacency. There had been no lasting effect of the experiences of 1848 on the cleanliness of the streets. Chester's water was still taken from a source in the River Dee below the city's sewage outlets, and there was still no permanent arrangement for removal of filth from the city. In May 1866 over 800 full privies and ashpits were reported to the Sanitary Committee as in need of immediate emptying, and the Council adopted temporary measures in response to the problem.[82] Much had been achieved through the operation of the Common Lodging Houses Act of 1851, but this legislation had not originated in Chester in response to the cholera epidemic and the Council had been content to rely on the lead from London. Hence cholera did not exert a powerful influence on public heath reform in early Victorian Chester and when it reappeared in 1866 it exposed just how little the authorities had achieved in the sphere of public health in the intervening years.

Notes

1 For public health reform during the period, see especially C. Hume, 'The Public Health Movement' in J. T. Ward (ed.), *Popular Movements, 1830–50* (London, 1970), 183–200; F. B. Smith, *The People's Health 1830–1910* (London, 1979); A. S. Wohl, *Endangered Lives: Public Health in Victorian Britain* (London, 1985); W. M. Faser, *A History of English Public Health, 1834–1939* (London, 1950).

2 See for example A. Briggs, 'Cholera and Society in the Nineteenth Century', *Past and Present*, no. 19 (1961); Smith, *The People's Health 1830–1910*; U. R. Henriques, *Before the Welfare State: Social Administration in Early Industrial Britain* (London, 1979), 120. For the impact of cholera, see also M. Pelling, *Cholera, Fever and English Medicine* (Oxford, 1976); R. J. Morris, *Cholera, 1832* (London, 1976); F. Cartwright, *A Social History of Medicine* (New York, 1977); M. Durey, *The Return of the Plague: British Society and the Cholera 1831–2* (Dublin, 1979); N. Longmate, *King Cholera: The Biography of a Disease* (London, 1966); Virginia Berridge, 'Health and Medicine' in F. M. L. Thompson (ed.), *The Cambridge Social History of Britain 1750–1950, Vol.3., Social Agencies and Institutions* (Cambridge, 1990), 171–243.

3 E. C. Midwinter, *Victorian Social Reform*, (London, 1968), 12.

4 *Registrar General's Report on the Mortality of Cholera in England* (1848–49). Extracts from statistics relating to the North West Division, 16. The 1841 population of Manchester was 192,403.

5 *Ibid.* The 1841 population of Liverpool was 223,003.

6 *Ibid.* The 1841 population of Chester was 49,097.

7 *Registrar General's Report on the Mortality of Cholera in England* (1848–49).

8 *Chester Chronicle*, 18 Feb. 1848.

9 *Ibid.*, 5 Oct. 1849.

10 *Report of the General Board of Health on the Epidemic Cholera of 1848 and 1849, Parliamentary Papers* (1850).

11 *Chester Chronicle*, 23 June 1848.

12 *Ibid.*, 8 Sept.1849.

13 Briggs, *Past and Present*, 19 (1961).

14 E. Gaskell, *Mary Barton* (London,1848), 68.

15 *Chester Chronicle*, 12 Oct. 1849.

16 *Report of the General Board of Health on Cholera, P.P.* (1850).

17 *Ibid.*, 144.

18 A. Briggs, *op. cit.*, (1961).

19 M. J. Kingman, 'Chester 1801–1861', (unpublished MA Thesis, University of Leicester, 1969), 21.

20 *Chester Chronicle*, 21 Feb. 1845.

21 Kristina Jeffes, 'The Irish in Early Victorian Chester: An Outcast Community?', Chapter 3 above.

22 C. R. Ellington, ed., 'A History of Cheshire', *The Victoria History of the Counties of England*, Vol.ll, 207–29.

23 Smith, *op. cit.*, 230.

24 *Ibid.*

25 *Chester Chronicle*, 7 Jan. 1848.

26 *Ibid.*, 30 June 1848.

27 *Ibid.*, 3 Nov. 1848.

28 *Ibid.*, 17 Nov. 1848

29 Extract from *The Lancet*, cited in the *Chester Chronicle*, 4 Aug. 1848.

30 *Chester Chronicle*, 29 June 1849.

31 *Ibid.*, 24 Aug. 1849.

32 *Ibid.*, 24 Nov. 1848.

33 *Ibid.*, 13 July 1849.

34 *Ibid.*, 22 Oct. 1849.

35 *Ibid.*, 30 March 1849.

36 *Ibid.*, 24 Nov. 1848.

37 F. Simpson, 'A Few Cheshire Worthies', *Chester Archaeological Society*, Vol. 28, (1928).

38 *The Second Report of the Royal Commission on the State of Large Towns and Populous Districts, with Appendix, Parliamentary Papers* (1845). Questions for Circulation.

39 This Act provided machinery for the automatic inclusion of all standard clauses previously included in Local Acts, thus making the process cheaper and simpler.

40 CRO CCB/47, Improvement Committee Minutes 1846–1851.

41 *Chester Chronicle*, 16 July 1847.

42 CRO CCB/47, 11 May 1849.

43 *Ibid.*, 8 June 1849.

44 *Ibid.*

45 *Ibid.*, 24 Aug. 1849.

46 *Ibid.*

47 *Ibid*, 10 Nov. 1848.

48 *Ibid*, 31 Aug. 1849.

49 N. Longmate, *op. cit.*, 155.

50 *Chester Chronicle*, 15 Dec. 1848.

51 CRO CCB/34,CCB/35, Special Committee Minute Books, 15 Aug. 1849.

52 *Report on the General Board of Health of the Epidemic cholera of 1848 and 1849. P.P.* (1850).

53 *Chester Chronicle*, 26 March 1849.

54 *Ibid.*, 11 May 1849.

55 *Ibid.*

56 *The Second Report on the State of Large Towns and Populous Districts, P.P.* (1845).

57 *Chester Chronicle*, 3 July 1846.

58 *Ibid.*, 11 May 1849.

59 M. Durey, *op. cit.*, 218.

60 Published in his pamphlets *On the Mode of Communication of Cholera* (1849) and *On the Mode of Transmission of Cholera* (1855).

61 *Supplement to The Second Report on the State of Large Towns and Populous Districts, P.P.* (1845).

62 CRO. The Water Works Clauses Act, 23 April 1847. Authorized the making of waterworks for supplying the towns with water.

63 *Chester Chronicle*, 24 Aug. 1849.

64 *Ibid.*, 14 Dec. 1849

65 *Ibid.*, 12 Dec. 1849

66 *Chester Courant*, 13 July 1849.

67 *The Second Report on the State of Large Towns and Populous Districts, P.P.* (1845), Answer to question 55.

68 *Chester Chronicle*, 16 July 1847.

69 *Ibid.*

70 *Ibid.*, 12 March 1849.

71 *Ibid.*, 19 March 1849.

72 *Ibid.*, 20 April 1849.

73 CRO CCB/34, Common Lodging House Committee. Minutes, 10 May 1849.

74 See Mary Glazier, 'Common Lodging Houses in Chester, 1841–71', Chapter 2 above.

75 *Chester Chronicle*, 18 Feb. 1848.

76 *Ibid.*, 18 Feb. 1848.

77 *Ibid.*

78 *Ibid.*, 13 July 1849.

79 Frances Wilbraham, *Streets and Lanes of a City* (1871), published under the *nom de plume* of Amy Dutton.

80 *Chester Chronicle*, 24 Aug. 1849.

81 *Report of the General Board of Health on Chester, P.P.* (1850).

82 *Chester Chronicle*, 12 May 1866.

5

Philanthropy and the Children of the Streets: The Chester Ragged School Society, 1851–1870

Roger Swift

The first half of the nineteenth century witnessed the rapid expansion of voluntary provisions for elementary education and by mid-century a plethora of charity schools, private adventure schools, Sunday Schools, and the day schools operated by the National Society (for Anglicans) and the British and Foreign School Society (for Nonconformists) offered a patchwork educational provision of variable quality to working-class children.[1] These voluntary developments in popular elementary education made all the more conspicuous the state of the children of the streets—the children of the very poor or the very demoralized who could not or would not attend existing elementary schools.[2] The foundation of the Ragged School Union in 1844 secured a wide coalition of religious interests under evangelical leadership to provide basic elementary education for these so-called 'ragged children'. Initially, classes were held on Sundays only but these were later extended to weekday evenings, staffed by volunteers and, with the coming of paid agents after 1844, to the daytime as well. Charles Dickens, an early supporter of the ragged school movement, described one such school in an article in *The Daily News* on 4 February 1846:

> The name [Ragged School] implies the purpose. They who are too ragged, wretched, filthy and forlorn, to enter any other

place; who could gain admission into no charity school, and who would be driven from any church door; are invited to come in here, and find some people not depraved, willing to teach them something, and show them some sympathy, and stretch a hand out, which is not the iron hand of Law, for their correction.[3]

By 1849 there were 82 Ragged schools, with 11,000 Sunday pupils and 8,000 day pupils plus 124 paid and 929 voluntary teachers, and the movement spread to most towns and cities in the United Kingdom during the 1850s. By 1867 there were in London alone 226 Sunday Ragged Schools, 204 Day schools, and 207 Evening schools, with an average attendance of 26,000.[4]

As an example of philanthropic endeavour, the work of the ragged schools was justified both on the grounds of compassion and social expediency—as an attempt to integrate into society those who would otherwise have turned to crime. Even the term 'ragged' is significant, carrying something of the connotation of the 'lumpenproletariat', and ragged children were regarded by contemporaries as the offspring of the submerged or outcast sectors of society. The concern of Lord Shaftesbury, one of the Ragged School Union's most prominent campaigners, was prompted in part by the fact that police statistics showed that almost half of persons taken into custody were without any occupation and a third could neither read nor write, thereby illustrating the relationship between poverty, ignorance and juvenile crime.[5] In June 1848 Shaftesbury promoted an emigration scheme for ragged school pupils which he saw, in part, as a solution to the problem of London's destitute children at a time when Australia in particular was clamouring for emigrants.[6] Mary Carpenter, whose pioneering work with ragged children in Bristol achieved national renown, also emphasized the role which ragged schools could play in the battle against juvenile crime. Carpenter advocated three types of ragged school for three types of child : free day schools, employing good teachers, for the mass of deprived and neglected children; industrial schools, with simple food and work training, for young vagrants and beggars (those in danger of falling into crime), with daily attendance enforced by court order; and boarding reformatories, run as family homes rather than penitentiaries, for convicted children.[7]

However, some contemporaries doubted their use. Henry Mayhew believed that ragged schools could not reform children who were unreformable; indeed, a ragged school education would, he argued, make them more skilful and artful criminals.[8] Dickens also had reservations about their utility, arguing that voluntary activity alone could not cope with the scale of the problem of the children of the streets. He also objected to the inevitable element of sabbatarianism and evangelism which informed the work of the Ragged School Union, commenting in September 1843 that 'no person, however well-intentioned, should perplex the minds of these unfortunate creatures with religious mysteries that young people with the best advantages can but imperfectly understand'.[9]

Nevertheless, as the Ragged School Union developed it became increasingly evident that its activities had to go beyond basic educational provision and during the 1850s it provided ragged school pupils with meals, penny banks, infant nurseries, clothing clubs and excursions. Ragged school graduates were found employment and accommodation in hostels.[10] At their peak in 1870 there were 250 ragged schools in London and about 100 in the provinces, with around 30,000 pupils and 400 paid teachers. After the 1870 Education Act most were absorbed by the School Boards, yet, as Michael Sanderson has observed, between 1840 and 1870 they were an important and underrated agency dealing with the rock-bottom illiteracy of the most degraded children too poor to come within the orbit of the voluntary schools, grants and HMIs.[11]

The origins of the ragged school movement in the City of Chester may be traced to 6 September 1851 when, according to the *Chester Chronicle*,

> a meeting of gentlemen favourable to the establishment of Ragged Schools in Chester was held in the large rooms at Messrs. Churton's auction mart in Foregate Street for the purposes of considering the best means of bringing such schools into operation in Chester with as little delay as possible.[12]

The new Society was initially known as 'The Chester Ragged School Institution', with the objective of 'the instruction of the children of the poor in general, more particularly that class who are prevented by their circumstances from all other means of instruction and improvement'.[13]

At the first meeting, which was chaired by the Rev. Chancellor Raikes, it was agreed that the management of the society and its financial affairs would be conducted by a Committee, elected at the Annual Meeting, consisting of a President, two Vice-Presidents, a Treasurer, an Honorary Secretary, an Auditor, all Clergymen and Ministers residing in the city of Chester who were subscribers, and 25 lay subscribers. The Committee was to meet each month, or oftener, five forming a quorum, and the services of the members were to be gratuitous. It was envisaged that the work of the Institution would be funded entirely by voluntary subscription and all subscribers of ten shillings per annum and donors of five pounds or more would be entitled to sit on the Committee and have the privilege of nominating candidates. Accordingly, a committee was formed to carry out the objects of the Society for the ensuing year and the Rev. Chancellor Raikes was duly elected President of the Society, with the Rev. W. B. Marsden, Vicar of St John's, and the Rev. F. Ford, Rector of St Peter's, as Vice-Presidents and Mr John Churton as Honorary Secretary.[14] Thereafter, the composition of the Society represented the elite of local landed and professional society. The Marquis of Westminster and the Right Rev. the Lord Bishop of Chester were patrons of the Society, whilst Lord Egerton of Tatton, the Lord Lieutenant of Cheshire, and the Very Rev. The Dean of Chester later became Vice-Presidents, as did local Members of Parliament, including J. Tollemache, MP, P. S. Humberston, MP, and Sir P. de M. Grey Egerton, MP. Among the foremost professional citizens of Chester who made notable contributions to the work of the Society were William Wardell, banker, of Abbotsfield; Henry Churton, surgeon and coroner, who served as Honorary Surgeon; John Churton, auctioneer, who served as Honorary Treasurer; Thomas Bowers, the Honorary Secretary; John Hicklin, editor of the *Chester Courant*; Joseph Oakes, linen draper and wholesaler; and Joseph Okell, land agent and surveyor.[15]

The first Annual Report of the Society, published in 1854 and prefaced with the entreaty 'Go out into the highways and hedges, and compel them to come in' (Luke XIV 23), provides some explanations for the establishment of a ragged school society in Chester.

First, the foundation of the Society needs to be placed firmly in the broader context of the development of the ragged school movement during the period. Indeed, the report acknowledged that ragged schools were:

> eminently useful and valuable, whether regarded in the light of philanthropy, patriotism or christianity, whether on the ground of benevolence, economy or duty . . . It is an ascertained fact that the outcasts of society, the most degraded children, may by God's blessing on the training afforded in our Ragged Schools, be reclaimed and converted into clean and orderly pupils, and become good citizens and consistent christians.[16]

Moreover, it was noted that such schools had become widely accepted in other cities, including London, Edinburgh, Liverpool, Birmingham and Bristol, hence it was a matter of civic pride as well as civic duty, that Chester, with its strong philanthropic traditions, should follow suit. Indeed, when the Chester Ragged and Industrial School Society was officially inaugurated at a civic ceremony attended by numerous local dignitaries on 10 November 1853, the Marquis of Westminster expressed the hope that the Society 'may form a link of that golden chain of benevolent institutions which draws society together, and which shall prove the glory and defence of our Country'.[17]

Second, the Society sought to meet both a perceived need and to fill a gap in existing elementary educational provisions in the city by providing schools for ragged children. The report acknowledged that 'few places are better supplied with schools suited to each class of the community than our own City'.[18] Indeed, the 1851 Education Census indicates that Chester boasted no fewer than 66 public schools (50 of which were supported by religious bodies), 91 private day schools, and 76 Sunday Schools.[19] Yet the Society observed that there were many poor children wholly uneducated and neglected living in the city and that Chester, like other densely populated places, 'abounds with instances of parental neglect and juvenile depravity'.[20] Moreover, these children were effectively excluded from gratuitous day schools such as the Blue Coat Hospital and similar institutions in the city—where admission depended on the previous good conduct of the children and the known character of their parents—by virtue of their lack of cleanliness, their want of decent clothing, and the notorious vice and immorality of their parents, who lacked material inducements to persuade their children to attend school instead of begging, hawking or stealing.[21]

Third, it was accepted that previous efforts to educate the children of the outcast poor by operating small schools in Chester on Sunday afternoons had been inadequate. These included schools run by the Misses Knill and Provis in Boughton, by Messrs Okell, Ewen and Henderson in Boarding School Yard, Lower Bridge Street, and by Mr Adams in Upper Northgate Street. Thus it was felt that 'a more combined effort was needed, and that the attention of the christian public should be directed to an evil which demanded a more continuous and more systematic agency to overcome'.[22]

Yet the report also suggests that a further motive of the Society was to attack juvenile delinquency in Chester at its roots by removing ragged children from the streets in order to inculcate habits of industry and honesty; in short, by moralising to the poorest of the poor. This objective was perhaps best encapsulated in the Annual Report of 1859, which stated:

> The prevention of habits leading to the commission of crime is far wiser and more hopeful than the mere attempt to reform criminals . . . Your Committee hope in these schools to sow the seeds of religious truth in the minds of the young belonging to the most destitute classes, often to orphans, or, worse than orphans, the children of parents lost to decency or morality, sunk in habits of sensuality, and without self-respect. Such children—aptly called 'City Arabs'—for whose welfare no special means of instruction were provided, now are invited to your schools; kindness and Christian charity welcome them to our open doors; their forlorn aspect, their rags and dirt, meet with no reproach . . . instruction in some of the industrial arts is given to such as seem best fitted for the exercise, enabling the youthful learners

to make themselves useful to their friends, and eventually to obtain an honest livelihood.[23]

Thus the prime aims of the Society were threefold: first, to offer Chester's largely uneducated street-children some form of elementary education; second, to provide them with industrial training which, it was hoped, would enable them to gain honest employment and become respectable members of society; third, and as a corollary of the former, to divert them from embarking on the slippery slope towards criminality.

At its meeting at the Auction Mart on Monday 15 September 1851 the Society resolved to establish two day schools immediately, one in Boughton and another in Bridge Street, with no child under the age of six to be admitted.[24] Land for the site of the former was obtained at the corner of Boughton and Hoole Lane by December 1851, and on 19 December the Committee expressed its cordial thanks to the Directors of the Shropshire Union Railway and Canal Company for their generous grant of a piece of land in Boughton for the purposes of a Ragged School and to Chester City Council 'for granting an Inclosure of the Waste Land at the end of Hoole Lane for the purposes of the Ragged School.'[25] Meanwhile, the Committee engaged temporary accommodation in a large room in St Olave Street and another in Crook Street, at a rental of £5 each, which were to be used for educational purposes only, with a view to preparing children for the industrial school.[26] The Society also engaged two experienced teachers for the new schools. Felix Thomas, formerly an assistant in the Birmingham Free Industrial School, commenced teaching in the Boughton School, whilst Thomas Pearshouse, formerly an assistant in a National School at Wolverly, Worcestershire, took charge of the school in Lower Bridge Street.[27]

The Boughton Ragged School and St Olave's Ragged School duly opened on Monday 5 January 1852, with children attending from 9.00 am–12.00 pm in the morning and 2.00–4.00 pm in the afternoon. St Olave's Ragged School occupied temporary premises in Lower Bridge Street prior to its move to permanent premises adjoining St Olave's Church on 1 March 1852.[28] An evening school was also opened in temporary premises in a large room rented for the purpose in Crook Street on 17 January 1852: it was used on three evenings per week between 6.30 and 9.30 pm (Monday, Wednesday and Friday) until the end of March, when the room at Boughton was enlarged and two evening classes were held there.[29] On 26 April 1852 Felix Thomas reported that 120 children (79 boys and 41 girls) had been recruited initially at Boughton School, although 25 of these had since left. Of those who had left, seven had gone begging, eight had moved to other schools, nine had gained employment, with two unaccounted for. Initial recruitment at St Olave's was 133 children (41 girls and 92 boys), of whom 32 had left. Of those who had left, three had gone begging, three had moved to Chester Workhouse, eleven had gained employment, five were unaccounted for. Of all the children attending, it was noted that there were 55 whose parents were receiving parish relief; 54 who were fatherless; 17 who were motherless; and 10 orphans. Thomas noted that the attendance at both evening schools was irregular, with 34 pupils attending Boughton School and 45 pupils attending Crook Street School, adding that the children were hoping that the evening schools would be closed for a few months during the Summer because many of them were kept at work until a late hour and could not attend the school before 8 o'clock, thus being obliged to leave altogether. Thomas also reported that each school was open on Sundays from 2 o'clock until 4 o'clock, although children who attended the day schools were encouraged to attend other schools on the Sabbath in order to accommodate 'any who may feel disposed to come who do not attend any Day School and who are too badly clothed to attend any other Sunday School'.[30] Other Cheshire towns followed Chester's example. In 1854 Stockport established a day school 'for destitute lads' which offered, in addition to academic studies, a range of industrial occupations including tailoring, shoe-making, and making clothes and bed linen, whilst Macclesfield established a ragged school for 100 pupils in 1856 which taught reading, writing, religious instruction and industrial activities, including knitting and clog-making.[31]

The Society was determined from the outset that only ragged children would be admitted to the new schools. On 30 August 1852 the Committee urged Thomas and Pearshouse to exercise an increased degree of caution as to the admission of pupils,[32] and duly resolved that 'the proper objects for admission be destitute orphans, destitute fatherless or motherless children, children who have been entirely neglected by their parents, up to ten years of age, and children who have been deserted by their parents, all of whom are to be six years old and upwards, and to be regularly entered upon the register of the schools'.[33] The Committee also resolved that children whose parents could provide for them but had neglected to do so for a period of six months could be admitted temporarily whilst inquiries were made as to whether they could be placed in some of the existing day schools.[34] Yet Felix Thomas observed that there were many ragged children in the city who did not take advantage of the new provisions:

> I cannot close these remarks without making known that there is to my knowledge a great many poor ignorant children who are not attending any Day or Evening School. I feel sorry when I meet with so many half-starved boys and girls in this city who are wandering from house to house selling rubbing-stones, firewood etc. I have requested many of them to attend my School and have been answered with a downcast look, 'Sir, I am obliged to go out and get some bread.[35]

The Committee also showed willing to maintain some of the most destitute children at the expense of the Society. In January 1855 it was reported that ten children were maintained at the expense of the Society,[36] and in February 1856 John Churton observed that 19 of the most destitute children were entirely clothed and fed at the expense of the Society.[37]

Admission rules were further revised in consequence of state legislation. The Industrial Schools Act of 1857 enabled vagrant children aged from 7 to 14 to be sent by Magistrates or Poor Law Guardians to industrial schools for training, with government grants covering half the costs of rent, teacher's salaries and school meals. Thus in October 1857 the Committee agreed to review the new legislation[38] and duly applied for a copy of the Act of Parliament to distribute among committee members.[39] In 1861 the Society resolved to have Boughton School certified with reference to the Industrial

Schools Act of 1861,[40] and in 1863 Chester ragged schools were granted status as Industrial Schools.[41] Thus it was reported in July 1864 that boys had been sent to the schools by the local magistrates for fixed term sentences.[42] The Reformatory and Industrial Schools Act of 1866 (which remained in force until the Children's Act of 1908) consolidated earlier legislation, specified the categories of children between the ages of 10 and 16 who could be placed in industrial schools, codified the dual system of voluntary control and Home Office inspection and established Home Office authority over industrial school buildings and rules. Moreover, children admitted under the terms of this Act had to be sufficiently clothed and fed, the dietary to be approved by HMI.[43] Thus the Annual Report of 1869 showed that the children admitted to the Chester ragged and industrial schools also included 'children found begging or exposed to beg, or wandering without any settled place of abode, or having no visible means of subsistence, or frequenting the company of reputed thieves, and associating with criminals and vicious persons' (all of whom could be sent by a Magistrate to a Certified Industrial School under Section 14 of the Act). In addition, children who had not been previously convicted of felony, but who had appeared before the Magistrates charged with an offence punishable by imprisonment, were sent to the industrial schools at the discretion of a Magistrate (as authorized by Section 15 of the Act), sometimes after having been sent to the workhouse on a temporary basis until a place was available at one of the local industrial schools.[44]

The Annual Reports of the Chester Ragged School Society provide a record, drawn from the admission registers, of the numbers of children who were admitted by the Society to its ragged schools. Table 5.1 presents a statistical analysis of those admitted between 1852 and 1870. It shows that some 2,551 children, comprising 1219 boys (47.8%) and 1332 girls (52.2%), were admitted to Boughton and St Olave's during the period. There were 1,211 admissions to Boughton School, comprising 564 boys (46.6%) and 647 girls (53.4%), whilst 1,340 children were admitted to St Olave's School, comprising 655 boys (48.9%) and 685 girls (51.1%).

The Annual Reports also contain information pertaining to the personal and familial circumstances of children who were admitted to

Table 5.1: Numbers of Children admitted, 1852–70

	Boughton		St Olave's		Total	
	No.	%	No.	%	No.	%
Boys	564	46.6	655	48.9	1219	47.8
Girls	647	53.4	685	51.1	1332	52.2
Total	1211	100	1340	100	2551	100

Source: CRO, Chester Ragged School Society Annual Reports, 1852–70.

the ragged schools. This evidence is not without its limitations. For example, the classifications which were employed were rather basic, comprising 'parentless', 'fatherless', 'motherless', 'deserted by father' (but not by the mother), 'father in prison or transported' (but not the mother), 'supported by father', 'both parents living' (which reveals nothing of their condition), and 'supported by the Parish'. Moreover, there were differences between Boughton School and St Olave's School in their methods of classifying children. For example, the categories 'deserted by father', 'father in prison', and 'supported by father' were initially deployed at Boughton, then discarded, but were hardly deployed at all at St Olave's. Similarly, the classification 'both parents living' was widely employed at St Olave's but hardly employed at Boughton. Finally, the returns are by no means comprehensive since the circumstances of some children were not recorded. Moreover, the returns shed little light on the extent to which the children of the itinerant Irish population of Boughton (described by Kristina Jeffes earlier in this volume) were admitted to the school. Nevertheless, these returns do provide some insights into the kind of children who attended Chester's ragged schools between 1852 and 1870, as Table 5.2 illustrates.

The table shows that of the 2,551 children who were admitted to the ragged schools at Boughton and St Olave's during the period, the personal circumstances of 2,349 children are recorded. Of these, 88 (3.7%) were orphans, 637 (27.1%) were fatherless, and 237 (10.1%) were motherless. In addition, 89 children (3.8%) had been deserted by their father and the fathers of 37 children (1.6%) were in prison. In

Table 5.2: Class of Children admitted, 1852–70

	Boughton		St Olave's		Total	
	No.	%	No.	%	No.	%
Parentless	50	4.8	38	2.8	88	3.7
Fatherless	346	33.5	291	22.1	637	27.1
Motherless	113	11.0	124	9.7	237	10.1
Deserted by Father	78	7.6	11	0.8	89	3.8
Father in Prison	34	3.3	3	0.2	37	1.6
Supported by Father	130	12.6			130	5.5
Both Parents living	57	5.5	724	55.1	781	33.3
Supported by Parish	225	21.7	125	9.3	350	14.9
Total	1033	100	1316	100	2349	100

Source: CRO, Chester Ragged School Society Annual Reports, 1852–70.

short, 1088 children (or 46.3% of all children whose personal circumstances are recorded) were deprived of either one or both parents. Although 781 children (at 33.9% by far the largest single category) had both parents living it seems reasonable to assume that these children were living in acute poverty (otherwise they would not have been admitted to the schools), although the returns do not indicate whether or not their parents were in receipt of outdoor relief from the Poor Law. However, 350 children (14.9%) were supported by the Parish. The overwhelming conclusion to be drawn from this material is that the children who attended Chester's ragged schools were, as the Society intended, drawn from the most deprived and destitute sectors of local working-class society.

The Annual Report for 1859 offers an interesting illustration of the kind of deprivation suffered by some of the children who were admitted to the Chester ragged schools, for it provided some case-studies, drawn from visits to the homes of the children themselves, 'which may be accepted as representing an average of the whole'. Thus one reads of:

A motherless child, mother confined to bed, and a sister aged 16 in a consumptive state—very destitute; a fatherless boy—one son at home aged 17, a great cripple, and another nearly as bad; two fatherless children (family of 6), a very clean, orderly place; a fatherless boy (6 of a family), in a most wretched condition; a fatherless child, deserted by her mother, lives with her grand-mother, a most pressing case for the dormitories; a family of eight—three at the school—father twenty weeks in the Infirmary (since dead), several of the children almost nude, and the whole in a most filthy and almost starving state.[45]

The Minutes of the Society, which include some references to the admission of specific children, reinforce this impression. One reads, for example, of applications made on 10 December 1852 to admit the sons of Bithel, a tailor, of St Olave Street, of Widow Jenkins, and of Gibson of St Olave Street to Boughton School. The Committee duly resolved that Bithel and Gibson could be admitted for one month each on probation, during which time they were to be supplied with food, that Mrs Bithel was required to produce a copy of the register of her marriage, and that Jenkins should be admitted into the school and 'enjoy all its privileges'.[46] In contrast, in July 1865 an application was made 'for the admission of two children of the convict Hesketh into the school to be placed upon the partial fed list; ordered that they be admitted'.[47] Other poor children were admitted to the school provided friends of relatives promised to help to support them. Thus in August 1864 the Committee resolved that 'The boy William Clarke be admitted to the school for three months, be instructed in tailoring, and receive two meals per day in the week, his father paying 1s. per week in advance for these advantages',[48] whilst in May 1865 it was resolved that Samuel Higham be admitted 'provided Mr Williams will undertake to pay 2s. 6d. per week towards the boys maintenance', and that 'the girl Jones be admitted', with the caveat that Mr H. Churton would be required to pay £8 per annum towards her maintenance'.[49] Children were also sent to the school by the Cheshire magistrates. On 14 July 1864 it was reported that 'The boy Weaver has been sent to the school by the Broxton magistrates for 6 months; a boy Scott from Northwich for 3 years and a girl Taylor from Birkenhead for four years',[50] and in the following week it was noted that 'Elizabeth Anne Burgoyne has been committed under the

Industrial Schools Act from Northwich for three years and John Basley has been sent from Runcorn for five years.[51]

What sort of curriculum did these children follow in Chester's ragged schools? In the context of academic studies, the curriculum was similar to that offered in Chester's day schools. Thus, as the Society reported in 1854,

> The education bestowed upon the poor children under our care is of a plain and useful character, based upon a knowledge of the Scriptures. Reading, Writing and Arithmetic are taught on weekdays, between the hours of 9 and 12 in the forenoon, and from 2 to 4.30 in the afternoon.[52]

By 1869 little had changed. The Annual Report recorded that 'The intellectual instruction comprised reading, Writing, Arithmetic 'and such other subjects as the classes may appear capable of learning with practical benefit'.[53] However, the Minutes show that the Society was determined from the outset that religious teaching in the schools should be undenominational. In 1854 the Committee noted that once ragged schools had been established in Chester 'a fear seemed to be entertained that an attempt was likely to be made to proselytize the children and to remove them from one branch of the christian community to another', and affirmed that religious instruction was taken from the Bible alone, and that no denominational bias was given to the children'.[54] The evidence suggests that this policy was adhered to. Thus Mr Bushell was able to claim at the Annual Meeting on 18 April 1870 that 'in the management of these schools the religious difficulty, of which they heard so much now in the discussions on voluntary elementary education, had not appeared', and recommended that a copy of the Annual Report be sent to Mr Forster 'in order that he might see that it was possible for gentlemen who differed in religious opinions to conduct a school without banishing the Bible or religious teaching from the school'.[55] Indeed, the Dean of Chester was moved to comment that:

> They stood upon a platform which secured the co-operation of Church people and Non-conformists; and it had been said that the religious difficulty of which they heard so much had not been

Table 5.3: Industrial Work at Boughton Industrial Ragged School, 1861

	Boys	Girls
Monday	1–4 Afternoon: Tailoring and Gardening	1–4 Afternoon: Housework
Tuesday	1–4 Afternoon: Tailoring and Gardening	2–4 Afternoon: Sewing and Knitting
Wednesday	1–4 Afternoon: Tailoring and Gardening	2–4 Afternoon: Sewing and Knitting
Thursday	1–4 Afternoon: Gardening and Shoemaking	2–4 Afternoon: Sewing and Knitting
Friday	1–4 Afternoon: Gardening and Shoemaking	1–4 Afternoon: Housework
Saturday	9–1 Morning: Gardening and Shoemaking	9–1 Morning: Housework

Source: CRO, RSS, Tenth Annual Report (1861), 11.

felt [in Chester]. Why, of course, it had not been felt. Good earnest men who meet together under a high motive to do good did not feel that difficulty.[56]

In contrast, industrial training formed an increasingly important role within the curriculum between 1852 and 1870. Indeed by 1869 the rules of the Society specified that industrial training 'shall be the principal object of the schools and shall be such as will form habits of labour, neatness, order, and general usefulness, rather than skilfullness in any particular calling'.[57] As Table 5.3 indicates, weekday afternoons and Saturday mornings were set aside for children to receive practical instruction in industrial work. Industrial training for the boys consisted initially of instruction in gardening and tailoring, to which shoemaking and woodsplitting were added during the 1860s. John Rigby was appointed to supervise gardening instruction and a tailor, George Bemain, was appointed to supervise the boys for the purpose of 'indoor work', which involved making and repairing clothes. It is clear a that the boys worked extremely hard: in 1855 they spent 25 weeks on this work, producing nine pairs of trousers, three jackets, four waistcoats, and 36 caps, and repairing 12 garments;[58] in

1857 they produced 19 pairs of trousers, 15 vests, 36 caps, five capes or mantles, five jackets and repaired 20 garments;[59] in 1858 they produced 32 pairs of trousers, 18 jackets, 12 vests, 30 caps and repaired 40 garments.[60] Industrial training for girls comprised instruction in housework, sewing and knitting. In June 1853 the Committee thanked Mrs Wardell for having promoted the industrial system in the girls' department of the Boughton School and recommended its adoption in St Olave's School,[61] and in September 1853 it was resolved that 'a Committee of Ladies would be most essential to the effectual carrying out of the proposed system of industrial training and feeding, and that the Secretary be requested to make application to Ladies who would be willing to become members of such a committee.[62] By 1854 arrangements had been made to teach the girls to sew, and Harriet Thomas, wife of Felix, was appointed sewing mistress and manager of the domestic department at Boughton School, with Elizabeth Pearshouse, wife of Thomas, performing a similar function at St Olave's School. Moreover, in consequence of these developments, the Committee established a Clothing Club for the children.[63]

Despite these developments, the Chester Ragged School Society faced two major problems in attempting to achieve its objectives. First, as a voluntary body, the Society constantly required sufficient funds to feed, clothe and educate ragged children and to improve and extend support facilities, including buildings. Indeed, the Annual Reports suggest that between 1852 and 1870 there was perennial concern over financial matters, with the result that the Society not infrequently lived a hand-to-mouth existence. Second, as the role and work of the Society developed so the number of children who received assistance increased, which in turn put increasing pressure on support services, including accommodation.

Initially, the Society was entirely dependent on income from donations and subscriptions. The Annual Reports suggest that income from these sources fluctuated between 1852 and 1870: for example, in 1852 the Society received 173 donations with a total value of £465.4.6 (which included £50 from Marquis of Westminster) and 264 subscriptions worth £234.3.0; In 1853 there were 29 donations, worth £61.11.3, and 229 subscriptions, worth £213.10.0; in 1859 income from donations totalled £40.17.6 and 217 subscriptions raised

£196.9.6; In 1869, income from 21 donations totalled £148.16.9 whilst 221 subscriptions raised £224.13.6.[64] These funds were, in themselves, inadequate. In 1859 the Treasurer, John Churton, observed that it took £8 to feed, clothe and educate a starving and ignorant child for a whole year, and called upon the citizens of Chester for greater financial support, adding 'What ample a reward for so small a sacrifice !'[65] In June 1860 it was reported that the Society was £120 in debt and that additional subscriptions and donations were required and 'the gentlemen of the press' were encouraged to publicize the issue with a view to encouraging subscriptions from those who had not yet subscribed or donated to the Society. The Lord Bishop of Chester was moved to comment:

> Now let us ask you about those little children who are left to run wild about our streets, whose religious education is neglected, and who are suffering in a worse way from neglect, ignorance, temptation and vice. What I ask you to do is to stretch out your hand [ie. money] and save them.[66]

The Society was forced to utilize additional means to supplement the income from donations and subscriptions. The institution of subscriptions to the Clothing Club brought in extra revenue, as did monies collected by Lady Collectors.[67] Income from sale of vegetables, firewood, clothing, shoes and other products of the Ragged Schools also boosted the coffers of the Society. In 1858 the Annual Report carried the following advertisement:

> Vegetables, grown on the land cultivated by the Boys, are constantly on Sale at the Boughton School. Orders will be punctually attended to, and Vegetables sent to any part of the City.[68]

Similar advertisements were carried in subsequent reports and in 1869 the Committee acknowledged that industrial work had 'as usual brought no small contribution to the funds; the vegetables have supplied the household and afforded a surplus for the market', adding that 'this branch of the school education is valuable not only in its financial aspect but in its useful training of the children and the habits of industry which it induces'.[69] Nevertheless, large donations from leading patrons often came to the rescue of the Society. Thus in 1859 a donation of £100 from William Atkinson Esq., of Ashton Hayes, was 'expended in conformity with the donor's wish in the erection of hot and cold baths, and otherwise providing the establishment with an efficient supply of water, cooking apparatus, washing appliances etc'.[70] Similarly, in 1867 the Committee reported—not for the first time—that the Marquis of Westminster had provided a donation which 'relieved them from all anxiety and enabled them to complete the work they had in hand'.[71]

The Society also welcomed material support from benevolent Cestrians and the Annual Reports frequently requested and specified 'acceptable presents' which would be 'gratefully acknowledged'. Thus in 1858 it was reported that 'presents of cast-off clothing would be acceptable; also, books for the formation of a school library',[72] whilst in 1869 it was reported that 'Contributions of coals, waste timber for converting into firewood, and books for a school library will be most acceptable; and three or four Store Pigs are much wanted'.[73] The 'acceptable presents' which the Society received, and which are listed in the Annual Reports, were wide-ranging. In 1859 these included an easel and blackboard donated by the Directors of the Church Institute and several parcels of books for the school library, parcels of left-off clothing, Easter buns and Christmas dinners.[74] In 1862 they included cauliflower and celery plants for the garden, parcels of left-off clothing, 48lbs of cheese, two store pigs and a bag of Indian meal for their food, 60 yards of calico, two hares and three couples of rabbits, books for the school library, a dinner of roast beef and plum pudding for Christmas Day (courtesy of Mr Sheriff Oakes), a weekly supply of dripping for making the children's Seed Bread, and a dozen garments for both boys and girls 'whose attendance and conduct had been most satisfactory during the year',[75] whilst in 1866 gifts included 60lbs of bun loaves, 9 couples of rabbits, books for the school library, and several parcels of left-off clothing.[76] In 1869 presents donated included 10 yards of flannel, one bag of marbles, Alphabet Cards and Scripture texts, nuts and oranges (in race week), buns (on breaking up), four petticoats, clogs and pinafores, four shirts and four chemises, and prizes for the 1st and 2nd classes, and the Committee conveyed its thanks to the Managers

Table 5.4: Dietary regime at Boughton School, 1859

	Breakfast	Dinner	Supper
Sunday	Coffee and Bread	Meat and Potatoes	Seed Bread
Monday	Seed Bread	Bread and Cheese or Dripping	Thickened Milk
Tuesday	Thickened Milk	Pea Soup	Seed Bread
Wednesday	Coffee and Bread	Cold Meat and Potatoes	Thickened Milk
Thursday	Thickened Milk	Rice Milk	Seed Bread
Friday	Seed Bread	Pea Soup	Bread and Treacle
Saturday	Thickened Milk	Cold Meat and Potatoes	Bread and Cheese

Source: CRO. RSS. Eighth Annual Report (1859), 9.

of the Grosvenor and Queen's Hotels for supplying the school with free broken meat, which had provided destitute children with partial feeding.[77] Indeed, gifts of foodstuffs were particularly appreciated by the Society, for the expense of providing free meals for the children was considerable, and in April 1870 the Society appealed for further donations to help feed the children in the schools because

> the scholars are many of them the children of most destitute parents and it can scarcely be expected that mental exertion or moral training can be anticipated from young children who are literally only one degree removed from a state of starvation.[78]

Not surprisingly, standard dietaries offered at the schools were both limited and monotonous and were similar to workhouse dietaries. As Table 5.4 illustrates, these comprised various combinations of coffee and bread, seed bread, and thickened milk for breakfast, meat and potatoes, pea or rice soup and bread and cheese for dinner, and seed bread, bread and cheese, bread and treacle or thickened milk for supper.

Central government grants undoubtedly enhanced the work of the Society. In June 1856 the Society was elated by 'the timely and liberal aid' afforded by the Committee of Council on Education when

Boughton School was submitted to government inspection and grant-aid was forthcoming. This in part encouraged the Society to build dormitories to accommodate 30 children (20 boys, 10 girls), which were finally completed in 1859. However, the Committee of Council grant was reduced from £148.6.3 in 1859.[79] to only £26.4.8 in 1860, when the Committee pointed out that the dormitories had been constructed largely due to this grant, adding:

> Are 30 of the most wretched children in the city, for which accommodation is now provided, to continue to ask for 'bread and received a stone ?' . . . Are neglected children, of whom there are yet a great many, to continue to grow up in the darkest ignorance?[80]

Nevertheless, with the implementation of the Revised Code, grant-aid from the Committee of Council was withdrawn in 1863 when Her Majesty's Inspectors Report on Boughton School stated that a grant of £64.12.7 had been made to the school and that this payment closed the account of the school with the Committee of Council on Education.[81] However, the acquisition of certified industrial school status by the Boughton School in 1863 in consequence of the Reformatory and Industrial Schools Act of 1861 provided the Society with an alternate source of central government funding. By 1869 payments made by the Home Office in support of certified cases who had been admitted to the school accounted for half the total income of the Society (£1,247 out of a total income of £2,430).[82]

In addition, local government grants occasionally supplemented central government funding. In January 1867 Cheshire County Quarter Sessions ordered that a contribution of £500 be made towards the enlargement of Boughton School under the terms of the Industrial Schools Act of 1866, provided the school received 40 certified children from the county in return.[83] Similar conditions underpinned County grants to Certified Industrial Schools at Macclesfield in December 1867[84] and Stockport and Birkenhead in October 1869.[85] Moreover, in 1869 it was reported that grants of £200 from Chester City Council and of the same from the County had financed further alterations and enlargements to Boughton and St Olave's during the previous year, enabling an additional number of

Table 5.5: Average Daily Attendances at Boughton and St Olave's 1852–67

School	Year															
	1852	'53	'54	'55	'56	'57	'58	'59	'60	'61	'62	'63	'64	'65	'66	'67
Boughton	56	58	39	55	54	54	54	50	52	61	60	61	67	74	88	103
St Olave's	68	64	41	51	37	27	71	74	44	73	64	61	76	75	74	73

Source: RSS Annual Reports 1852–67

children to be admitted, and thereby keeping pace with 'the increased wants of an increasing population'.[86]

The need to provide accommodation for utterly destitute children was another problem which faced the Society. In 1854 Felix Thomas observed that dormitories had been provided in some ragged schools in London, Birmingham and Liverpool and recommended their construction at Boughton School at an estimated cost of about £200.[87] Accordingly the Society provided four 'friendless boys' with lodgings as a temporary expedient,[88] and in July 1856 the Committee resolved to erect dormitories, although the final cost was almost £900.[89] By 1860 the Society was providing board, lodging and clothing for the most destitute children, with dormitories which afforded accommodation for 20 boys and 15 girls in 'neat and commodious schools'.[90] By the 1860s, however, the Committee also became increasingly concerned at the inability of Boughton and St Olave's to cater effectively for the needs of non-boarders, who comprised the bulk of the children who attended these schools. Indeed, Table 5.5 suggests that average daily attendances at Boughton and St Olave's rose substantially between 1863 and 1865.

Accordingly, on 12 December 1865 the Committee resolved to establish a third ragged school in Chester 'without delay',[91] and on 19 December it decided to purchase suitable property in Princess Street, comprising two houses which belonged to the Ecclesiastical Commissioners and four adjacent cottages, at a total cost of £495.[92] Following a public appeal for funds, the property was purchased in June 1866,[93] and renovations were completed by May 1868.[94] The Committee appointed a schoolmaster, Edward Reynolds, at a salary of £70 per annum, and the Bishop Graham Memorial School opened on 3 August with 30 children,[95] and by February 1869 there were 104 children registered at the school.[96] In March 1869 the Committee resolved that industrial work should be carried out at the school,[97] and additional property on the west side of the School was purchased for £235 in April 1869.[98] At the end of its first year in operation, it was reported that the average daily attendance at the school had been 96,[99] thereby relieving substantially the pressure of numbers on Boughton and St Olave's.

How far had the Chester Ragged School Society achieved its essential objectives in regard to elementary educational provisions, industrial training and the reformation of juvenile offenders on the eve of the 1870 Education Act?

Qualitative evidence pertaining to the educational achievements of the Society is of variable quality and value. The Minutes and Annual Reports of the Society contain references to the quality of ragged school educational provisions but these are clearly partial, subjective, often self-congratulatory. Neither do they shed any light on the perceptions of the parents of ragged children in regard to the quality of their education. In short, these sources tend to paint a rosy picture of sustained academic progress between 1852 and 1870. In 1854, for example, the Committee reported that

> a considerable measure of success has attended the teaching and training. Orderly habits prevail to a considerable extent, the minds of the children are imbued with much sound Scriptural truth, and the progress of many of the pupils (who have no other advantages) in reading, writing and accounts, are highly credi-table,[100]

whilst the Minutes contained several letters from former ragged school pupils which praised the schools for their educational achievements.[101] In 1856 the Committee stated that it had 'every reason to rejoice in the progress made by the children, and to feel satisfied with the unwearied diligence exhibited by the Masters . . . to promote their advancement in religious, moral and useful learning';[102] in 1857 it attributed the sound state of the Schools to 'the sound instruction, forbearing treatment, and well-considered system which continue to mark the proceedings of the Masters';[103] and in 1858 it reported that 'much good is being done by these schools, by imparting instruction to that class of neglected children'.[104] References to the achievements of individual children, which were sometimes included in the Annual Reports, also endorse this image. Thus in 1855 Felix Thomas reported that James King, originally from Edinburgh, and Joseph Rowland, of Cheshire, were initially 'entirely ignorant, friendless, and destitute; specimens of neglect of mind and body; their homes, the street; their only friends for food and shelter, public sympathy', but were now 'progressing most satisfactorily; both are now able to read the Scriptures, write and cast accounts'.[105] Yet the more objective reports of inspections of the schools by external examiners on the eve of the 1870 Education Act also testify to academic progress. For example, Henry Rogers, Assistant HMI, visited Boughton School on 24 September 1869, noting 'the good order and kindly discipline of the School' and concluding 'My first visit has afforded me much satisfaction. The premises and arrangements are very complete. The children passed a very creditable examination, and were all apparently making satisfactory progress. A large number of children enter almost entirely ignorant, and it requires the exercise of much time and much patience to get them forward'.[106] The Rev. Sidney Turner, HMI, submitted a further report on Boughton School on 29 March 1870, reporting 'everything in excellent order. The appearance of the children very satisfactory, and the teaching carried on very efficiently'.[107] The Dean of Chester, J. S. Howson, who conducted the annual examinations at St Olave's School and the Bishop Graham Memorial School, was similarly impressed by the educational standards attained by these schools, reporting in December 1869 that St Olave's was 'in a most satisfactory condition as regards both teaching and discipline', and that he was 'much gratified in all respects' with the Bishop Graham School.[108]

Quantitative evidence endorses these impressions. From its inception, the Society maintained a record of the degree of literacy of ragged children on their admission to, and departure from the schools at Boughton and St Olave's and this information was published in each Annual Report. Although the classification which was employed was somewhat crude, comprising variations on the categories 'could

Table 5.6: Literacy of Children admitted, 1852–70.

| | Boughton | | St Olave's | | Total | |
	No.	%	No.	%	No.	%
Read and Write Well	82	6.8	175	13.0	257	10.1
Read and Write	64	5.3	127	9.5	191	7.5
Read a little	395	32.9	337	25.2	732	28.8
Illiterate	661	55.0	701	52.3	1362	53.6
Total	1202	100	1340	100	2542	100

Source: CRO. RSS. Annual Reports 1852–70.

not read at all', 'could read a little', 'could read and write', and 'could read [and/or] write pretty well', an analysis of these aggregate statistics provides some measure of the extent to which the Society achieved its educational aims between 1852 and 1870. Table 5.6 details the degree of literacy of 2,542 children who were admitted to Boughton and St Olave's between January 1852 and December 1869 (i.e. 99.6% of all admissions during the period). It suggests that 1,362 children (53.6%) were illiterate and that 732 (28.8%) could only read a little. In short, 2,094 children (82.4%) admitted by the Society were, as might well be expected, initially either illiterate or semi-literate. In contrast, only 448 children (17.6%) were defined as literate.

Table 5.7 details the degree of literacy of 2,053 children who left Boughton and St Olave's during the same period. Of these, 485 (23.6%) were defined as illiterate on their departure, 449 (21.9%) could read a little, 463 (22.2%) could read and write, and 656 (31.9%) could read and write well. Although these statistics are open to interpretation, they would appear to suggest that the degree of literacy of children who attended Chester's ragged schools between 1852 and 1870 improved substantially, for 1,568 children (76.4%) were literate by the time they left school. Of course, it could be argued that 934 children (45.5%) were either illiterate or semi-literate when they left, but when this is set against the fact that 82.4%

Table 5.7: Literacy of Children on Departure, 1852-70.

	Boughton		St Olave's		Total	
	No.	%	No.	%	No.	%
Read and Write Well	334	33.8	322	30.3	656	31.9
Read and Write	304	30.7	159	14.9	463	22.6
Read a little	94	9.5	355	33.4	449	21.9
Illiterate	257	26.0	228	21.4	485	23.6
Total	989	100	1064	100	2053	100

Source: CRO. RSS. Annual Reports 1852-70.

of children were illiterate or semi-literate when admitted, the statistics still bear testimony to remarkable progress.

The Annual Reports abound with commendatory references to the merits of industrial training. In 1859 the Committee reported that it could trace 150 former pupils who were supporting themselves by 'honest labour',[109] and in January 1860 the Society organized a reunion of former ragged school children at the Corn Exchange—a sight which, it was observed, 'could melt a heart of stone, strengthen one weak in faith or gladden the heart of a philanthropist'—and it was noted that only two of the 170 persons who attended were without employment and that 57 of the young women were employed as domestic servants.[110] In 1864 the Committee reported that it could 'trace very many of the old scholars performing well their parts in life, with several, indeed, occupying positions of trust and responsibility',[111] whilst in 1869 the Committee was moved to comment that it looked back 'with deep thankfulness on the progress made in the cause of industrial education since the Chester Ragged Schools were first set on foot'.[112] These comments notwithstanding, a more valuable index of the success of the Society in preparing ragged children for 'honest labour' may be found in the aggregate returns compiled annually by the Society in regard to the destinations of pupils on their leaving school. The destinations of pupils were enumerated within seven categories, comprising 'to other schools'

Table 5.8: Destinations of Children, 1852–70

	Boughton		St Olave's		Total	
	No.	%	No.	%	No.	%
To other schools	230	23.3	333	29.5	563	26.6
Obtained work	360	36.5	445	39.4	805	38.0
To begging	21	2.1	5	0.4	26	1.2
To the Workhouse	54	5.8	41	3.6	95	4.5
Not Known	217	22.1	211	18.7	428	20.3
Left Chester	93	9.4	83	7.3	176	8.3
Others	10	1.0	12	1.0	22	1.1
Total	985	100	1130	100	2115	100

Source: CRO. RSS. Annual Reports 1852–70.

(which were unspecified), 'obtained work' (although the range of occupations is not recorded), 'to begging', 'to the Workhouse', 'not known', 'left Chester' (for unspecified destinations) and 'others' (also unspecified).

Table 5.8 details the aggregate returns in regard to the destinations of pupils who left Boughton and St Olave's between 1852 and 1870. It shows that of the 2,115 children who left the schools during this period, 805 (38%) obtained employment, although information relating to the kind of employment which was obtained by both boys and girls, or, indeed, to the permanence of that employment, is lacking. Moreover, 563 children (26.6%) moved to other day schools in Chester, which perhaps illustrates the academic progress made by many ragged school pupils whilst attending the schools. Taken together, these figures suggest that the Society achieved a measure of success in providing nearly 65% of its pupils with a better start in life. However, the destinations of 626 children (29.7%) remain unknown, concealed within the categories 'not known', 'left Chester' and 'others'. Some of these children may well have secured employment, whilst others returned to their former street-life in other towns, resorting to begging—as did 26 former pupils of Chester's ragged schools—or to crime.

The Annual Reports also suggest that the Society believed that Ragged and Industrial Schools were indispensable in the fight against juvenile delinquency in Chester. First, it was held that those who were sent to such schools were less likely to commit further offences thereafter because they had lost both their criminal connections and their criminal skills, whilst their prospects for honest employment were better because they had experienced regular training in the schools. At the Annual Meeting of the Society in June 1860, Mr J.Rogers claimed that since the neglected poor constituted an ignorant, criminal, and dangerous section of the community, it was in the duty and interest of everyone to aid in diminishing their number by providing Ragged Schools—'the very best thing for protecting the young against the evils that they were often subjected'—whilst the Rev. Chapman observed that Chester's ragged schools had already rescued a large number of children, adding that if the people did not support the children in these schools, they would unquestionably be compelled to support them in prison.[113] The Rev. Dr Miller, Honorary Canon of Worcester Cathedral and Rector of St Martin's, Birmingham, who also attended the meeting, added that:

> Crime was not only dangerous but costly. Surely the experience they had with regard to all their philanthropic institutions in the present day was the best argument that could be adduced in illustrating that the juvenile population during the last 25 years had become greatly improved. What would have been the state of England now, in a political, social, moral, intellectual, and commercial point of view, if these societies were not in existence? The proper education of the young was of the utmost importance, for if children were not educated in schools they were educated in the streets, every day, by the great enemy of souls, which too frequently placed them in the dock before magistrates, as criminals.[114]

Second, it was argued that children had been removed from the scene of criminal life before they had become hardened, thus breaking the progression from minor offender to major offender. This had a number of benefits, according to William Wardell:

By taking hold of these people [ragged children] before the law interfered with them the country and the nation at large would be benefited. The social position of the community and their happiness depended upon the character of the people, because if the lower classes were left to themselves the property and lives of those above them would be insecure, whereas if the religious and moral condition of the people were as it ought to be, all would be safe.[115]

Similarly, in welcoming the passing of the Industrial Schools Act of 1870, the Committee was moved to comment that:

Formerly it was impossible to deal with many of these [ragged] children, whom they now saw there clothed and well fed, who were in positions of great danger. It was impossible to deal with them till they became criminals. But now, instead of waiting for the cure, prevention stepped in; and whenever it was found that children were begging, or associating with evil companions, not properly cared for by their parents, or in a position which was calculated to lead them into crime, the magistrates had power to send them to industrial schools.[116]

Finally, it was argued that attendance at such schools reduced the number of juveniles appearing before the courts by taking some of them, including gang leaders, out of circulation. Thus Mr P. S. Humberston, a Chester JP and MP, observed in 1859 that:

Since the schools have been in operation, the amount of juvenile depravity has been diminished, and that it was now very rarely that any children were brought up to the police court charged with such offences as, on the case being proved against them, caused them to be imprisoned, and the whole credit of this is to be attributable to the operations of the ragged schools.[117]

Significantly, Humberston's comments foreshadowed the conclusions of the *Report of the Royal Commission on Reformatories and Industrial Schools* of 1884, which credited such schools with breaking up the gangs of young criminals in the larger towns; ending the training of boys as professional thieves; rescuing juvenile criminals from becoming habitual or hardened offenders; and preventing large numbers of children from entering a career of crime.[118]

The Chester Ragged Industrial School Society undoubtedly made a significant contribution to the education and welfare of the 'children of the streets' in Chester between 1851 and 1870. As such, it offers an interesting illustration of some of the motives for, and consequences of philanthropic endeavour in mid-Victorian England, most notably in the context of the social control of the children of the poor. Although the Society continued to operate after 1870, the advent of compulsory state elementary education during the final decades of the nineteenth century severely curtailed its range of activities. Boughton Industrial School was eventually closed by the Ragged School Society in 1908 due to declining numbers and became the joint responsibility of Cheshire County Council and Chester City Council in 1911, serving as a reformatory until 1929. In 1876 the Ragged School Society handed over responsibility for St Olave's Ragged School to St Olave's parish and in 1879 it became St Michael's with St Olave's Infant School, whilst the Bishop Graham Memorial School eventually closed in 1915.[119]

Notes

1 For the growth of the voluntary system, see especially G. Sutherland, *Elementary Education in the Nineteenth Century* (London, 1971), 3–26; E. C. Midwinter, *Nineteenth Century Education* (London, 1982),18–28; G.Sutherland, 'Education', in F. M. L. Thompson (ed.), *The Cambridge Social History of Britain 1750–1950* (Cambridge, 1990), vol. 3, *SocialAgencies and Institutions*, 119–70.

2 G. Himmelfarb, *The Idea of Poverty: England in the Early Industrial Age* (London, 1984), 374–75.

3 *The Daily News*, 4 Feb. 1846. Dickens had been appalled by what he had seen at the Field Lane Ragged School, in London's Saffron Hill, which he first visited on behalf of Ms Frances Burdett-Coutts in 1843, andwhich formed the basis of this article. Dickens saw the voluntary Ragged School movement as a rather unsatisfactory stop-gap in what was essentially a national problem. He believed that such schools, which symbolized the twin

phantoms of Ignorance and Want, were mere palliatives and that general action of a concerted kind was required. For further details, see P. Ackroyd, *Dickens* (London, 1990), 427–30.

4 For further details on the growth of Ragged Schools, see J. H. Y. Briggs, 'Ragged Schools', in Sally Mitchell (ed.), *Victorian Britain: An Encyclopedia* (London, 1988), 661–62. See also M. G. Jones, *The Charity School Movement* (London, 1964), 154–62; D. Owen, *English Philanthropy 1660–1960* (London, 1964), 146–51; J. Walvin, *A Child's World: A Social History of English Childhood 1800–1914* (London, 1982), 110–23, 149–58.

5 J. L. and B. Hammond, *Lord Shaftesbury* (London, 1923), 231–35.

6 G. Battiscombe, *Shaftesbury: A Biography of the Seventh Earl, 1801–1885* (London, 1974), 205–06. His idea was to send promising ragged school boys aged 14 and upwards who had been taught crafts such as tailoring and cobbling in school and ragged girls who could gain employment as domestics to Australia and start a new life. However, Parliament provided a grant of 1500 for one year only, which was not repeated.

7 J. Manton, *Mary Carpenter and the Children of the Streets* (London, 1976), 81–111. Mary Carpenter opened her first ragged school in the poor district of Lewin's Mead, Bristol, in August 1846. She sought to individualize the learning experience and to secure employment for ragged school pupils. Religious teaching was unsectarian (an unorthodox and revolutionary innovation) and the curriculum ranged beyond the three Rs, including History and Geography. In 1852 Carpenter gave evidence to the Select Committee of the House of Commons on Criminal and Destitute Children (PP. 515), whose findings influenced the passing of the Young Offenders Act of 1854 (17 and 18 Vict., c.86) which provided for the establishment of reform schools, open to government inspection, for juvenile offenders. In 1862 Carpenter opposed Robert Lowe's Revised Code and the system of 'Payment by Results' on the grounds that ragged schools would inevitably not reach the required standards and would continue to be automatically deprived of government grants. For further details, see especially I. Pinchbeck and M. Hewitt, 'Vagrancy and Delinquency in an Urban Setting', in M. Fitzgerald, G. McLennan and J. Pawson (eds.), *Crime and Society: Readings in History and Theory* (London, 1981), 198–216; see also Himmelfarb, *The Idea of Poverty*, 378–83.

8 H. Mayhew, *The Morning Chronicle*, 19 March 1850. Mayhew attributed the criminal propensities of street children to '[1] the conduct of parents, masters and mistresses; [2] the companionship and associations formed in tender years; [3] the employment of children by costermongers and others who live by street traffic, and the training of costermongers'

children to a street life; [4] orphanhood, friendlessness, and utter desti-
tution; [5] vagrant dispositions and tastes on the part of children, which cause
them to be runaways': H. Mayhew, *London Labour and the London Poor*
(London, 1861), vol. 1, 468–69. For further details on Mayhew's attitude to
ragged schools, see especially A. Humphreys, *Travels into the Poor Man's
Country: The Work of Henry Mayhew* (Athens, 1977), 56–60.

9 N. Philip and V. Neuburg (eds.), *Charles Dickens: A December Vision:
His Social Journalism* (London, 1986), 88–94. The instalment of *Bleak
House* which described the death of Jo, the poor crossing–sweeper, brought
Dickens some hostile comments from the Ragged School Union at its annual
meeting at Exeter Hall in May 1853. For further details, see also Philip
Collins, *Dickens and Education*, (London, 1964), 86–93; N. Pope, *Dickens
and Charity* (New York, 1978), 177–81.

10 J. H. Y. Briggs, 'Ragged Schools', in Mitchell (ed.), *Victorian Britain*
(London, 1988), 661–62.

11 M. Sanderson, *Education, Economic Change and Society in England,
1780–1870* (London, 1983), 21. After 1870 ragged schools had to reassess
their role and activities in the light of the 1870 Education Act and
environmental improvement in many cities. Some closed, but others continued, for education was neither free (until 1880) nor compulsory (until 1891).
In 1893 the RSU was relaunched as the Shaftesbury Society, focusing on
work with disabled children, practical instruction of destitute boys on the
training ship *Arethus*, and missions for poor families in inner-city slums. For
further details, see especially H. W. Schupf, 'Education for the Neglected:
Ragged Schools in Nineteenth Century England', *History of Education
Quarterly*, vol. 12., 162–83.

12 *Chester Chronicle.*

13 Chester City Record Office [hereafter CRO], DES/23/5, Ragged
School Society [hereafter RSS], First Annual Report (1854), 4. The name of
the association was subsequently altered to 'The Chester Ragged and
Industrial School Institution' in consequence of the Industrial Schools Act of
1857 (20 and 21 Vict., c.48). Later it became 'The Chester Certified Ragged
Industrial School Society' following the passing of the Reformatory and
Industrial Schools Act of 1866 (29 and 30 Vict. c.118).

14 CRO, DES 23/1, RSS, Managing Committee Minute Book [hereafter
Minutes], 15 Sept. 1851; the first committee comprised the Revs F. Ford, W.
H. Massie, W. P. Hutton, R. Thomas, W. B. Marsden, J. Haworth, W.
Evans, J. Williams, R. Knill; Messrs Wardell, Ewart, Colley, Roberts,
Rogers, Harper, H. Churton, Morris, Simpson, Beck, Peters, Bowers,
Dickson, Hope, Sumner, Brown, Titherington, Smith, Parker, J.Churton,

180   ROGER SWIFT

Hassall, Chivas, Boydell, J.Price, Hicklin, Evans, A. Churton, Oakes, Okell, Wilcox, Williams, Henderson, Ewen, Darkin, Jones and Pullan. See also CRO, RSS, First Annual Report (1854), 4.

15 S. Bagshaw, *History, Gazetteer and Directory of the County Palatine of Chester* (Sheffield, 1850), 96–110.

16 RSS, First Annual Report (1854), 6.

17 *Ibid.*, 12.

18 *Ibid.*, 5.

19 *Education Census: England and Wales* (1851), Summary Tables, Division VIII, 168, Section 459 (Great Boughton). For further details on the origins of the Chester ragged schools, see also J. C. Fowler, 'The Development of Elementary Education in Chester, 1800–1902' (unpublished MA Thesis, University of Liverpool, 1968), 121–26.

20 RSS, First Annual Report (1854), 5.

21 *Ibid.*, 6.

22 *Ibid.*

23 RSS, Eighth Annual Report (1859), 6.

24 RSS, Minutes, 15 Sept. 1851.

25 *Chester Courant*, 24 Dec. 1851.

26 RSS, Minutes, 19 Dec. 1851.

27 RSS, First Annual Report (1854), 7.

28 RSS, Minutes, 26 Apr. 1852.

29 *Ibid.*

30 *Ibid.*

31 D. Wardle, 'Education before 1903' in B. Harris (ed.), *VCH, A History of Cheshire*, vol. III (Oxford, 1980), 209.

32 RSS, Minutes, 30 Aug. 1852.

33 *Ibid.*, 25 Nov. 1853.

34 RSS, First Annual Report (1854), 4.

35 RSS, Minutes, 26 Apr. 1852.

36 *Ibid.*, 26 Jan. 1855.

37 *Chester Chronicle*, 9 Feb. 1856.

38 RSS, Minutes, 18 Oct. 1857.

39 *Ibid.*, 14 Dec. 1857.

40 *Ibid.*, 22 Aug. 1861.

41 *Ibid.*, 3 July 1863.

42 *Ibid.*, 14 July 1864. By 1866, of 45 children in the Boughton School as inmates, no fewer than 41 were certified cases: Minutes, 18 July 1866. A strict disciplinary code was laid down for these children and the range of punishments included forfeiting of rewards and privileges; lessening the

quality or quantity of food; confinement in a separate room or light cell for up to three days; moderate flogging with a school cane or rod. However, no child could be wholly deprived of food and was entitled, when confined, to a half a pound of bread and either gruel or milk and water twice daily plus a sufficient quantity of warm clothing or covering. All punishments were registered in a book kept for the purpose which was submitted to the Committee at its monthly meeting: Eighteenth Annual Report (1869), 4.

43 Manton, *Mary Carpenter and the Children of the Streets*, 159–75.

44 RSS, Eighteenth Annual Report (1869), 5. N.B. This report indicates that a medical officer was appointed to visit the schools periodically. in order to ensure that children suffering from infectious diseases were not admitted.

45 RSS, Eighth Annual Report (1859), 7.

46 RSS, Minutes, 10 Dec. 1855.

47 *Ibid.*, 19 July 1865.

48 *Ibid.*, 19 Aug. 1864.

49 *Ibid.*, 29 May 1865.

50 *Ibid.*, 14 July 1864.

51 *Ibid.*, 20 July 1864.

52 RSS, First Annual Report (1854), 10.

53 RSS, Eighteenth Annual Report (1869), 4.

54 RSS, First Annual Report (1854), 7.

55 Report of Chester Ragged School Society Annual Meeting, 18 April 1870, Eighteenth Annual Report (1969), 30–31.

56 *Ibid.*

57 *Ibid.*, 4.

58 RSS, Third Annual Report (1855), 7.

59 RSS, Seventh Annual Report (1858), 8.

60 RSS, Eighth Annual Report (1859), 8.

61 RSS, Minutes, 18 June 1853.

62 *Ibid.*, 29 Sept. 1854.

63 RSS, First Annual Report (1854), 11.

64 RSS, First Annual Report (1854), 13–20; Eighth Annual Report (1859), 13–16; Eighteenth Annual Report (1869), 18–25.

65 RSS, Eighth Annual Report (1859), 12.

66 *Chester Chronicle*, 30 June 1860.

67 Thus, for example,in 1859 income from 61 subscriptions to the clothing club amounted to £18.7.6: RSS, Eighth Annual Report (1859),13–16; In 1869 income from 82 subscriptions to the clothing club amounted to £21.8.0, with £65.12.5 collected by Lady Collectors: Eighteenth Annual Report (1869), 18–25.

68 RSS, Seventh Annual Report (1858), 11.
69 RSS, Eighteenth Annual Report (1869), 8.
70 RSS, Eighth Annual Report (1859), 6–7.
71 RSS, Eighteenth Annual Report (1869), 6.
72 RSS, Seventh Annual Report (1858), 11.
73 RSS, Eighteenth Annual Report (1869), 26.
74 RSS, Eighth Annual Report (1859), 17.
75 RSS, Eleventh Annual Report (1862), 10.
76 RSS, Fifteenth Annual Report (1866), 9.
77 RSS, Eighteenth Annual Report (1869), 10–15.
78 Ibid., 10.
79 RSS, Eighth Annual Report (1859), 10.
80 RSS, Ninth Annual Report (1860), 11.
81 RSS, Minutes, 23 April 1863.
82 RSS, Eighteenth Annual Report (1869) 10.
83 Cheshire County Record Office [hereafter CCRO], QAM/4, Reformatories and Industrial Schools for Juvenile Offenders, Committee Minute Book 1858–1914, 5 January 1867.
84 Ibid., 30 Dec. 1867.
85 Ibid., 18 Oct. 1869.
86 RSS, Eighteenth Annual Report (1869), 7.
87 RSS, Third Annual Report (1854), 8.
88 RSS, Fourth Annual Report (1855), 9.
89 RSS, Minutes, 14 July 1856.
90 W. White, Directory of Cheshire (Sheffield, 1860), 93–94.
91 RSS, Minutes, 12 Dec. 1865.
92 Ibid., 19 Dec. 1865.
93 Ibid., 5 June 1866.
94 Ibid., 12 May 1868.
95 Ibid., 4 Aug. 1868.
96 Ibid., 5 Feb. 1869.
97 Ibid., 31 March 1869.
98 Ibid., 30 April 1869.
99 Ibid., 13 Dec. 1869.
100 RSS, First Annual Report (1854), 10.
101 RSS, Minutes, 19 Feb. 1854; 29 Nov. 1854.
102 RSS, Third Annual Report (1854), 7.
103 RSS, Sixth Annual Report (1857), 7.
104 RSS, Seventh Annual Report (1858), 10.
105 RSS, Third Annual Report (1854), 9.

106 RSS, Eighteenth Annual Report (1869), 8.
107 *Ibid.*, 8.
108 *Ibid.*, 10–11.
109 RSS, Eighth Annual Report (1859), 6.
110 RSS, Ninth Annual Report (1860), 10.
111 RSS, Thirteenth Annual Report (1864), 5.
112 RSS, Eighteenth Annual Report (1869), 8.
113 *Chester Chronicle*, 30 June 1860.
114 *Ibid.*
115 *Ibid.*
116 RSS, Eighteenth Annual Report (1869), 30.
117 RSS, Eighth Annual Report (1859), 6.
118 *Royal Commission on Reformatories and Industrial Schools, Parliamentary Papers* (1884) xiv, 10. See also J. J. Tobias, *Crime and Industrial Society in the Nineteenth Century* (London, 1967), 249–52.
119 A. M. Kennett, *Chester Schools* (Chester, 1973), 13, 20 and 67.

6

'Black Sunday': Skeleton Army Disturbances in Late Victorian Chester

Julian Reed-Purvis

Historians have generally accepted that the second half of the nineteenth century witnessed a marked decline in the use of riot as an expression of popular discontent.[1] However, as David Jones has illustrated, one exception to this trend came with the foundation of the Salvation Army by William Booth in 1878, for the subsequent activities of the Salvationists resulted in numerous public disorders caused by groups that were given the title of 'Skeleton Armies', a term first coined during anti-Salvationist disturbances in Weston Super Mare in 1881.[2] Victor Bailey has shown that there were regional variations in the pattern of these disorders: between 1879 and 1882 the riots centred largely on the North, the North West, the Midlands and South Wales; between 1881 and 1882 disorders were most prevalent in the Home Counties, Wiltshire, Somerset and Devon; finally, there were riots in Sussex and Kent between 1883 and 1885.[3] Moreover, the Skeleton Armies possessed some common characteristics. They dressed up in uniforms, carried dishcloths on broom handles, and chanted far from pious 'rough' hymns, with the intention of mocking the processions and practices of the Salvationists. Preachers were shouted down by abuse, and sundry items, including refuse and cow manure, were hurled at the Salvationists as they marched, as was the case in the Isle of Wight and Honiton in Devon. The Skeletons often drew upon large numbers, and in Folkestone it was estimated that 700 roughs marched alongside the

Salvationists. The membership of the Skeleton Armies was drawn from the lower orders, most commonly labourers, semi-skilled workers and shop assistants. Public houses often played a major role in recruitment and, in many cases, incitement to riot. However, unlike the object of their disdain, the Skeletons did not possess a national organization and their activities appear to have resulted from purely local conditions. Nevertheless, as Donald Richter has observed, Skeleton Army disturbances posed considerable difficulties for both the Home Office and the provincial magistracy in regard to the maintenance of law and order during the early 1880s.[4]

The most serious anti-Salvationist violence occurred in 1882—when 56 buildings were attacked and 669 Salvationists were assaulted—particularly in small provincial towns such as Honiton, Frome and Salisbury.[5] The city of Chester was not immune from these disturbances. On Sunday 26 March 1882, a detachment of the Salvation Army was attacked by a mob in Boughton. For weeks afterwards the local press was dominated by the riot, which virtually paralysed Boughton and witnessed a number of very serious injuries to members of the Salvation Army. The *Chester Chronicle* described the events in Boughton as 'Black Sunday',[6] and the riot, which received national coverage in *The Guardian*,[7] bore many of the hallmarks of a Skeleton Army disturbance. The events surrounding 'Black Sunday', which disturbed the peace of a relatively tranquil provincial cathedral city, are worthy of closer scrutiny, for they provide an insight into contemporary social attitudes in late-nineteenth century Chester.

The Salvation Army was founded from the Christian Mission by William Booth and his wife Catherine in 1878. Booth had been born into an Anglican family but had converted to Wesleyan Methodism, where he quickly became associated with the Reformist Evangelicals, known as the Methodist Connection, and it was in London that Booth found his destiny whilst substituting for a fellow Wesleyan clergyman in Whitechapel. Booth had been deeply unhappy with his occupation as a church minister, and his first encounter with the London poor gave him a sense of mission to save a huge section of the British population that seemed to know nothing of the Almighty. It was here, amidst 'the denizens of Darkest England',[8] that Booth decided to concentrate his work in the East End. This area of London was one of great poverty and was renowned for its drunkenness, and from the start Booth campaigned for temperance among the population, holding his first meeting outside the *Blind Beggar* public house in Whitechapel. The degree to which the East End was dominated by drink is shown by the fact that every fifth shop sold gin; indeed, for many of the poorest inhabitants, alcohol and the public house provided the sole source of enjoyment and entertainment. Despite the inevitable abuse that he received, Booth persevered, establishing other 'stations' in the East End, and thanks to subscriptions from wealthy patrons he was able to buy a headquarters for his mission in Aldgate. By 1875 the Christian Mission had thirty-two stations and had succeeded in winning over thousands of converts.[9]

Booth intended that his mission should be a militant one. His objective was to spread God's word and to provide, for those who were saved, a community in which to worship the Almighty. Together with his son Bramwell, Booth also sought to relieve poverty, and the Mission provided soup kitchens where the poor could avoid the temptations of the public house and innovations such as Christian 'free and easies'. It was whilst drawing up a constitution for the sect that Booth hit upon the idea of a 'Salvation Army', a designation which neatly encapsulated his ideas, for he had always regarded his mission in the sense of a military campaign against sin, a concept which was perfectly suited to an age dominated by imperialism. Booth's followers were his troops, and the movement subsequently used military ranks (Booth became its first 'General'), language and organization, which were regarded as the best means of maintaining discipline and clearness of purpose.[10]

However, the activities of the Salvation Army caused resentment within the communities that they attempted to save. Their condemnation of intemperance and the public house, as well as other forms of popular entertainment, inevitably provoked hostility in working-class districts. Booth's methods also upset the working class, as he felt that any means of attracting the attention of the wicked was acceptable; hence there were to be no half measures, for faith had to be absolute and the message needed to be heard above the din of other distractions. Thus the Army would launch an 'attack' on an area by singing hymns, clapping, shouting and loudly showing emotion. For many, the Salvation Army's methods and beliefs seemed to be self-righteous. Those who were converted to the sect were placed in the mercy seat and were often paraded around the area. The inevitable emphasis was on how their faith had improved their lives. One other area which may well have helped to stimulate resentment amongst the masses was the equal role allocated to both men and women in the Salvation Army, in contrast with Anglicanism and Catholicism, which did not allow women to conduct services and prescribed only a limited role for them. So, to many, the active participation of women in the Salvation Army was at best unusual, and at worst unacceptable. Thus from the outset there were dangers for the Salvation Army in working amidst the poorest elements of Victorian society: the very concept of an 'army' could be misinterpreted to provoke an aggressive reaction, whilst the methods used by the Salvationists to draw attention to themselves upset the peace and quiet of many towns. In particular, their attack on intemperance and their emphasis on how their members' lives had been improved by turning their backs on friends, associates, and the traditional forms of working-class entertainment, inevitably provoked resentment, as the disorders which involved the Skeleton Armies illustrated.

The Salvation Army commenced its activities in Chester on 26 November 1881, but it was not until the evening of Wednesday 26 January 1882 that its activities provoked public concern when, together with some Primitive Methodists, the Salvationists marched through Saughall and the residents of the village complained about the noise generated by Salvation Army hymns.[11] Several days later, a letter from 'An Angry Citizen' was published in the *Chester Courant*. This letter is worth quoting, for it illustrates some of the popular contemporary criticisms which were levelled at the Salvation Army:

> Sir, A detachment of the Salvation Army, now in this city, are allowed nightly to parade streets shouting and singing, to the serious inconvenience of the public. If a man has a restive horse he must hold him fast by the heads to prevent him bolting on account of the noise. If a pedestrian is going in the opposite

direction he must get into a doorway or out of the street until the Army of 'Blood and Fire Soldiers' pass.

How long are the authorities to countenance such obstruction? Let the Army conduct their services in the places they have taken for that purpose. They may there shout their war whoops, do their marching and counter-marching, drill and exhibit their recruits to their hearts' content, but to allow them to parade the narrow and crowded thoroughfares of the city, shouting their songs at such an ear-splitting pitch, argues supineness on the part of the authorities. Only on Wednesday evening past, at the end of Northgate Street, both the tramcar and the Bache Bus were blocked and had to wait until the Army and its followers passed; and then had to walk some distance to prevent collision with the rear.

If an unfortunate fish-hawker puts down her basket on the street to sell her fish, how soon she is pounced upon; or if a shopkeeper has a box or bale for a short time on the footpath, how soon and swift punishment follows; or if an unfortunate publican entertains a friend on Christmas Eve, down comes Justices' justice upon him, and the verdict, 'You are fined 5 and costs, in default, one month's imprisonment with hard labour', is delivered with most impressive solemnity.

Now, Mr Editor, what is sauce for the goose should be sauce for the gander, and if the law is strictly and swiftly enforced and in some instances strained to constrict for small offences, why is this huge obstruction patted on the back and allowed to exist ? I think it shows the necessity of a stipendiary magistrate for the city, one who knows the law and can think for himself.[12]

Nevertheless, the initial success of the Salvationists in Chester was revealed by the large congregations who attended the Sunday services held at the Pavilion Skating Rink in City Road and the *Chester Chronicle* observed:

A glance at the character of the service and the class of people taking part in it may not be uninteresting. And from the outset, unqualified credit may be given to the members for industry. The services on a Sunday number no fewer than four, the first taking place at 7.00 in the morning, the second at 10.00 and the third at 3.00 and the fourth in the evening. The Pavilion Rink, a building erected during the short-lived mania for roller-skating, is capable of accommodating four or five thousand people, and when it was stated that it was on Sunday filled at each service, it will be readily conceived, setting aside the question of whether it will be lasting or beneficial, how great the influence in which has been obtained over the classes who find the services suitable.[13]

The activities of the Salvation Army in Chester were boosted by General William Booth's visit to the city in early March 1882, when large crowds watched the Salvationists, replete with brass band, process from Chester Railway Station to the city centre. During his visit, Booth presented the new standard to the Chester Corps of the Army and duly addressed crowded Salvationist meetings in the Pavilion Rink during the weekend.[14] Booth's visit was not accompanied by anti-Salvationist disorders but during the following week Jeremiah Morris, of Chester, and John Fletcher, of Altrincham, were apprehended and charged with indecent and riotous behaviour after interrupting a Salvationist meeting at the Pavilion Rink, using offensive language and assaulting a Salvation Army officer. The two men, who had clearly been the worse for drink at the time, were duly convicted and sentenced to fourteen days' imprisonment, with hard labour, for causing the disturbance, and seven days' imprisonment for the assault.[15]

Before each Sunday morning service the Salvationists gathered at the Fountain in Boughton and marched to the Pavilion Rink. However, unlike Saughall, the working-class district of Boughton possessed a notorious reputation for rowdy behaviour and had been the scene of disturbances during the General Election of 1880. Moreover, as Kristina Jeffes has shown in her study of Irish settlement in Chester during the early Victorian period, the district had long contained a substantial Irish Catholic population,[16] who were famed, according to the *Chronicle*, for their love of 'hilarity and enjoyment'.[17] The Salvation Army regarded Boughton as an ideal focus for their activities in Chester, for many of the residents were clearly in need of salvation, but the Army also recognized that

Salvationist processions through the district might provoke opposition from some of the inhabitants. Nevertheless, on Sunday 26
March, the Army gathered as usual at the Boughton Fountain. The
procession was led by the 'Captain', Miss Miriam Falconbridge. The
meeting had added significance as the Standard Bearer, Henry
Speed, carried the colours of the Chester Station which had been
presented by William Booth. The possession of the new standard
appears to have emboldened the Salvationists, for they decided to
incorporate Boughton into their route rather than to skirt around the
district, which had been their normal practice hitherto. Accordingly,
they advanced along the Tarvin Road, down Cecil Street, and up
Christleton Road, singing their hymns as they marched, accompanied
by two policemen, Sergeant Price and Inspector Farrell. As Henry
Speed later recalled :

> I was in the procession when it formed at Boughton on Sunday. I
> counted two hundred and seventy five at the corner of Seaville
> Street. We came in the direction of Chester with this force and
> had a large banner. We were singing one of our hymns as we
> came along. When we got to the end of Steven Street, we saw a
> crowd of people there, and they made across the street to
> interrupt us. They did not block it There was no noise then, but
> one or two of them drew up their sleeves and were getting ready
> just as we were nearing them.[18]

At this point, the policemen ordered the crowd, which numbered
between five and seven hundred persons, to part and a way was made.
However, once the police had passed through, volleys of stones,
ashes and cinders, paper bags filled with sawdust and pepper, rotten
eggs, oranges and turnips were hurled at the Salvationists, and cries
of 'Aim at the Zulu' (evidently a reference to the Standard Bearer,
Henry Speed) and 'Hit the Zulu Queen' (Captain Falconbridge) were
uttered. Throughout this onslaught the Army members made no
attempt to retaliate and eventually succeeded in passing down Steven
Street. However, near the bridge over the Shropshire Union Canal in
Sellar Street, the crowd was reinforced by the arrival of a group of
roughs who had been awaiting the procession on the canal towpath,
and the disorders escalated. Miss Falconbridge was struck on the

head by a stone, rendered unconscious, and conveyed to the nearby home of a fellow-Salvationist, Mr Lawson, where she received medical attention; both police officers were hit by stones; and a partially-sighted Salvationist, Henry Thompson, was hit on the head and left in danger of losing his sight completely. Fighting broke out and several marchers were injured, whilst one innocent passer-by who expressed disgust at the proceedings was set upon and thrown into the Canal. Amidst the chaos, Henry Speed led the procession into Brook Street and ultimately to relative safety at the Pavilion Rink.

During the middle of the afternoon a large crowd gathered in Boughton. Estimates vary as to its size, but it was certainly larger than the mob that had initiated the morning disorders, for its ranks contained many women and children. This crowd, which proceeded to march along the Boughton Road in the direction of the Pavilion Rink, displayed all the trappings of a Skeleton Army. The marchers sang parodies of Salvationist hymns and some of the women brandished brooms and umbrellas, to which they had attached dishcloths and shawls for the purpose of mimicking Salvation Army flags. These theatricals were intended to mock and insult the methods and beliefs of the Salvationists.[19]

Police reinforcements, commanded by the Chief Constable, G. L. Fenwick, were duly despatched to Boughton in an attempt to defuse a potentially serious disturbance and, despite angry cries of 'pitch into 'em', Fenwick and Sergeant Murphy succeeded in persuading the crowd to disperse. However, the district remained far from tranquil for the rest of the day, and the *Courant* reported that Boughton:

> was a scene of uncontrolled rowdyism, unoffending passers-by who were in any way suspected of being attached to the Army were assaulted and abused.[20]

The Salvationists managed to complete their services for the day but several were attacked on leaving the Pavilion, whilst the house of Mr Dawson, who had been injured during the morning, had its window-panes smashed by volleys of stones.

The preliminary examination of those accused of taking part in the

Boughton disturbance took place at an overcrowded Police Court on 30 March 1882. The *Chronicle* reported:

> Altogether some twenty three individuals were charged with participating in the riots, and their physiognomy was on the whole most stupid and in many cases of brutal character . . . One or two were young people who might possibly have participated in the riot through youthful wantonness led by older companions. But the majority were unmistakenly roughs of decidedly criminal appearance; some of the women were sallow-faced and of a low type of physique, but most of the men were big, hulking, powerful fellows and included some of the most troublesome characters in the town.[21]

The majority of those charged, including four women, had Irish names, and the dim view that the Bench took of the affair was shown by their refusal to allow bail for those who had voluntarily surrendered themselves to the Court. The main testimony was provided by Sergeant Price, who gave a detailed account of the events of the morning of 26 March 1882. For their part, the defendants strenuously protested their innocence, claiming either that although they had been present during the disturbances they had not thrown any missiles or that they had been elsewhere at the time of the riot.[22] The proceedings were not without their lighter side. One Irish woman, Mrs Dermondy, whose age and respectability evidently distinguished her from her co-defendants, was dressed in her Sunday best and appeared greatly shocked by her predicament. The *Courant* reported that her feelings 'found vent in sundry helplessness, raising of the hands, and whispers of 'Dear . . . dear . . .' She stated that she had not thrown stones during the riot but had merely been looking after her 'poor little children', whom she feared would be trampled by the crowd. However, a witness subsequently stated that he had seen 'the poor little innocent Mrs Dermondy' throw a turnip at the Salvationists.[23] The court was adjourned until the following day, when the hearing began in sensational fashion. The Chairman of the Bench, Sir Thomas Frost, who was also the Mayor of Chester, read out an anonymous letter which he had received, signed 'Revenge and

Death', a phrase which mocked the 'Blood and Fire' motto of the Salvation Army. The letter threatened:

> We (the secret brotherhood of Chester) hear that you will occupy the Chair tomorrow in the hearing of the attack on the Salvation Army, and we (the Secret Brotherhood) under-signed—that is revenge and death—solemnly vow and swear that if you pronounce one or any of the prisoners guilty you and all your brother magistrates will answer with your lives.[24]

The Bench had also received letters from Canon Cholmondeley and William Booth. Cholmondeley strongly attacked the methods and provocative tactics of the Salvationists, claiming

> the Salvation Army is no peaceful guild: it is an organised propagandism and an active proselytising body whose aims interfere directly with that usual orderly and regular attendance at church and chapel.[25]

In contrast, the tone of General Booth's letter was more conciliatory and, whilst pleading for clemency to be shown to those accused of riot, Booth acknowledged that the tactics of the Army might have contributed to the disturbances:

> That the magistrates of Chester take so sensible a view of their duties towards those who merely seek in all order and peace to labour for the good of others, and of course I cannot presume to advise you, who are responsible for order in Chester, as to the exercise of your authority . . . I do venture to plead for your mercy towards our assailants of Sunday last. Their conviction will surely say enough as to the efficiency of the City authorities and will surely be an adequate warning to such persons in Chester, or their punishment, will I fear, lead to more conflict and troubles, if not in Chester, at any rate elsewhere. In any case I have instructed our officers that they are not to approach Boughton, or any other neighbourhood inhabited mainly by the Roman Catholics, with any procession or any such move likely to result in irritating a people with whom we have the most earnest desire to get upon friendly terms with as soon as possible.[26]

The Bench heeded Booth's message: of the 23 defendants, ten were bound over to keep the peace and seven, including the 'respectable' Mrs Dermondy, were discharged. However, a hard core of eight rioters were committed for trial at the Chester Quarter Sessions. These comprised four labourers (Thomas Jordan, aged 31; Edward Hughes, 31; Michael Minton, 25, and Patrick Tansey, 22), three masons (Edward Moran, 28; Robert Davies, 26, and John Brannigan, 30) , and a tailor (Owen McGough, 22).[27] Nevertheless, feelings still ran high and one witness, John Newman, was assaulted as he left the Court House.[28]

The trial of the ringleaders took place at the Quarter Sessions in the Town Hall on Tuesday 11 April before Sir Thomas Frost and Horatio Lloyd, the Recorder, who stated that the Salvation Army was entitled to legal protection, irrespective of their religious convictions, and that he intended to administer fair and impartial justice. Lloyd added that all the elements of a riot had been present during the disturbances and that those charged had either assaulted members of the Salvation Army or had been witnessed at the disturbance. Mr Higgins, the defending solicitor, argued that, with the exception of Jordan, the evidence against the accused was unreliable and in many cases exaggerated, adding that it would have been very difficult for the accused to have participated in the affrays at both Steven Street and Seller Street Bridge. Evidence for the prosecution was provided by several members of the Salvation Army, including Henry Speed, who identified several stone throwers; Henry Thompson, the man left in danger of going blind; and Robert Dutton, who testified that 40 missiles were thrown at his house on the evening of the 26 March, one almost killing his daughter. Accordingly, guilty verdicts were returned against Jordan, Hughes, Minton, Moran and McGough— who were each required to provide sureties of 20s to keep the peace for six months—whilst Tansey, Davies and Brannigan were discharged. In the aftermath of the trial the sentences were criticized for their leniency, and it was argued that the rioters had been allowed to perpetrate a very serious crime without appropriate punishment.[29] In contrast, more thoughtful observers recognized that the imposition of relatively lenient sentences was more likely to facilitate a return to normality since, in the event of further disorders those involved knew that the Court would punish them much more severely. The extent to which the Recorder was influenced by the plea for leniency from William Booth and other Salvationists is unclear. The main aim of the authorities had been to preserve law and order and to ensure that there was no repetition of the disturbances; moreover, as the *Chronicle* observed, this had been achieved, and without the authorities being perceived as overtly sympathetic to the interests of the Salvationists, who had provided much of the evidence in court.[30] The reaction of the Salvation Army to the disorders was, in general, conciliatory and, on the advice of Chief Constable Fenwick, who was widely considered to be an ally of the movement, the Army agreed to postpone a proposed march by the Handbridge Detachment.[31]

Correspondence in the *Chronicle* and the *Courant* suggests that public reactions to the riot and its aftermath were mixed. Both newspapers suggested that the riot had done much to damage the reputation of Chester, an important tourist centre, as a law-abiding city, and urged that strong and firm action should be taken to punish such 'dastardly and unwarrantable conduct.'[32] Moreover, in calling on the civic authorities to maintain both law and order and religious tolerance in the city, they also concurred that whilst the Salvation Army had acted foolishly by marching through Boughton it was nevertheless their right to do so. Indeed, most correspondents to the local press were broadly sympathetic to the rights of the Salvationists and were hostile towards those they held responsible for the riot, namely the Irish Catholics of Boughton. In this context it worth noting that the work of the Salvation Army amongst the lower orders had been welcomed by many in Chester, including John Saul Howson, the Dean of Chester, who praised the attempts of the Army to relieve poverty and discourage drunkenness as something for which 'every Christian heart must truly and earnestly rejoice',[33] and the Reverend R.D. Thomas, who refuted the allegations made against the Army by Canon Cholmondeley.[34] One correspondent praised the Salvationists for providing 'something more homely than most of our churches have to offer', whilst another was moved to comment that the only quarrel the Salvationists had was with the Devil, and that by their attack on the procession the Catholics had shown their religion to be more intolerant and demonstrative than that of the Salvation Army.[35] Councillor Bromley, the member for Boughton, who had visited the Salvationists in the wake of the disorders, was also quick to distance himself from the rioters and to praise publicly the work of the Army in the area. In so doing, Bromley was acknowledging that there were also many respectable citizens in the Boughton area, to whom disorder constituted a threat to both property and the person.[36] Yet by addressing the Salvationists in his ward, Bromley was in effect also acknowledging the role of local Irish Catholic 'roughs' in fomenting disorder. Indeed, one correspondent to the *Courant* maintained that the Salvation Army had a perfect right to march through Boughton, asking 'How long are the Irish in Boughton to be allowed to believe that whenever they choose they can with impunity defy the law;'[37] another described Boughton as 'Little Ireland minus the Coercion Act',[38] whilst a letter in the *Chronicle* pointed to the hypocrisy of Roman Catholics, who enjoyed full religious tolerance and who had themselves held a procession during the recent visit of Lord Denbigh to Saltney.[39] Indeed, the prejudice which some correspondents displayed towards the Irish Catholics was considerable, as a letter published in the *Chronicle* on 1 April illustrated:

The attack of the Irish Papists of Boughton on the unoffending Salvationists ill be handed down as another proof of the development which the human mind is capable of under the influence of Popish learning. We should not shut our eyes to the fact that the affair is but a natural outcome of a system of dogmatic teaching of a Church which has ever proved itself antagonistic to real liberty and which has instilled in the minds of its notaries that persecution is a justifiable means of prompting the interests of the Church. Surely the Irishmen who howl for liberty must be the most arrogant hypocrites. Let us hope that this event, painful as it is in demonstrating the arrogance and intolerance of the Irish contingent of our population, may serve to resuscitate our drooping Protestantism and enable us to keep a more faithful look-out on the watch towers and, in the exercise of wise discretion, see that the Protestant position of our own countrymen are not sacrificed in consideration of our deeper problems offered by the people.[40]

Comments such as this suggest that some Cestrians were unable to distinguish between the acts of the rougher elements who appeared in court, and the views and behaviour of law-abiding Catholics. As one Catholic observed, a riotous Catholic was a bad Catholic, whilst another was critical of the *Chronicle*'s partial coverage of the disturbances, adding that those involved 'seldom or never enter a place of worship and may be termed the very residuum of the Catholic population.'[41]

Yet the Salvation Army was not entirely exempted from criticism. The strongest attack on the Army and its methods was made by Canon Cholmondeley at the Sunday morning mass at St Werburgh's Roman Catholic Church on 2 April. Cholmondeley observed:

We regret to hear of the proceedings of last Sunday, we hope such conflict may be avoided in the future, and our advice to our people is don't join in the attacks, for you may be sure of one thing, you will give strength and sympathy to a cause which we are sure you would not willingly help. The best thing is to take no notice of revivalists. Let them walk until they are tired, and sing until they are hoarse. We have seen this sort of thing before; it has that appearance of religion, which takes with some people for a time, and then dies out. Let it die out, but if you interfere you will only keep it alive. Don't go near them, and it will pass along the street; take not the smallest notice of it than if it did not concern you.[42]

Cholmondeley continued his attack on the Salvation Army in a letter to the *Courant* on 5 April, stating that the Army was fundamentally aggressive—unlike 'peaceful organizations such as the Forresters Lodge or the Oddfellows Lodge'—and that its avowed aim of 'blocking Satan in his stronghold' in Boughton was provocative. Indeed, the Canon expressed his fear that if the Army processed through Boughton again, 'it would be impossible to say what horrors or miseries would occur'.[43] Other correspondents to the local press wrote in similar vein: one described the Salvationists as a 'troop of wild, ignorant, raw recruits who blocked the streets and indulged in blasphemy and desecration',[44] whilst another blamed the Salvationists for the disturbance and pointed out that the Catholic procession in Saltney was a gala occasion, and did not, 'day after day, weary and annoy others with nauseating repetitions of words and music.'[45] A particularly strong criticism of the Salvationists was that in their services and their attitude they appeared elitist and self-righteous— 'modern day Pharisees', according to one correspondent,[46] whilst another observed:

> Have not the peaceable inhabitants the right to protection ? That the poor, ignorant and thoughtless children should be taught to blaspheme and discredit the Sabbath is shocking. Let those erratics keep their own buildings so that the quiet, sober-minded people may enjoy their Sundays in peace and safety.[47]

Neither was the brewing trade, and particularly local publicans, excluded from responsibility for the disorders, as one perceptive correspondent to the *Chronicle* observed on 1 April:

> Facts are coming to light now, that whilst the riot on Sunday morning was by the Irish in Boughton, the real movers were the publicans. It appears from what I can gather now that Catholic and the Irish feeling among the lower classes in Boughton has been a good deal stirred up by the influence of the lower-class publicans, whose business has been at a low ebb owing to the work of the Salvation Army amongst many of the late frequenters of their low taverns and drink shops. Many of the publicans at Boughton and Seller Street neighbourhoods are very wrath at the loss of their business which they are beginning to feel.[48]

Moreover, it was rumoured that the bags of flour and sawdust which had been thrown at the Salvationists had been prepared in public houses in Boughton, that many of the 'roughs' who took part in the disorders had been primed with beer beforehand, and that some Boughton publicans had been seen marching with the crowd.[49]

In assessing the causes of 'Black Sunday', it is clear that the Salvation Army bore some responsibility for the disorders. Boughton was an area that possessed an established reputation for drunken and disorderly behaviour and, whilst this was no doubt an attraction to the Salvationists, who wished to combat what they regarded as sinful behaviour, their decision to alter their route to encompass an area containing a large number of Irish Catholics was both reckless and provocative, reflecting a lack of sensitivity for the feelings of the working-class populace. The leader of the Army on that day, Miriam Falconbridge, was no stranger to conflict, having been previously involved in a riot in Salisbury, and Norman Murdoch has argued that middle-class leaders of Salvation Army detachments, such as 'Captain' Falconbridge, failed completely to relate to or understand the nature of the communities in which they worked.[50] Indeed, Stuart Mews has suggested recently that the Salvation Army was largely responsible for these disturbances: 'Sometimes, it was the Army which seemed to be looking for trouble. At Chester, they deliberately chose to march into the Irish quarter, despite police requests to keep out. The Irish matched the flags and bugles of the Army by turning out in force, armed with cudgels and stones and carrying flags of various kinds. Later that day, about 1000 Irish marched to the Salvationist headquarters in the converted ice rink to storm the building.'[51] However, this over-simplistic interpretation is open to criticism on several counts. First, Boughton was not an 'Irish quarter' *per se*, for its working-class populace, both 'rough' and 'respectable', was not exclusively Irish; second, the crowds which took part in the disturbances were not composed exclusively of Irish people; third, the Irish did not storm the Pavilion Rink; fourth, the police did not request the Salvation Army to desist from marching into Boughton until after the riot had occurred; finally, the course of events clearly indicates that the disturbances constituted something more than a pitched battle between Salvationists and Irish Catholics.

Yet some of the 'rougher' elements of the Boughton populace were also responsible for the disturbances, for there was sufficient evidence to suggest that the riot had been carefully planned, and with the active connivance of local publicans. One Salvationist, who refused to be named, subsequently informed the *Chester Chronicle* that he had been warned by a Catholic friend on Saturday 25 March not to parade at the Fountain on 26 March.[52] The testimony of

Sergeant Price and Henry Speed also confirmed that a large crowd of roughs had intended to intercept the Army on their usual route, and had lain in wait at Bishops Field. Moreover, it was the arrival of this group at the Seller Street Bridge that exacerbated the violence which contributed to most of the injuries sustained by the Salvationists during the day. In this context, Bailey's explanation of the emergence and subsequent activities of the Skeleton Armies in terms of the opposition of brewers and publicans to the Salvation Army, coupled with popular disapproval of the Salvationists' 'moral imperialism' and local community resistance to organizations from outside, is particularly relevant to an analysis of the Boughton disorders.[53]

Thus the riot can hardly be explained in terms of a spontaneous reaction to the presence of the Salvation Army and the violence of the Boughtonites may well be explained in terms of a perceived attack on their neighbourhood culture, within which pub-culture loomed large, rather than any direct threat posed by the Salvationists to their religious convictions. Indeed, there is much evidence to suggest that the riot was fomented by drink. The Salvationists looked upon Boughton as a stronghold of Satan, largely because of its reputation for drunkenness. Yet the public house was integral to popular culture in the district and the constant attacks on intemperance contributed in no small part to the growth of hostility among sections of the Boughton working classes towards the Army and all that it represented. The main instigators of the riot appear to have been local publicans whose trade was threatened by the growing success of the Army in winning converts to temperance. The whole incident was planned in public houses and the fact that the mob was primed with beer in part explains the ugly scenes of 26 March. The role played by drink in the disturbance was highlighted further by the subsequent actions of the magistrates, who considered closing the pubs in Boughton on the following Saturday in order to prevent a repetition of the violence.[54] Moreover, it is also evident that most of the people who were subsequently charged with participating in the disorders were young, and it is possible that—when combined with strong drink—their youth got the better of them. Thus what began simply as an attempt to insult the Salvationists developed into something far more serious.

Yet the activities of the Salvation Army also upset the social equilibrium in the communities, including Boughton, in which they operated: as quiet sabbatarians, abstinence advocates, non-smokers, anti-feathers and fashion, the Army represented a pietistic tradition at considerable odds with those they came to save. Moreover, the Salvation Army attempted to be non-denominational, which often aroused hostility amongst the adherents of traditional faiths, including Roman Catholicism. Norman Murdoch has shown that in Liverpool the Salvationists operated in Catholic and, more particularly, Irish Catholic communities, and the Irish not only regarded their activities as an interference in their way of life but were also sensitive to what they perceived to be an attack on their Catholic faith.[55] Moreover, as Bailey has illustrated, working-class opposition to the Salvation Army occasionally derived from Irish Catholic sentiment, contributing to disorders in Bolton in 1882 and Birkenhead in 1883,[56] and it is likely that at least some of the Irish Catholics who participated in the Boughton riot were motivated by religious sentiment. Moreover, the way in which Catholics and, in particular, Irish Catholics, were discriminated against was one of the most revealing aspects of the Boughton disturbance.[57] Even in an ancient city such as Chester, the Irish were viewed with suspicion because of their supposed drunkenness and their adherence to a religion that set them apart from the majority Protestant community, and the attack on the Salvationists allowed Protestant bigots to condemn publicly Catholicism, albeit at a time when anti-Catholic feeling, a feature of mid-Victorian England, had diminished substantially.[58]

Yet the Chester disturbances need also to be considered in relation to local law-enforcement agencies. The civil authorities in Chester clearly failed to anticipate the events of Sunday 26 March. Indeed, the *Chronicle* commented 'It is surprising that the authorities who are primarily responsible for the public peace, should by their inaction, allow such unseemly disturbances as that caused by the Salvation Army to be brought about.'[59] The provision of only two policemen in Boughton on the day of the riot proved hopelessly inadequate, facilitating the escalation of the disorders and contributing to the serious injuries sustained by the Salvation Army at the hands of the mob. Indeed, on 30 March, when it was feared that the Salvation

Army would hold another procession on the following Sunday, the Chester Magistrates urged the Watch Committee to provide the Chief Constable with a sufficient number of men from the Cheshire County Constabulary to assist the city force in maintaining the peace.[60] In the event, these forces were not summoned in view of the subsequent postponement of the procession. However, on 21 April the Watch Committee recommended the establishment of a police station in Boughton to be occupied permanently by one police-sergeant,[61] and on 27 July 1882 the Machine House at Boughton was converted into a police station.[62]

The reaction of the provincial magistracy to anti-Salvationist disturbances during the 1880s differed across the country. In the South of England the Salvationists complained that the magistrates were reluctant to deal firmly against their attackers because they were in sympathy with the Skeletons, as in Poole and Eastbourne where the magistrates actually ridiculed the beliefs of the Salvationists.[63] In contrast, Murdoch has argued that in dealing with disturbances in Liverpool in 1882, the main concern of the civil authorities was to maintain public order without partiality.[64] A far more common reaction of the civil authorities in seeking to restore the public peace was to ban Salvationist processions or, as in Chester, to request the Army not to march in order to prevent any future confrontations. Indeed, this policy, coupled with the sentences imposed on the leading participants in the Boughton riot, proved successful in Chester, for public right of way was confirmed, freedom of speech and religious toleration were preserved, and those guilty of public affray and riot were identified and punished. Henceforth, there were no major attacks on the Salvation Army in Chester, although on 3 May two juveniles, Francis James and Thomas Peers, were each fined 1s., with 2s.6d. costs, for throwing stones at Salvationists at the Pavilion Rink on 29 April,[65] and the Chester Bench emerged from 'Black Sunday' with its independence and integrity intact, an example that other Justices of the Peace would have done well to emulate.

Anti-Salvationist violence during the 1880s had a profound impact on the subsequent development of the Salvation Army. William Booth's vision of an evangelical assault upon sin and wickedness in every town and city in the land was restrained, and his methods subsequently modified. Indeed, Murdoch has argued that the attack on the Army in Liverpool in 1879 was instrumental in this. As General Booth's letter to the Chester magistrates illustrated, he was aware that the causes of the disorders in Chester were very similar to those which had occurred in Liverpool three years earlier, and the reaction of working-class communities, including Irish Catholics, to the Salvation Army subsequently forced Booth to win converts through new means, namely social provision, something for which the Army is rightly praised up to the present day. The riot in Boughton may have played a small part in contributing to this change of policy.

Notes

1 John Stevenson, *Popular Disturbances in England 1700–1870* (London, 1979), 275–300.

2 D. Jones, *Crime, Protest, Community and Police in Nineteenth Century Britain,* (London, 1980), 123.

3 Victor Bailey, 'Salvation Army Riots, the "Skeleton Army" and Legal Authority in the Provincial Town', in A. P. Donajgrodzki (ed.), *Social Control in Nineteenth Century Britain* (London, 1977), 231–53.

4 For an examination of the problems which anti-Salvation Army disturbances posed for the Home Office and the provincial magistracy, see Donald Richter, *Riotous Victorians* (London, 1981), 73–86: 'Dirty Dick's Army'.

5 Bailey, *op. cit.,* 234.

6 *The Chester Chronicle,* 1 April 1882. For the Boughton Riots, see also Julie Gascoyne, 'Anti-Salvation Army Riots in Late Victorian England, with special reference to Chester' (unpublished BA dissertation, Chester College of Higher Education), 1982; Pamela Machin, 'The antagonism encountered by the Salvation Army during the early 1880s, with particular reference to the Riot in Boughton, Chester in March 1882' (unpublished BA dissertation, Chester College of Higher Education), 1984; see also Gordon Watkinson's paper, 'The Boughton Riots, 1882', copies of which are deposited in Chester City Record Office and the Salvation Army Archives, London.

7 *The Guardian,* 29 March 1882.

8 W. Booth, *In Darkest England and the Way Out* (London, 1890), 15.

9 For the Salvation Army, see especially Gillian Ball, 'The Salvation

Army' in Sally Mitchell (ed.), *Victorian Britain: An Encyclopaedia* (London, 1988), 691–92; R. Robertson, 'The Salvation Army: the persistence of sectarianism', in B. R. Wilson (ed.), *Patterns of Sectarianism* (London, 1967), 49–105; R. Sandall, *The History of the Salvation Army 1865–78*, 4 vols (London, 1947); G. Hanks, *God's Special Army: The Story of William Booth* (London, 1980).

10 Gerald Parsons, 'Emotion and Piety: Revivalism and Ritualism in Victorian Christianity' in G. Parsons (ed.), *Religion in Victorian Britain,* Vol. 1, *Traditions* (Manchester, 1988), 213–34;

11 *The Chester Courant*, 28 Jan. 1882

12 *Ibid.*

13 *Chester Chronicle*, 6 April 1882.

14 *Chester Courant*, 14 March 1882.

15 *Ibid.*, 12 April 1882.

16 For the growth of the Irish community of Boughton, see Kristina Jeffes, chapter 3 above.

17 *Chester Chronicle*, 29 March 1882.

18 *Ibid.*, 1 April 1882.

19 *Chester Courant*, 29 March 1882

20 *Ibid.*

21 *Chester Chronicle,* 5 April 1882

22 *Ibid.*, 1 April 1882

23 *Chester Courant*, 29 March 1882.

24 *Chester Chronicle*, 1 April 1882.

25 *Ibid.*

26 *Ibid.*

27 Chester City Record Office. Quarter Sessions Papers. Calendar of Prisoners, April 1882.

28 *Chester Chronicle*, 1 April 1882.

29 *Chester Courant*, 19 April 1882

30 *Chester Chronicle*, 22 April 1882

31 *Ibid.*, 5 April 1882

32 *Chester Courant*, 29 March 1882.

33 *Chester Chronicle*, 5 April 1882.

34 *Chester Courant*, 29 March 1882

35 *Chester Chronicle*, 29 March 1882

36 *Chester Courant*, 29 March 1882

37 *Ibid.*, 29 March 1882.

38 *Chester Chronicle*, 1 April 1882.

39 *Ibid.*, 29 March 1882.

40 *Ibid.*, 1 April 1882

41 *Ibid.*

42 *Ibid.*, 5 April 1882

43 *Chester Courant*, 5 April 1882.

44 *Chester Chronicle*, 1 April 1882

45 *Ibid.*

46 *Ibid.*, 8 April 1882.

47 *Ibid.*, 1 April 1882

48 *Ibid.*

49 *Ibid.*

50 Norman H. Murdoch, 'Salvation Army Disturbances in Liverpool, England, 1879–1887', *Journal of Social History*, 25/8 (Spring 1992), 575–93; see also Norman H. Murdoch, 'From Militancy to Social Mission: The Salvation Army and Street Disturbances in Liverpool, 1879–1887', in J. Belchem (ed.), *Popular Politics, Riot and Labour: Essays in Liverpool History, 1790–1940* (Liverpool, 1992), 160–72.

51 Stuart Mews, 'The General and the Bishops: Alternative Responses to Dechristianisation', in T. R. Gourvish and Alan O'Day (eds.), *Later Victorian Britain, 1867–1900* (London, 1988), 214.

52 *Chester Chronicle*, 29 March 1882.

53 Bailey, *op. cit.*, 234.

54 *Chester Chronicle*, 5 April 1882.

55 Murdoch, 'From Militancy to Social Mission . . .', 164.

56 Bailey, *op cit.*, 252.

57 For contemporary anti-Catholic and anti-Irish feeling, see especially Roger Swift and Sheridan Gilley (eds.), *The Irish in the Victorian City* (London, 1989), notably the editors' introduction; see also Roger Swift, *The Irish in Britain 1815–1914: Perspectives and Sources* (Historical Association, London, 1990), 29–31.

58 For further details, see especially E. R. Norman, *Anti-Catholicism in Victorian England* (London, 1968); D. G. Paz, *Popular Anti-Catholicism in Mid-Victorian England* (Stanford, 1992).

59 *Chester Chronicle*, 1 April 1882.

60 Chester City Watch Committee Minutes, 1 April 1882.

61 *Ibid.*, 21 April 1882.

62 *Ibid.*, 27 July 1882.

63 Bailey, *op. cit.*, 243.

64 Murdoch, *op. cit.*, 161.

65 *Chester Courant*, 3 May 1882.

7

'An Observant American in England': Henry James on Victorian Chester

Chris Walsh

In May 1872 a twenty-nine year old Henry James, with one minor novel to his name, started on his fifth tour of Europe, in the company of his Aunt Kate and his sister Alice. The journey across the Atlantic in the Cunarder *Algeria* took just nine days, but James experienced no seasickness, unlike his companions. After disembarking at Liverpool, and booking tickets for his aunt and sister to return to America in October (he was staying longer in Europe), James took his relatives straight to Chester. For on this occasion he was travelling with a commission to write a number of impressionistic travel sketches for an American weekly, *The Nation*. The itinerary of the James party thereafter—selectively chronicled by James—took them through the midlands and the south-west of England to London, before heading on to Paris and the continent. The first essay in the sequence appeared under the title, 'A European Summer. I. Chester', in *The Nation* on 4 July 1872. It was later reprinted, as 'Chester', in a collection of travel pieces, *English Hours* in 1905. The complete text is reproduced below as Appendix I.[1]

An account of Henry James on Victorian Chester may seem a slightly unusual choice of topic. Shades, perhaps, of a somewhat arcane, though perfectly worthy, study of James by Jorg Hasler entitled *Switzerland in the Life and Work of Henry James*. Hasler's comments in the opening pages of his monograph, where he takes 'due note of the real proportions and of the relative unimportance of Switzerland for James', suggest a defensive or apologetic posture.[2] But why should this be so? Switzerland does, after all, feature quite prominently in the fictional and non-fictional writings of James— enough to justify a brief consideration of the subject at least. The answer probably has to do with a sense that other topographical claims on the attention of Jamesian scholars are weightier in their significance: America, England, Italy, and France are obviously richer quarries. The same might be felt about Chester: not only is Chester itself, in its Victorian phase, as Roger Swift points out in his introduction to this volume, a city neglected by today's nineteenth-century historians (even though it is, visibly and overwhelmingly, a Victorian city if it is anything), but the literary treatment of Chester is similarly neglected—books and articles on the Victorian city and the nineteenth-century novel typically deal with London or the northern industrial cities, yet they almost wholly ignore Chester. John Henry Raleigh in his article, 'The Novel and the City', describes James, surprisingly perhaps, as 'the leading literary connoisseur of cities' in the nineteenth century,[3] but when we turn to John Kimmey's account of 'Henry James and the Victorian City',[4] in which he describes James as 'a unique writer about the Victorian city',[5] it comes as something of a shock to see that Chester is not so much as mentioned. For, as we shall see, in addition to his essay on Chester, James also set the opening of one of his last major novels—*The Ambassadors* (1903)— in this much visited but under-explored Victorian city. And it might be instructive to place alongside the findings of those primarily interested in the social history of Victorian Chester elsewhere in this volume the impressions and words of a contemporary *literary* source, to see what may be learnt by taking a rather different, critical approach.

For James, at any rate, a sketch of Chester was an appropriate way of beginning his series of travel essays for the discerning American reader, if only because it was likely to be the first attractive English cathedral city steeped in history the American tourist would encounter on arriving in the country. But at this point we should perhaps pause to reflect on the context—or, rather, contexts—in which James's travel essays of the early 1870s were written. In purely personal terms, it might be noted that he was writing partly to supplement the income from his father so that he could continue to stay in Europe for as long as he wished. So his journalistic offerings had to be accessible, and they had to captivate and hold on to the attention and interest of his American readers (flattering their knowledge, on occasion, no doubt, in the process of informing); certainly he could not afford to upset them: he had to tread warily where vulnerable national susceptibilities and prejudices were involved. So he was writing to sell (not always a prime concern with the later novelist); but he had no wish to sell out, as far as his own genuinely felt, and carefully thought through, responses to England and the English, to Europe and the Europeans, were concerned. What he had to do was to relate to the ambivalence which most Americans felt towards their European roots and ancestry—to European culture and history, and its institutions and conventions. This was not so difficult, for he himself shared much of the ambivalence, though he was actually more of an Anglophile than most of his fellow Americans at that time (and was eventually to become a naturalized British citizen in 1915, just a year before his death). 'It's a complex fate being an American', James once commented, 'and one of the responsibilities it entails is fighting against a superstitious valuation of Europe.'[6] The America/Europe theme (sometimes referred to as the 'International theme') was to prove to be a major preoccupation of James's novels and short stories, of course, but it appears in these early travel sketches also, the essay on Chester being no exception. In the event, James probably hit a good few nails on their heads, as far as his readers were concerned. Certainly the accounts of his travels which James wrote proved to be popular enough for two other American magazines (the *Atlantic* and the *Galaxy*) to readily publish similar pieces. Back in America, James was steadily making a name for himself; meanwhile, the financial rewards helped to enable James to prolong his sojourn in Europe.

So much for the context of writing, publishing, and reading the essay, 'Chester'. But what of the broader historico-cultural context of England in 1872? What kind of world was James visiting and purporting to describe? The other essays in this volume elaborate in detail on the socio-economic traits of the locality and region. But what of the national picture? How was the country as a whole perceived as faring? 'To generalize is to be an idiot', claimed William Blake (in a generalising mode himself). Concise summaries of a period inevitably tend to sound pat, even glib, and are to some extent misleading. But it is difficult, looking back, not to see this mid-Victorian phase as a time of equipoise and transition. Nobody then knew it, but Victoria's reign was rather more than half over, Gladstone's great administration was nearing its close, and the days of Britain's supremacy as the greatest of imperial world powers were already numbered. A more technological and democratic world was being shaped: in 1872 while Edison was busy perfecting the electric telegraph, the (Secret) Ballot Act was in the process of being given parliamentary approval. A year earlier, in 1871, Stanley's venture into darkest Africa had culminated in the finding of Livingstone, the Franco-Prussian War had come to an end, religious tests had been abolished at Oxford, Cambridge, and Durham, and trades unions had (at last) been made legal. Two years earlier, in 1870, the Elementary Education Act had been passed, and entry to the Civil Service had been thrown open to competition. It was, in short, a time of innovation; change was in the air. But there was also the sense that the old world was giving place to a new world. This was felt by some to be a cause for rejoicing—to such people the fresh prospects were exciting. Others, though, looked back at the vanishing past with regret and nostalgia, and ahead to the dazzling new future with gloom and despondency. Carlyle's apocalyptic essay, 'Shooting Niagara— And After?' of 1867, with its strongly anti-democratic note, was greeted by nods of assent by not a few, but most of his middle-class, educated, British readers considered Carlyle's polemic to be ill-judged, and out of step with the temper of the age. In the eyes of many, democracy was well on its inexorable way, and was a development to be welcomed rather than condemned. And America was leading the way there, as in much else. The balance of power, too, would before long shift to America, whose star was rising. Meanwhile, Victorian cities such as Chester (with its Roman roots and medieval associations) were increasingly coming to be seen more as part of an earlier age, than as part of the thriving technologicoindustrial world which seemed to beckon from just around the corner.

Some of these feelings, insights and changing perceptions were given expression in the literature and art of the period. The literary and arts world was, of course, the world in which Henry James was to spend the remaining forty-four years of his life. Significantly, 1871 had seen the first Impressionist exhibition in France; a year later, on the English side of the Channel, Whistler was painting *Old Battersea Bridge*. In 1871 Ruskin's *Fors Clavigera* began publication, a scathing critique of the unacceptable face of Victorian bourgeois capitalism; Trollope's fictional treatment of a similar theme, in *The Way We Live Now* was to follow in 1874–75. The main literary landmarks of 1872 itself include the start of Forster's *Life of Dickens* (Dickens had died in 1870); Butler's dystopian travelogue, *Erewhon*; Hardy's pastoral idyll, *Under the Greenwood Tree*; and Eliza Lynn Linton's curious politico-religious fiction, *The True History of Joshua Davidson*. Tennyson finally finished his latter-day chronicles of King Arthur, *Idylls of the King*; and the greatest English novel of the century, George Eliot's *Middlemarch*, was also published in 1872 in volume form. Eliot's novel, in depicting Coventry and the English midlands in the period of turmoil leading up to the first Reform Act of 1832, was an eloquent, brilliantly intelligent and judicious meditation on the march of progress. Describing the novel as 'a treasure-house of detail, but . . . an indifferent whole', Henry James asked: '[i]f we write novels so, how shall we write History?'.[7]

The question posed by James there is not without relevance to his essay on Chester. How should a writer attempt to record and sum up (in less than ten pages) his impressions of a city such as Chester? James's solution to the problem was to structure the essay, quite simply, around the three key facets of the city which would immediately strike anyone visiting it in 1872 for the first time—the walls, the Rows, and the Cathedral. After an introductory paragraph, James in effect conducts the reader on a guided tour of, first, the Roman walls of Chester, and, secondly, its famous Rows. There then follows a discussion of English manners, and some thoughts on the crowdedness of English cities, using Chester as an example. He concludes the essay with a sketch of the Cathedral, and an account of hearing

Charles Kingsley preach therein. Badly summarized thus, the essay sounds more straightforward than it is; but the simplicity is—as so often with James—deceptive.

Consider the opening lines of the essay, which strike a sufficiently characteristic note:

> If the Atlantic voyage be counted, as it certainly may, even with the ocean in a fairly good humour, an emphatic zero in the sum of one's better experience, the American traveller arriving at this venerable town finds himself transported, without a sensible gradation, from the edge of the New World to the very heart of the Old. It is almost a misfortune, perhaps, that Chester lies so close to the threshold of England; for it is so rare and complete a specimen of an antique town that the later-coming wonders of its sisters in renown—of Shrewsbury, Coventry, and York—suffer a trifle by comparison, and the tourist's appetite for the picturesque just loses its finer edge. Yet the first impressions of an observant American in England—of our old friend the sentimental tourist—stir up within him such a cloud of sensibility that while the charm is still unbroken he may as well dispose mentally of the greater as of the less.[8]

The tone , from the outset is measured, urbane, deft, and quietly authoritative. This is partly a matter of James's syntax, with its convolutions and high degree of subordination: the neo-Johnsonian periods appear to roll effortlessly off the page, but the reader has to work to trace the line of James's thought. Part of the difficulty of reading this passage is knowing how to interpret certain words and phrases; James's lexical choices often seem laden with meaning, but the process of disambiguation can be fraught. How are we to make sense, for example, of the reference to Chester as 'so rare and complete a specimen of an antique town'? Is this to be read as a glowing (but nonetheless subjective) approbation? Or as an objective (if a trifle vague) characterization? The account, in other words, needs to be read with care and circumspection: the nuances of thought and feeling, the inflections of voice and tone, the subtle caveats and delicate ironies—all these features combine to offer a literary perspective on a Victorian city which is as 'rare', if hardly as 'complete', as the object of James's meticulous scrutiny.

The prose style of Henry James (especially in his later writings) achieved a certain notoriety for its prolixity, complexity and obscurity. The essay on Chester is similarly dense in places. Here is a typical example, from the second half of the introductory paragraph:

> I have been playing at first impressions for the second time, and have won the game against a cynical adversary. I have been strolling and restrolling along the ancient wall—so perfect in its antiquity—which locks this dense little city in its stony circle, with a certain friend who has been treating me to a bitter lament on the decay of his relish for the picturesque. 'I have turned the corner of youth,' is his ceaseless plaint; 'I suspected it, but now I know it—now my heart beats but once where it beat a dozen times before, and that where I found sermons in stones and pictures in meadows, delicious revelations and intimations ineffable, I find nothing but the hard, heavy prose of British civilization.' But little by little I have grown used to my friend's sad monody, and indeed feel half indebted to it as a warning against cheap infatuations.[9]

James is an allusive writer, who favours a certain indirect mode of presentation. The quotation from Shakespeare's *As You Like It* above ('sermons in stones'), if considered alongside the Latin tags from Lucan and Virgil later in the essay, indicates how James is interested not merely in providing empirical observations and physical descriptions, but in conveying his complex imaginative understanding of the city of Chester and its (to him, distinctive) ethos. All perceptions are relative, and necessarily tinged, to some extent, with emotion. James recognizes this, and crafts a rich literary style to correlate with such a state of affairs. Not all readers find James's style easy to cope with; certainly patience is a useful virtue to possess when reading James in full flow. Indeed, Henry James's older brother William (the pragmatist philosopher and coiner of the term 'stream of consciousness') criticized James's travel essays for their 'over-refinement and elaboration', commenting that their 'style ran a little more to *curliness* than suited the average mind'; he urged him to be more

'Newspaporial'.[10] But his younger brother—a novelist and critic in the making—was trying to evolve a style of his own; he had, as he put it, 'a mortal horror of seeming to write thin'.[11] And for James the ideal prose style for travel essays consisted of 'tissue[s] of images and pictures' as the essayist tries to do justice to, in the words of James's biographer, Leon Edel, 'the works of nature and the works of man . . . the flow of life into art, the flow of art into life'.[12]

Another marked feature of the essay is James's creation of a distinctive 'point of view' throughout. In the above extract, for example, James, writing in the first person, is able to play off his delight in the antique and the picturesque by introducing as foil his 'cynical' friend who speaks, in almost Wordsworthian terms, of 'the hard, heavy prose of British civilization'. In fact, James's attention to point of view in his travel essays parallels his experimentation as a writer of novels and short stories, and his formal interests as a critic and theorist of fiction. He knows how much depends on the perspective from which material is presented to the reader—whether the material in question be fictional or historical. In his travel sketches, rather than writing explicitly and straightforwardly *in propria persona*, James refers to himself obliquely as (variously) 'the American traveller', 'the observant American', 'the contemplative observer', 'the restless analyst', or (most suggestively) 'the sentimental tourist'. This undoubtedly gives him a certain latitude when it comes to expressing views about which he may feel a certain ambivalence. (Arguably, James learnt the value of such an oblique approach from the Victorian with the completest mastery of the ironic dramatic monologue form, Robert Browning.) He prefers to present himself, in other words, as an outsider figure—a 'grateful alien' or 'observant stranger'—who is objective yet sympathetic.[13] He depicts himself not as a mere detached cataloguer of facts and figures, but as someone learning from experience, undergoing an education. As Kimmey comments, James 'judges and discriminates as well as records and reports. The object is to consider intellectually and capture imaginatively the turbulent scene before him . . . he speaks of himself as "the habitual observer, the preoccupied painter, the pedestrian prowler" . . . that is, he is a student, and artist, and a copious mental note taker. He is one who gathers impressions and lets the city "assault" his imagination'.[14] For example, in James's description of 'the brave little walls of Chester', he is clearly impressed by the walls for the opportunity they offer to surround—literally and metaphorically—'the little swarming towered and gabled town within'. He continues:

> The wall enfolds the place in a continuous ring, which, passing through innumerable picturesque vicissitudes, often threatens to snap, but never fairly breaks the link; so that, starting at any point, an hour's easy stroll will bring you back to your station. I have quite lost my heart to this charming creation . . . [15]

He moves on to give a detailed physical description of the walls, from their 'Roman substructure' upwards and outwards. He prizes the walls' ruggedness and irregularity, the accessibility and spaciousness of the walkway, and—above all—the variety and unexpectedness of the many views of Chester life which the walls afford the pedestrian. James elaborates on this last aspect:

> It is full of that delightful element of the crooked, the accidental, the unforeseen, which, to American eyes, accustomed to our eternal straight lines and right angles, is the striking feature of European street scenery. An American strolling in the Chester streets finds a perfect feast of crookedness—of those random corners, projections and recesses, odd domestic interspaces charmingly saved or lost, those innumerable architectural surprises and caprices and fantasies . . . An American is born to the idea that on his walks abroad it is perpetual level wall ahead of him, and such a revelation as he finds here of infinite accident and infinite effect gives a wholly novel zest to the use of his eyes.[16]

For James, a walk around Chester's walls essentially defamiliarizes those habitual, everyday views of reality which most unreflecting observers may be supposed to hold. And this is—at least by implication—a key point of James in this essay. It is all too easy to take reality for granted. One justification for writing a literary, aesthetic appreciation of Chester, is that the reader may be enabled to look afresh at, and reconsider, aspects of the Victorian city which might otherwise be overlooked or glossed over. So James's essay stresses the unusualness of the perspectives the walls of Chester have to offer. At the same time, he is at pains to emphasize the pictorial beauty of a traditional scene such as that in which

> the rambling wall . . . skirts the edge of the cathedral grave-yard, and sweeps beneath the great square tower and behind the sacred east window of the choir . . . the best standpoint for feeling how fine an influence in the architectural line . . . is the massive tower of an English abbey, dominating the homes of men; and for watching the eddying flight of swallows make vaster still to the eye the large calm fields of stonework.[17]

A few lines before the above quotation, James mentions—entirely appropriately—the 'magic in some of the early pages' of Dickens's *David Copperfield* (1849–50) and George Eliot's *The Mill on the Floss* (1860), for it is the Englishness of the Cestrian *mise en scène* (to use, paradoxically enough, a favourite phrase of James, employed elsewhere in the essay), which James implies is so sought after by the American tourist, yet so taken for granted by the English inhabitants of Chester. The literary allusions, here, serve to heighten the reader's self-consciousness of the 'composedness' of the scene. The essay's point of view at this juncture is complex, layered.

It is instructive to compare the description of the walls in the essay with James's account of thirty years later in his novel *The Ambassadors*:

> The tortuous wall—girdle, long since snapped, of the little swollen city, half held in place by careful civic hands—wanders in narrow file between parapets smoothed by peaceful generations, pausing here and there for a dismantled gate or a bridged gap, with rises and drops, steps up and steps down, queer twists, queer contacts, peeps into homely streets and under the brows of gables, views of cathedral tower and waterside fields, of huddled English town and ordered English country. Too deep almost for words was the delight of these things for Strether . . .[18]

Thus the ambassadorial American Lambert Strether, on a forced 'ramble . . . on the ramparts' with the intelligent, cosmopolitan

Maria Gostrey. The passage is strikingly similar to the meditation on the walls in this essay. The notion of the wall as a 'girdle' (though now 'long since snapped'), the pleasing irregularities of the circuit, the sudden glimpses into 'homely streets', and—above all—the sense of the Englishness of it all, and the 'delight' Strether experiences as a result: all these elements have their equivalents in the 'Chester' essay proper. The reality of Victorian Chester, for James, it would seem, was most vividly grasped by examining the 'tissue of images and pictures' which present themselves to the observant American tourist on his walk around the city's walls.

Two chapters later in *The Ambassadors* 'the wicked old Rows of Chester' come under the scrutiny of Strether's stolid lawyer compatriot, Waymarsh, who is much struck by their queerness, as he 'leaned on an old balustrade that guarded the edge of the Row', taking in 'a particularly crooked and huddled street-view'.[19] This is a partial perspective (in both senses of 'partial'). But, again, it is one which has a parallel in the essay on Chester. There the Rows are described as 'an architectural idiosyncrasy which must be seen to be appreciated'. James continues:

> They are a sort of Gothic edition of the blessed arcades and porticoes of Italy, and consist, roughly speaking, of a running public passage tunnelled through the second storey of the houses.[20]

Again, as with James's account of the walls, there follows a detailed description of the actual physical construct of the Rows, so that the reader who has never seen them for himself may be able to imagine (if not appreciate) them. The Rows, even more than the walls, it would seem, have changed considerably since James's time. His use (again) of the word 'specimen' is followed by some thoughts on the 'rich and intelligent restorations of the old facades' by 'the actual townsfolk' whose 'elaborate and ingenious repairs attest a highly informed consciousness of the pictorial value of the city'. Indeed, James writes effusively about this aspect of the city:

> If the picturesque be measured by its hostility to our modern notions of convenience, Chester is probably the most romantic

city in the world . . . Chester is still an antique town, and medieval England sits bravely under her gables.[21]

Here James comes close to contradicting an earlier point he made when he referred to the picturesque and convenient walls. But he is at least as much a realist as he is a romantic; he would certainly seem to have few illusions about Chester's rudimentary heritage industry when he remarks that he suspects 'much of this revived innocence of having recovered a freshness that never can have been, of having been restored with usurious interest'.[22] This ushers in a meditation on the past human inhabitants of the Rows, where James is perhaps following the advice of his brother, who urged him to develop the human theme more; but, more probably, this is the future novelist in the making, with his profound capacity for human sympathy. This is social history of a kind—the absence of hard facts and figures notwithstanding. James projects himself imaginatively into Chester's medieval past, and the result is not unilluminating.

But James is not, of course, concerned primarily with Chester's past, as the next section of the essay, in which he considers 'the fine differences in national manners', makes plain. Here he is obviously writing for his American readers:

The tone of things is somehow heavier than with us; manners and modes are more absolute and positive; they seem to swarm and to thicken the atmosphere about you. Morally and physically it is a denser air than ours. We seem loosely hung together at home as compared with the English, every man of whom is a tight fit in his place. It is not an inferential but a palpable fact that England is a crowded country . . . wherever you go the population has overflowed.[23]

This is not only true of city life (always 'there is a crowd and hubbub in Chester'), but applies also to rural England, for '[t]he English landscape is always a "landscape with figures" '. And in this section James switches his attention away from the 'scenic' Rows, with their 'elegant' shop-fronts, to a consideration of Chester's contemporary human inhabitants, observing that 'everywhere you go you are accompanied by a vague consciousness of the British child hovering about your knees and coat-skirts, naked, grimy, and portentous'.[24] Portentous of what, exactly? James develops his theme a little further:

> When you think of the small profits, the small jealousies, the long waiting, and the narrow margin for evil days implied by this redundancy of shops and shopmen, you hear afresh the steady rumble of that deep keynote of English manners, overscored so often, and with such sweet beguilement, by finer harmonies, but never extinguished—the economic struggle for existence.[25]

In his introduction to James's *English Hours*, Leon Edel describes the travel essays as both documentary and painterly. 'Like most great novelists he accepts the world—in such societies 'such things are', as [James] remarks in *The Ambassadors*. His concern is with concrete and palpable reality.'[26] But while conceding that James 'does not turn his eyes completely away from the visible poverty and the slums', Edel stresses how much he saw himself as 'a very polite and even cautious tourist', for

> James is not a Tocqueville or a Bryce; he is certainly not an economist or social scientist; nor does he attempt a scientific critique of British institutions. He travels for the delight of his senses; he relishes the old, the picturesque, the noble antiquities, the idea of continuity and preservation—the sense of history that lives within the beauties and the ugliness of the land.[27]

This suggests something of the value of James's essay on Chester for today's socio-cultural historian of the Victorian period: reading the essay, it is possible to pick up an intelligent, sensitive observer's *sense* of Chester's (and England's) Victorian present, measured against its past, and against the conditions of a contrasting culture such as America's. Archive materials in city and county record offices—very valuable though they obviously are—do not always provide the kinds of sensory, aesthetic, and emotional data which we need to fill out *our* sense of the reality we think of as Victorian Chester, Victorian England.

James's sense of the artistry of buildings and city—his aesthetic appreciation of pictorial scenes—culminates in his evocative, impressionistic depiction of Chester Cathedral—freshly restored by 'Mr Gilbert Scott, ruthless renovator', it nevertheless produces 'to an American . . . the proper vibrations'[28]; this is followed by his distinctly muted response to hearing 'Canon Kingsley' preach, before concluding the essay with the slightly tongue-in-cheek comment that perhaps 'it takes passionate pilgrims, vague aliens and other disinherited persons to appreciate the "points" of this admirable country'[29]. Again, the interest is more in the human figures who crowd the canvas, than in the splendid backdrop itself. Life matters more than art, as his remarks on the 'landscape with figures', quoted above, imply. The crowdedness of Chester, we saw, made at least as strong an impression on James as the beauty of its architecture. The emphasis throughout the essay, in fact, is a conservative one: James stresses order, enclosure, form, tradition. Bonney MacDonald writes interestingly on James's preoccupation with restriction and privacy in his English sketches of the 1870s, arguing that James presents an 'ideal of privacy after confronting the overly public and crowded texture of British life' as he equates 'England's private and inaccessible charms not only with hidden landscapes and cramped interiors, but also with imaginative license and increased artistic freedom'; thus he 'locates a wealth of suggestion in England's landscape of enclosure and privacy'.[30] This reminds us, quite rightly, that what we are dealing with here, of course, is interpretation, not brute fact. Indeed, properly speaking, what else is there to deal with? For no 'facts' come to the human brain unmediated—sans language, sans context, sans value, sans anything. James's essay is an *interpretation* of Victorian Chester, which we attempt to interpret in turn. Therein lies for us both its interest, and its challenge.

T. S. Eliot, another American writer who settled in England and became a British citizen, wrote of his illustrious predecessor:

> . . . the fact that, an American, his view of England—a view which very gradually dissolves in his development—was a romantic view, is a small matter. His romanticism implied no defect in observation of the things he wanted to observe; it was not the romanticism of those who dream because they are too lazy or too fearful to face the fact; it issues, rather, from the

imperative insistence of an ideal which tormented him. He was possessed by the vision of an ideal society; he saw (not fancied) the relations between the members of such a society. And no one, in the end, has ever been more aware—or with more benignity, or less bitterness—of the disparity between possibility and fact.[31]

James's essay on Chester, as we have seen, is a piece of romantic realism. In interpreting Victorian Chester, in attempting to make some kind of sense of what, in his eyes, was a unique phenomenon, James presents us with a view of an interesting and important nineteenth-century city. His essay, in its perceptiveness, sensitivity, and manifest intelligence, brilliantly recreates the Chester of 1872 for today's cultural and social historians of the Victorian period. Our knowledge of the city of Chester in that phase of its history would undoubtedly be the poorer without James's valuable essay to guide us.

Appendix I

Henry James, 'Chester'

from *English Hours* [1905], ed. Leon Edel [Oxford and New York, 1981], pp. 35–43

If the Atlantic voyage be counted, as it certainly may, even with the ocean in a fairly good humour, an emphatic zero in the sum of one's better experience, the American traveller arriving at this venerable town finds himself transported, without a sensible gradation, from the edge of the New World to the very heart of the Old. It is almost a misfortune, perhaps, that Chester lies so close to the threshold of England; for it is so rare and complete a specimen of an antique town that the later-coming wonders of is sisters in renown—of Shrewsbury, Coventry, and York—suffer a trifle by comparison, and the tourist's appetite for the picturesque just loses its finer edge. Yet the first impressions of an observant American in England—of our old friend the sentimental tourist—stir up within him such a cloud of sensibility that while the charm is still unbroken he may perhaps as well dispose mentally of the greater as of the less. I have been playing at first impressions for the second time, and have won the game against a cynical adversary. I have been strolling and restrolling along the ancient wall—so perfect in its antiquity—which locks this dense little city in its stony circle, with a certain friend who has been treating me to a bitter lament on the decay of his relish for the picturesque. 'I have turned the corner of youth,' is his ceaseless plaint; 'I suspected it, but now I know it—now that my heart beats but once where it beat a dozen times before, and that where I found sermons in stones and pictures in meadows, delicious revelations and intimations ineffable, I find nothing but the hard, heavy prose of British civilization.' But little by little I have grown used to my friend's sad monody, and indeed feel half indebted to it as a warning against cheap infatuations.

I defied him, at any rate, to argue successfully against the effect of the brave little walls of Chester. There could be no better example of that phenomenon so delightfully frequent in England—an ancient property or institution lovingly readopted and consecrated to some modern amenity. The good Cestrians may boast of their walls without a shadow of that mental reservation on grounds of modern ease which is so often the tax paid by the romantic; and I can easily imagine that, though most modern towns contrive to get on comfortably without this stony girdle, these people should have come to regard theirs as a prime necessity. For through it, surely, they may know their city more intimately than their unbuckled neighbours—survey it, feel it, rejoice in it as many times a day as they please. The civic consciousness, sunning itself thus on the city's rim and glancing at the little swarming towered and gabled town within, and then at the blue undulations of the near Welsh border, may easily deepen to delicious complacency. The wall enfolds the place in a continuous ring, which, passing though innumerable picturesque vicissitudes, often threatens to snap, but never fairly breaks the link; so that, starting at any point, an hour's easy stroll will bring you back to your station. I have quite lost my heart to this charming creation, and there are so many things to be said about it that I hardly know where to begin. The great fact, I suppose, is that it contains a Roman substructure, rests for much of its course on foundations laid by that race of master-builders. But in spite of this sturdy origin, much of which is buried in the well-trodden soil of the ages, it is the gentlest and least offensive of ramparts; it completes its long irregular curve without a frown or menace in all its disembattled stretch. The earthy deposit of time has, indeed, in some places climbed so high about its base that it amounts to no more than a causeway of modest dimensions. It has everywhere, however, a rugged outer parapet and a broad hollow flagging, wide enough for two strollers abreast. Thus equipped, it wanders through its adventurous circuit; now sloping, now bending, now broadening into a terrace, now narrowing into an alley, now swelling into an arch, now dipping into steps, now passing some thorn-screened garden, and now reminding you that it was once a more serious matter than all this by the extrusion of a rugged, ivy-smothered tower. Its final hoary humility is enhanced, to your mind, by the freedom with which you may approach it from any point in the town. Every few steps, as you go, you see some little court or alley boring toward it through the close-pressed houses. It is full of that delightful element of the crooked, the accidental, the unforeseen, which, to American eyes, accustomed to our eternal straight lines and right angles, is the striking feature of European street scenery. An American strolling in the Chester streets finds a perfect feast of crookedness—of those random corners, projections and recesses, odd domestic interspaces charmingly saved or lost, those innumerable architectural surprises and caprices and fantasies which lead to such refreshing exercise a vision benumbed by brownstone fronts. An American is born to the idea that on his walks abroad it is perpetual level wall ahead of him, and such a revelation as he finds here of infinite accident and infinite effect gives a wholly novel zest to the use of his eyes. It produces, too, the reflection—a superficial and fallacious one perhaps—that amid all this cunning chiaroscuro of its *mise en scène*, life must have more of a certain homely entertainment. It is at least no fallacy to say that childhood—or the later memory of childhood—must borrow from such a background a kind of anecdotal wealth. We all know how in the retrospect of later moods the incidents of early youth 'compose', visibly, each as an individual picture, with a magic for which the greatest painters have no corresponding art. There is a vivid reflection of this magic in some of the early pages of Dickens' 'Copperfield' and of George Eliot's 'Mill on the Floss', the writers having had the happiness of growing up among old, old things. Two or three of the phases of this rambling wall belong especially to the class of things fondly remembered. In one place it skirts the edge of the cathedral graveyard, and sweeps beneath the great square tower and behind the sacred east window of the choir. Of the cathedral there is more to say; but just the spot I speak of is the best standpoint for feeling how fine an influence in the architectural line—where theoretically, at least, influences are great—is the massive tower of an English abbey, dominating the homes of men; and for watching the eddying flight of swallows make vaster still to the eye the large calm fields of stonework. At another point, two battered and crumbling towers, decaying in their winding-sheets of ivy, make a prodigiously designed diversion. One inserted in the body of the wall and the other connected with it by a short crumbling ridge of masonry, they contribute to a positive jumble of local colour. A shaded mall wanders at the foot of the rampart; beside this passes a narrow canal, with locks and barges and burly watermen in smocks and breeches; while the venerable pair of towers, with their old red sandstone sides peeping through the gaps in their green mantles, rest on the soft grass of one of those odd fragments of public garden, a crooked strip of ground turned to social account, which one meets at every turn, apparently, in England—a tribute to the needs of the 'masses'. *Stat magni nominis umbra*. The quotation is doubly pertinent here, for this little garden-strip is adorned with mossy fragments of Roman stonework, bits of pavements, altars, baths, disinterred in the local soil. England is the land of small economies, and the present rarely fails to find good use for the odds and ends of the past. These two hoary shells of masonry are therefore converted into 'museums', receptacles for the dustiest and shabbiest of tawdry back-parlour curiosities. Here preside a couple of those grotesque creatures, *à la* Dickens, whom one finds squeezed into every cranny of English civilization, scraping a thin subsistence, like mites in a mouldy cheese.

Next after its wall—possibly even before it—Chester values its Rows, an architectural idiosyncrasy which must be seen to be appreciated. They are a sort of Gothic edition of the blessed arcades and porticoes of Italy, and consist, roughly speaking, of a running public passage tunnelled through the second storey of the houses. The low basement is thus directly on the drive-way, to which a flight of steps descends, at frequent intervals, from this superincumbent verandah. The upper portion of the houses projects to the outer line of the gallery, where they are propped with pillars and posts and parapets. The shop-fronts face along the arcade and admit you to little caverns of traffic, more or less dusky according to their opportunities for illumination in the rear. If the picturesque be measured by its hostility to our modern notions of convenience, Chester is probably the most romantic city in the world. This arrangement is endlessly rich in opportunities for amusing effect, but the full charm of the architecture of which it is so essential a part must be observed from the street below. Chester is still an antique town, and mediaeval England sits bravely under her gables. Every third house is a 'specimen'—gabled and latticed, timbered and carved, and wearing its years more or less lightly. These ancient dwellings present every shade and degree of historical colour and expression. Some are dark with neglect and deformity, and the horizontal slit admitting light into the lurking Row seems to collapse on its dislocated props like a pair of toothless old jaws. Others stand there square-shouldered and sturdy, with their beams painted and straightened, their plaster whitewashed, their carvings polished, and the low casement covering the breadth of the frontage adorned with curtains and flower-pots. It is noticeable that the actual townsfolk have bravely accepted the situation bequeathed by the past, and the large number of rich and intelligent restorations of the old facades makes an effective jumble of their piety and their policy. These elaborate and ingenious repairs attest a highly informed consciousness of the pictorial value of the city. I indeed suspect much of this revived innocence of having recovered a freshness that never can have been, of having been restored with usorious interest. About the genuine antiques there would be properly a great deal to say, for they are really a theme for the philosopher; but the theme is too heavy for my pen, and I can give them but the passing tribute of a sigh. They are cruelly quaint, dreadfully expressive. Fix one of them with your gaze, and it seems fairly to reek with mortality. Every stain and crevice seems to syllable some human record—a record of lives airless and unlighted. I have been trying hard to fancy them animated by the children of 'Merry England', but I am quite unable to think of them save as peopled by the victims of dismal old-world pains and fears. Human life, surely, packed away behind those impenetrable lattices of lead and bottle-glass, just above which the black outer beam marks the suffocating nearness of the ceiling, can have expanded into scant freedom and bloomed into small sweetness.

Nothing has struck me more in my strolls along the Rows than the fact that the most zealous observation can keep but uneven pace with the fine differences in national manners. some of the most sensible of these differences are yet so subtle and indefinable that one must give up the attempt to express them, though the omission leave but a rough sketch. As you pass with the bustling current from shop to shop, you feel local custom and tradition—another tone of things—pressing on you from every side. The tone of things is somehow heavier than with us; manners and modes are more absolute and positive; they seem to swarm and to thicken the atmosphere about you. Morally and physically it is a denser air than ours. We seem loosely hung together at home as compared with the English, every man of whom is a tight fit in his place. It is not an inferential but a palpable fact that England is a crowded country. There is stillness and space—grassy, oak-studded space—at Eaton Hall, where the Marquis of Westminster dwells (or I believe can afford to humour his notion of not dwelling), but there is a crowd and a hubbub in Chester. Wherever you go the population has overflowed. You stroll on the walls at eventide and you hardly find elbow-room. You haunt the cathedral shades, and a dozen sauntering mortals temper your solitude. You glance up an alley or side-street, and discover populous windows and doorsteps. You roll along country roads and find countless humble pedestrians dotting the green waysides. The English landscape is always a 'landscape with figures'. And everywhere you go you are accompanied by a vague consciousness of the British child hovering about your knees and coat-skirts, naked, grimy, and portentous. You reflect with a sort of physical relief on Australia, Canada, India. Where there are many men, of course, there are many needs; which helps to justify to the philosophic stranger the vast number and the irresistible coquetry of the little shops which adorn these low-browed Rows. The shop-fronts have always seemed to me the most elegant things in England; and I waste more time than I should care to confess to in covetous contemplation of the vast, clear panes behind which the nether integuments of gentlemen are daintily suspended from glittering brass rods. The manners of the dealers in these comfortable wares seldom fail to confirm your agreeable impression. You are thanked with effusion for spending twopence—a fact of deep significance to the truly analytic mind, and which always seems to me a vague reverberation from certain of Miss Edgeworth's novels, perused in childhood. When you think of the small profits, the small jealousies, the long waiting, and the narrow margin for evil days implied by this redundancy of shops and shopmen, you hear afresh the steady rumble of that deep keynote of English manners, overscored so often, and with such sweet beguilement, by finer harmonies, but never extinguished—the economic struggle for existence.

The Rows are as 'scenic' as one could wish, and it is a pity that before the birth of their modern consciousness there was no English Balzac to introduce them into a realistic romance with a psychological commentary. But the cathedral is better still, modestly as it stands on the roll of English abbeys. It is of moderate dimensions, and rather meagre in form and ornament; but to an American it expresses and answers for the type, producing thereby the proper vibrations. Among these is a certain irresistible regret that so much of its hoary substance should give place to the fine, fresh-coloured masonry with which Mr Gilbert Scott, ruthless renovator, is so intelligently investing it. The red sandstone of the primitive structure, darkened and devoured by time, survives at many points in frowning mockery of the imputed need of tinkering. The great tower, however—completely restored—rises high enough to seem to belong, as cathedral towers should, to the far-off air that vibrates with the chimes and the swallows, and to square serenely, east and west and south and north, its embossed and fluted sides. English cathedrals, within, are apt at first to look pale and naked; but after a while, if the proportions be fair and the spaces largely distributed, when you perceive the light beating softly down from the cold clerestory and your eye measures caressingly the tallness of columns and the hollowness of arches, and lingers on the old genteel inscriptions of mural marbles and brasses; and, above all, when you become conscious of that sweet, cool mustiness in the air which seems to haunt these places as the very climate of Episcopacy, you may grow to feel that they are less the empty shells of a departed faith than the abodes of a faith which may still affirm a presence and awaken echoes. Catholicism has gone, but Anglicanism has the next best music. So at least it seemed to me, a Sunday or two since, as I sat in the choir at Chester awaiting a discourse from Canon Kingsley. The Anglican service had never seemed to my profane sense so much an affair of magnificent intonations and cadences—of pompous effects of resonance and melody. The vast oaken architecture of the stalls among which we nestled—somewhat stiffly and with a due apprehension of wounded ribs and knees—climbing vainly against the dizzier reach of the columns; the beautiful English voices of certain officiating canons; the little rosy 'king's scholars' sitting ranged beneath the pulpit, in white-winged surplices, which made their heads, above the pew-edges, look like rows of sleepy cherubs; every element in the scene gave it a great spectacular beauty. They suggested too what is suggested in England at every turn, that conservatism here has all the charm and leaves dissent and democracy and other vulgar variations nothing but their bald logic. Conservatism has the cathedrals, the colleges, the castle, the gardens, the traditions, the associations, the fine names, the better manners, the poetry; Dissent has the dusky brick chapels in provincial by-streets, the names out of Dickens, the uncertain tenure of the *h*, and the poor *mens sibi conscia recti*.

Differences which in other countries are slight and varying, almost metaphysical, as one may say , are marked in England by a gulf. Nowhere else does the degree of one's respectability involve such solid consequences, and I am sure I don't wonder that the sacramental word which with us (and, in such correlatives as they possess, more or less among the continental races) is pronounced lightly and facetiously and as a quotation from the Philistines, is uttered here with a perfectly grave face. To have the courage of one's mere convictions is in short to have a prodigious deal of courage, and I think one must need as much to be a Dissenter as one needs patience not to be a duke. Perhaps the Dissenters (to limit the question to them) manage to stay out of the church by letting it all hang on the sermon. Canon Kingsley's discourse was one more example of the familiar truth—not without its significance to minds zealous for the good old fashion of 'making an effort'—that there is an odd link between large forms and small emanations. The sermon, beneath that triply consecrated vault, should have had a builded majesty. It had not; and I confess that a tender memory of ancient obligations to the author of 'Westward Ho!' and 'Hypatia' forbids my saying more of it. An American, I think, is not incapable of taking a secret satisfaction in an incongruity of this kind. He finds with relief that even mortals reared as in the ring of a perpetual circus are only mortals. His constant sense of the beautiful scenic properties of English life is apt to beget a habit of melancholy reference to the dead-blank wall which forms the background of our own life-drama; and from doubting in this fantastic humour whether we have even that modest value in the scale of beauty that he has sometimes fondly hoped, he lapses into a moody scepticism as to our place in the scale of 'importance', and finds himself wondering vaguely whether this be not a richer race as well as a lovelier land. That of course will never do; so that when after being escorted down the beautiful choir in what, from the American point of view, is an almost gorgeous ecclesiastical march, by the Dean in a white robe trimmed with scarlet and black-robed sacristans carrying silver wands, the officiating canon mounts into a splendid canopied and pinnacled pulpit of Gothic stonework and proves—not an 'acting' Jeremy Taylor, our poor sentimental tourist begins to hold up his head again and to reflect that so far as we *have* opportunities we mostly rise to them. I am not sure indeed that in the excess of his reactions he is not tempted to accuse his English neighbours of being impenetrable and uninspired, to affirm that they do not half discern their good fortune, and that it takes passionate pilgrims, vague aliens and other disinherited persons to appreciate the 'points' of this admirable country.

Notes

1 Quotations from, and references to, this essay are taken from Henry James, *English Hours* (1905), ed. Leon Edel (Oxford and New York, 1981), 35–43.

2 Jorg Hasler, *Switzerland in the Life and Work of Henry James* (Basle, 1966), 10.

3 John Henry Raleigh, 'The Novel and the City: England and America in the Nineteenth Century', *Victorian Studies*, vol. 11 (1968), 325.

4 This is the title of the introductory chapter in John Kimmey, *Henry James and London: The City in his Fiction* (New York, 1991).

5 *Ibid.*, 18.

6 Cited by George Perkins in his entry on Henry James in *The Novel to 1900*, intro. A. O. J. Cockshut (London and Basingstoke, 1980), 166.

7 The review is reproduced in David Carroll (ed.), *George Eliot: The Critical Heritage* (London, 1971), 353–59.

8 *English Hours*, 35.

9 *Ibid.*

10 Leon Edel, *Henry James: The Conquest of London 1870–1883* (London, 1962), 70–71.

11 *Ibid.*, 71.

12 *Ibid.*, 72. Hence, in Edel's view, James's eye for architecture, 'for buildings by which man has asserted his creative power'; to James a great building was 'the greatest conceivable work of art. More than any other it represents difficulties annulled, resources combined, labour, courage and patience' (73).

13 The parallel here is not with the foreign chronicler of English history (as in, say Halévy's *History of the English People in the Nineteenth Century*), but with the 'flâneur', fascinatingly discussed by John Rignall in his *Realist Fiction and the Strolling Spectator* (London and New York, 1992).

14 Kimmey, 5.

15 *English Hours*, 36.

16 *Ibid.*, 37.

17 *Ibid.*

18 Henry James, *The Ambassadors*, ed. Christopher Butler (Oxford and New York, 1985), 10.

19 *The Ambassadors*, 28–29.

20 *English Hours*, 38.

21 *Ibid.*

22 *Ibid.*, 39.

23 *Ibid.*, 40.

24 *Ibid.*

25 *Ibid.*, 40–41.

26 'Introduction' to *English Hours*, ix.

27 *Ibid.*, vii. Later in the introduction, Edel suggests that James 'sees the Victorian world as organized to preserve and reinforce respect for traditional institutions and that these are accepted on the whole by an entire society as a tacit social contract' (xi).

28 *English Hours*, 41.

29 *Ibid.*, 43.

30 Bonney MacDonald, 'Henry James's *English Hours*: Private Spaces and the Aesthetics of Enclosure', in Daniel Mark Fogel (ed.), *A Companion to Henry James Studies* (Westport, CT and London, 1993), 395–406.

31 Taken from 'A Prediction', reprinted in Leon Edel (ed.), *Henry James; A Collection of Critical Essays* (Englewood Cliffs, NJ, 1963), 55–56.

Appendix
Victorian Chester:
Brief Chronology

1830   Erection of St Paul's Church, Boughton.

1831   Publication of Joseph Hemingway's *A History of the City of Chester*.

1832   Cholera epidemic.

1832   Princess Victoria opens the Grosvenor Bridge, designed by Thomas Harrison.

1835   Chester City Assembly becomes the Council of the Borough of Chester under the terms of the Municipal Corporations Act of 1835.

       Mechanics' Institute founded in St John Street.

1836   Watch Committee, with responsibility for borough policing, established by the City Council under the terms of the Municipal Corporations Act.

       Establishment of Poor Law Guardians in accordance with the Poor Law Amendment Act of 1834.

1839   Diocesan Teacher Training College opened in Parkgate Road.

1840   Opening of railway lines from Chester to Birkenhead (Chester & Birkenhead Railway) and Crewe (Chester & Crewe Railway), with two railway termini situated at Hoole/City Road.

1842   Post Office erected in St John Street.

       W. E. Gladstone lays foundation stone of Diocesan Teacher Training College.

1845   Chester Improvement Act gives the Council the same powers as those exercised by Local Boards under the Public Health Acts, and provides for the better paving, lighting and improving of the Borough of Chester and for the establishment of new market places.

1847   Typhus epidemic.

Chester Theatre opened in the Commercial Hall, Foregate Street, accommodating 1,500 persons.

The Chester Literary Improvement Society established in Nicholas Street.

1848   General Railway Station opens in City Road, amalgamating the two previous termini, and serving the London & North Western, Chester & Holyhead, Shrewsbury & Chester, Chester & Birkenhead, and the Birkenhead, Lancashire and Cheshire Junction railways.

Cholera epidemic.

Sanitary Committee formed, under Nuisance Removals and Disease Prevention Acts of 1848.

Chester Cemetery Act sanctions the foundation of the Overleigh Cemetery, the property of the Chester Cemetery Company.

1849   Founding of The Architectural, Archaeological and Historic Society of Chester, Cheshire and North Wales.

Chester Public Swimming and Shower Baths opens on a site adjoining the Water Tower.

Common Lodging House Committee established for the purpose of local regulation and supervision of lodging houses.

1851   Foundation of The Chester Ragged School Institution.

Chester brought under the terms of the Common Lodging Houses Act of 1851.

Publication of Thomas Pullin's French/English guidebook to Chester.

1852   Queen's Park Suspension Bridge opens.

1853   Erection of Trustee Savings Bank building in Grosvenor Street, designed by James Harrison to house the Chester Savings Bank (est. 1817).

Inauguration of The Chester Ragged and Industrial School Society.

1855   The Theatre Royal in Northgate Street rebuilt by James Harrison as the Music Hall, accommodating 1,000 persons.

1856   Publication of Thomas Hughes' *The Strangers Handbook to Chester and its Environs.*

1858   Opening of the Great Boughton Union workhouse at Boughton Heath.

1859   Establishment of Chester Penny Savings Bank in St Bridget's School House, Grosvenor Street.

1861   Building of Queens Hotel in City Road.

1862   Old Exchange Building in Northgate Street damaged by fire and demolished.

1863   The Marquis of Westminster finances the rebuilding of the old Royal Hotel, subsequently renamed The Grosvenor Hotel, in Eastgate Street.
       New Public Market opens in Northgate Street.

1866   Cholera epidemic.

1867   Second Marquis of Westminster presents Grosvenor Park to the City.
       Charles Dickens reads from his own work at the Music Hall.
       Unsuccessful attempt by about 1500 members of the Fenian Brotherhood to seize Chester Castle and capture arms.

1868   Beginnings of alterations to Chester Cathedral by Sir George Gilbert Scott.

1869   New Town Hall in Northgate Street opened by Edward, Prince of Wales.
       Erection of the Volunteer Drill Hall, Albion Street, headquarters of the Second Volunteer Battalion (Earl of Chester's) Cheshire Regiment.

1870   Charles Kingsley appointed Canon of the Cathedral.

1871   Founding of Chester Society of Science, Literature and Art (President, Charles Kingsley).

1872   Henry James visits Chester.
       Chester constituted an Urban Sanitary Authority under the Public Health Act of 1872.

1875   Northgate Railway Station opens.

1876   The Mechanics' Institute, now a Public Library and Reading Room, opens as a Free Library.
       Erection of new Post Office building, St John Street.

1877   First Roman Catholic ordination since the Reformation takes place at St Werburgh's Church.

1879   First horse-drawn tram service, from the General Railway Station to Saltney.

1882   Erection of the Royalty Theatre in City Road.
Anti-Salvation Army disturbances in Boughton.

1883   Foundation of Chester Liberal Club in Watergate Street.

1884   Chester Improvement Act extends the powers of the Council, both as an Urban Sanitary Authority and as a Municipal Authority; provisions include the consolidation of the City of Chester into one parish, the improved provision for the levying of rates, the issue of corporation stock, provision as to markets and fairs, the lifting of tolls from the Dee bridges, and the consolidation and amendment of the previous Improvement Act.

1885   Change from a two member to a one member constituency after boundary changes in consequence of the Redistribution of Seats Act of 1885.

1886   Grosvenor Museum opens in Grosvenor Street.
Foundation of Chester Conservative Club in Little St John Street.

1887   Typhoid epidemic: 360 reported cases in Chester between 1887 and 1889.

1888   Chester becomes a County Borough under the Local Government Act of 1888.

1890   Manchester, Sheffield and Lincolnshire Railway Company station opened in Liverpool Road.

1892   The Duke of Westminster presents Edgar's Field, Handbridge, to the Council as a public park.

1893   The Prince of Wales visits the Royal Agricultural Society's Show at Hoole.

1897   Queen Victoria's Diamond Jubilee celebrations.

1899   Eastgate Clock, designed by John Douglas, erected to commemorate the Diamond Jubilee.

1903   Train service electrified.

Select Bibliography

Primary Sources

Cheshire County Record Office
Chester Chronicle
Chester Courant
Cheshire Sheaf
S. Bagshaw, *History, Gazetteer and Directory of the County Palatine of Chester* (Chester, 1850).
W. White, *Directory of Cheshire* (Sheffield, 1860).

Chester City Record Office
Parry & Son, *The Chester Directory* (1840).
James Pigot, *The Commercial Directory* (1818–20).
Pigot & Co., *The Commercial Directory of Cheshire* (1822).
Wardle & Bentham, *The Commercial Guide* (1814–15).
Breweries: Documents relating to Bridge Street Brewery.
Documents relating to Chester Northgate Brewery Company.
Burrell Ltd., Ledger, 1883–1890.
Canals: 1828 Agreement—E O Wrench & Props., Ellesmere and
            Chester Canal.
Ellesmere Canal Props., Report to the General Assembly 27 Nov.
1805.
Cemetery Act 1848.
Cemetery Records: Overleigh, 1887–1889
City Council: Assembly Book 1848–1854
            Council Minutes 1845–1890
            Proceedings under Chester Improvement Act 1846
            Special Committee Minutes 1849–1857
Committees: Common Lodging Houses, 1851–1872.
            Improvement, 1846–1851.

Sanitary, 1840–1857.
Watch, 1854–1857.
MOH Reports: Dr G. Ballard, to Local Government Board, 1890.
Dr G. Kenyon, concerning the River Dee, 1894.
Annual Reports, 1887–1889, 1908, 1910–1912, 1919.
Quarter Sessions File, 1882.
Ragged School Society, Annual Reports and Minutes, 1851–1875.
Royal Infirmary, Minutes of Board Meetings, 1846–1854.
Waterworks Act, 1857.
Waterworks Clauses Act, 1847.
Waterworks Company, Reports and Acts, 1826–1930.
Census Returns and Abstracts, 1831–1881.

Chester City Library
Associated Lead Manufacturers Ltd., *Chester Works* (typescript,1957).
Chester, Wrexham and North Wales Trustee Savings Bank 150th. Annual Report, 1817–1967 (1967).

Clwyd County Record Office
Flintshire Oil and Cannel Co., Saltney: Deeds etc., 1877–1887.
Henry Wood & Co., notes and advertisement on Company.
Register: Railway Employees at Mold Junction, 1864–1927.

Parliamentary Papers
Report of the Royal Commission on the Condition of the Poorer Classes in Ireland: Appendix G, The State of the Irish Poor in Great Britain (1836).
Report of the General Board of Health on Chester (1845).
Report of the General Board of Health on the Cholera Epidemic of 1848 and 1849, with Maps and Diagrams (1850).
Health of Towns Report (1847).
First Report of the Royal Commission on the Housing of the Working Classes (1884–1885).
Fifteenth Annual Report of the Local Government Report (1886–1887)
Sixteenth Annual Report of the Local Government Report (1888–1889).

Public Health Acts (1872, 1897).
Report of the Royal Commission on Reformatories and Industrial Schools (1884).
Registrar General's Annual Reports (1849, 1887–1888, 1888–1889).
Registrar General's Annual Report on the Mortality of Cholera in England (1848–1849).
Second Report of the Royal Commission on the State of Large Towns and Populous Districts (1845).
Education Census, England and Wales (1851).

Secondary Sources

Local Studies
[i] *Books*
P. J. Aspinall and D. M. Hudson, *Ellesmere Port: The Making of an Industrial Borough* (1982).
P. E. Baughan, *Regional History of the Railways of Great Britain, Vol.XI, North and Mid-Wales* (Newton Abbot, 1980).
R. M. Bevan, *The Roodee: 450 Years of Racing in Chester* (Northwich, 1982).
B. Bracegirdle, *Engineering in Chester: 200 years of progress* (Chester,1966).
P. Broster, *The Chester Guide* (1782).
I. Callister, *The Chester Grosvenor: A History* (Chester, 1983).
Chester Northgate Brewery Co. Ltd., *A Guide to Chester and District* (Chester, n.d., c.1930).
B. D. Clark (ed.), *Saltney and Saltney Ferry: A Short Illustrated Guide* (Chester, 1988).
B. D. Clark (ed.), *Saltney and Saltney Ferry: A Second Illustrated History* (Chester, 1989).
G. A. Cooke, *Topographical Description of Chester* (1830).
C. S. Davies, *Agricultural History of Cheshire* (Manchester,1960).
A. H. Dodd, *The Industrial Revolution in North Wales* (Cardiff, 1971).
A. Dutton, *Streets and Lanes of a City* (1871).
C. R. Ellington (ed.), *The Victoria History of the Counties of England: A History of Cheshire, Vol.2* (Oxford, 1980).

G. L. Fenwick, *A History of the Ancient City of Chester* (1896).

K. Goulbourne and G. Jackson, *Chester: A Portrait in Old Pictures and Postcards, Vol.1* (1987), *Vol.2* (1988).

B. Harris, *Chester* (Bartholomew City Guide, 1979).

S. Harrison, 'The Port of Chester', in A. M. Kennett (ed.), *Chester: 1900 Years of History* (Chester,1979).

J. Hemingway, *A History of the City of Chester* (1831).

M. H. O. Hoddinott, *A Site Development History of the Chester Leadworks of Messrs. Walker, Parker & Co., 1800–1900.*

H. Hughes, *Chronicle of Chester: the 200 years 1775–1975* (London, 1975).

T. Hughes, *Strangers Handbook to Chester* (Chester,1856; Manchester,1972).

A. H. John (ed.), *Minutes relating to Messrs. Samuel Walker & Co., Rotherham Iron Foundries and Steel Refiners 1741–1829, and Messrs. Walker, Parker & Co., Lead Manufacturers 1788–1893* (1951).

A. M. Kennett, *Chester Schools* (Chester,1973).

A. M. Kennett (ed.), *Georgian Chester: Aspects of Cestrian History from 1600 to 1837* (Chester, 1987).

A. M. Kennett (ed.), *Chester and the River Dee: An Illustrated History of Chester and its Port* (Chester, 1982).

G. Lloyd, *Notes on Henry Wood & Co. Ltd.* (Chester, 1964).

N. Moore, *Chester Clocks and Clockmakers* (1975).

G. Ormerod, *History of the County Palatine and City of Chester* (1882).

N. Pevsner and E. Hubbard, *The Buildings of England: Cheshire* (London,1971).

Presbyterian Church Magazine, *City Road Presbyterian Church, Chester* (1993).

Robinson, Son & Pike (pub.), *Chester in 1892* (Brighton, 1892).

St Paul's Church Magazine, *St. Paul's, Boughton, Chester* (1987).

St Werburgh's Church Magazine, *Catholicism in Chester, A Double Centenary 1875–1975* (Chester, 1975).

Saltney and Saltney Ferry History Group, *Saltney and Saltney Ferry: A Third Illustrated History* (Chester, 1992).

F. Simpson, *A History of Chester Free Library* (Chester,1931).

F. Simpson, *Church and Chapel Notes, Chester.*

F. Simpson, *Presbyterian Church of Wales, City Road, Chester, 1865–1965: Commemoration of the Centenary* (1964).

M. E. Sturman, *Catholicism in Chester, A Double Centenary* (1975).

D. Sylvester and G. Nulty (eds.), *The Historical Atlas of Cheshire* (1958).

A. T. Thacker and C. Lewis (eds.), *The Victoria History of the County of Cheshire [VCH]: Vol. V, The City of Chester* (Oxford, in press, 1996).

D. Thomas, *Visitors Guide to Chester* (1852).

J. Tomlinson, *Victorian and Edwardian Chester* (Deeside, 1976).

C. J. Williams, *Industry in Clwyd: An Illustrated History* (Hawarden, 1986).

[ii] *Articles*

H. E. Boulton, 'The Chester Infirmary', *Chester Archaeological Society*, vol.47 (1960).

R. Craig, 'Shipping and Shipbuilding in the Port of Chester in the Eighteenth and early Nineteenth Centuries', *Transactions of the Historic Society of Lancashire and Cheshire*, cxvi (1966).

K. Davies, 'The Growth and Development of Settlement and Population in Flintshire, 1801–1851', *Journal of the Flintshire Historical Society*, xxv (1972–73).

K. Davies, 'The Growth and Development of Settlement and Population in Flintshire, 1851–1891', *J. Flints. H. S.*, xxvi (1973–74).

K. Davies, 'The Growth and Development of Settlement and Population in Flintshire, part lll, 1891–1931'. *J. Flints. H. S.*, xxvii (1975–76).

M. J. Groombridge, 'The City Guilds of Chester', *Journal of the Chester and N. Wales Architec. Archaeol. and Hist. Society*, xxxix.

C. Hargreaves, 'Social Areas Within the Walls of Chester, 1861', *Journal of the Cheshire Archaeological Society*, 65 (1982).

W. Harrison, 'Development of the Turnpike System in Lancashire and Cheshire', *Transactions of the Lancashire and Cheshire Antiquarian Society*, iv (1886).

L. and M. Hillis, 'The Chester Whiteware Manufactory', *Northern Ceramics Society Journal*, vol. 4 (1980–81).

G. C. Lerry, 'The Industries of Denbighshire, Part I', *Transactions of the Denbighshire Historical Society*, vi.

G. C. Lerry, 'The Industries of Denbighshire from Tudor Times to the Present Day, Part III: More Recent Developments', *Trans. Denbighs. H. S.*, viii (1959).

S. I. Mitchell, 'Retailing in Eighteenth and early Nineteenth Century Cheshire', *T.H.S.L.C.*, vol. 130 (1980).

F. Neal, 'The Birkenhead Garibaldi Riots of 1862', *T.H.S.L.C.*, vol. 131 (1982).

D. Nuttall, 'A History of Printing in Chester', *Journal Chester Arch. Society*, liv.

G. W. Place, 'The Repatriation of Irish vagrants from Cheshire, 1750–1815', *Journal of the Chester Arch. Society*, vol. 68 (1986).

R. E. Porter, 'The Marketing of Argicultural Produce in Cheshire in the Nineteenth Century', *T.H.S.L.C.*, cxxvi (1976).

P. S. Richards, 'The Hawarden Bridge, Shotton, Chester, Iron and Steelworks of Messrs.

John Summers & Co.', *Journal Flints. H. S.*, 25 (1972–73).

E. A. Shearing, 'Chester Canal Projects', *Journal Railway and Canal H. S.*, xxviii.

F. Simpson, 'A Few Cheshire Worthies', *Journal Chester Arch. Society*, vol. 28 (1928).

F. Simpson, 'The River Dee', *Journal Chester Arch. Society*, xiv (1908).

G. C. Spence, 'Notes on Clay Tobacco Pipes and Clay Pipe Makers in Cheshire', *Trans. Lancs. and Chesh. Antiquarian Society*, liv.

J. Williams, 'The Irish in the 'East Cheshire Silk Industry', *T.H.S.L.C.*, vol. 136 (1986).

General Studies

[i] *Books*
P. Ackroyd, *Dickens* (London,1990).
A. Adburgham, *Shops and Shopping, 1800–1914* (1981).

W. Albert, *The Turnpike Road System in England, 1663–1840* (1972).

D. Alexander, *Retailing in England during the Industrial Revolution* (1970).

W. A. Armstrong, 'Mid Nineteenth-Century York', in P. Laslett and R. Wall (eds.), *Household and Family in Past Time* (Cambridge, 1977).

P. S. Bagwell, *The Railwaymen: The History of the National Union of Railwaymen* (London, 1963).

D. Baines, *Emigration from Europe 1815–1930* (1991).

D. E. S. Baines, 'Labour Supply and the Labour Market, 1860–1914', in R. C. Floud and D. McCloskey (eds.), *The Economic History of Britain since 1700, Vol 2; 1860 to the 1970s* (Cambridge, 1981).

N. Barber, *Where Have all the Breweries gone? A Directory of British Brewery Companies* (n.d., c.1980).

G. Battiscombe, *Shaftesbury: A Biography of the Seventh Earl, 1801–1885* (London, 1975).

BBC Third Programme Talks, *Ideas and Beliefs of the Victorians* (London, 1949).

J. Belchem (ed.), *Popular Politics, Riot and Labour: Essays in Liverpool History 1790–1940* (Liverpool, 1992).

J. Belchem, *Industrialization and the Working Class: The English Experience, 1750–1900* (London, 1991).

G. Best, *Mid-Victorian Britain, 1851–1875* (London, 1971).

C. Booth, *In Darkest England and the Way Out* (London, 1890).

A. Briggs, *The Age of Improvement* (London, 1959).

A. Briggs, *Victorian Cities* (London, 1990).

A. Briggs, *Victorian People* (London, 1965)

J. Burnett, *A Social History of Housing, 1851–1985* (London, 1986).

J. Caird, *English Agriculture* (1850–51).

T. Carlyle, *Chartism* (1839; London, 1972).

D. Carroll (ed.), *George Eliot: The Critical Heritage* (London, 1971).

F. Cartwright, *A Social History of Medicine* (New York, 1977).

S. D. Chapman, *A History of Working Class Housing: A Symposium* (Newton Abbott, 1971).

R. Christiansen, *A Regional History of the Railways of Great Britain, Vol.7; the West Midlands* (Newton Abbot, 1973).

K. Clark, *The Gothic Revival* (London, 1974).

G. Kitson Clark, *The Making of Victorian England* (Oxford, 1962).

B. Coleman, *The Church of England in the mid-Nineteenth Century* (Columbia, NY, 1978).

G. Crossick and H. G. Haupt (eds.), *Shopkeepers and Master Artisans in Nineteenth Century Europe* (London, 1984).

L. P. Curtis, *Apes and Angels: The Irishman in Victorian Caricature* (Newton Abbot, 1971).

S. J. Davies, 'Classes and Police in Manchester 1829–1880', in A. J. Kidd and K. W. Roberts (eds.), *City, Class and Culture: Studies of Cultural Production and Social Policy in Manchester* (Manchester, 1985).

D. Davis, *A History of Shopping* (1966).

G. Davis, *The Irish in Britain, 1815–1914* (Dublin, 1991).

A. P. Donajgrodzki (ed.), *Social Control in Nineteenth Century Britain* (London, 1977).

M. Durey, *The Return of the Plague: British Society and the Cholera 1831–2* (Dublin, 1979).

H. J. Dyos and M. Wolff (eds.), *The Victorian City: Images and Realties, 2 vols.* (London,1973).

L. Edel, *Henry James: The Conquest of London, 1870–1883* (London, 1962).

L. Edel (ed.), *Henry James: A Collection of Critical Essays* (New Jersey, 1963).

C. Hamilton Ellis, *British Railway History, 1830–1876.*

F. Engels, *The Condition of the Working Classes in England* (1844; Oxford, 1958).

D. M. Fogel (ed.), *A Companion to Henry James Studies* (London, 1993).

B. Ford, *Victorian Britain* (Cambridge, 1992).

R. F. Foster, *Modern Ireland, 1600–1972* (London, 1988).

A. Fox, *A History of the National Union of Boot and Shoe Operatives, 1874–1958* (Oxford, 1958).

D. Fraser (ed.), *The New Poor Law in the Nineteenth Century* (London, 1976).

W. M. Frazer, *A History of English Public Health, 1834–1939* (London, 1950).

E. Gaskell, *Mary Barton* (1848).

S. Gilley, 'English attitudes to the Irish in England, 1780–1900', in C. Holmes (ed.), *Immigrants and Minorities in British Society* (London, 1978).

H. S. Goodhart-Rendell, *English Architecture since the Regency* (London, 1989).

E. Gouldie, *Cruel Habitations: A History of Working-Class Housing, 1780–1918* (London, 1974).

T. R. Gourvish and Alan O'Day (eds.), *Later Victorian Britain, 1867–1900* (London, 1988).

C. Hadfield, *The Canals of the West Midlands* (Newton Abbot, 1985).

J. L. and B. Hammond, *Lord Shaftesbury* (London, 1923).

G. Hanks, *God's Special Army: The Story of William Booth* (London, 1980).

J. E. Hartley, *The Irish in Scotland* (Cork, 1943).

B. Harrison, *Drink and the Victorians: The Temperance Question in England, 1815–1872* (London, 1971).

J. F. C. Harrison, *Early Victorian Britain, 1832–1851* (London, 1979).

J. F. C. Harrison, *Late Victorian Britain, 1870–1901* (London, 1990).

J. F. C. Harrison, *Learning and Living: A Study in the History of the Adult Education Movement* (London, 1961).

J. Hasler, *Switzerland in the Life and Work of Henry James* (Basle, 1966).

G. R. Hawke, *Railways and Economic Growth in England and Wales, 1840–1870* (Oxford, 1970).

U. R. Q. Henriques, *Before the Welfare State: Social administration in early industrial Britain* (London, 1979).

M. Hickman and M. Hartigan, *The History of the Irish in Britain: a Bibliography* (London, 1986).

G. Himmelfarb, *The Idea of Poverty: England in the Early Industrial Age* (London, 1984).

F. H. Hinsley (ed.), *The New Cambridge Modern History, 1870–1890* (Cambridge, 1979).

G. O. Holt, *A Regional History of the Railways of Great Britain, Vol 10; The North-West* (1978).

E. Hopkins, *A Social and Economic History of the English Working Classes* (London, 1982).

P. Howell and I. Sutton, *The Faber Guide to Victorian Churches* (London, 1989).

E. Hubbard, *The Work of John Douglas* (London, 1991).

P. Hudson, *The Industrial Revolution* (London, 1972).

R. S. Inglis, *Churches and the Working-Class of Victorian England* (London, 1974).

J. A. Jackson, *The Irish in Britain* (London, 1963).

H. James, *English Hours* (1905), ed. L. Edel (Oxford and New York, 1981).

H. James, *The Ambassadors*, ed. Christopher Butler (Oxford and New York, 1985).

D. Jones, *Crime, Protest, Community and the Police in Nineteenth-Century Britain* (London, 1982).

J. P. Kay, *The Moral and Physical Condition of the Working Classes Employed in the Cotton Manufacture in Manchester* (1832).

T. Kelly, *George Birkbeck: Pioneer of Adult Education* (Liverpool, 1957).

T. Kelly, *A History of Adult Education in Great Britain* (Liverpool, 1957).

B. Kemp, *English Church Monuments* (London,1980).

P. Kidson, P. Murray and P. Thompson, *A History of English Architecture* (London, 1979).

J. Kinmey, *Henry James and London: The City in his Fiction* (New York, 1991).

N. Kirk, 'Ethnicity, Class and Popular Toryism, 1850–1890', in K. Lunn (ed.), *Hosts, Immigrants and Minorities: historical responses to newcomers in British society* (Folkestone, 1980).

L. Lees, *Exiles of Erin: Irish migrants in Victorian London* (Manchester, 1979).

N. Longmate, *King Cholera: The Biography of a Disease* (London, 1966).

W. J. Lowe, *The Irish in Mid-Victorian Lancashire* (London, 1989).

F. McKenna, *The Railway Workers, 1840–1970* (Where?, When?).

J. Manton, *Mary Carpenter and the Children of the Streets* (London, 1976).

G. Marsden (ed.), *Victorian Values: Personalities and Perspectives in Nineteenth-Century Society* (London, 1990).

P. Mathias, *The Retailing Revolution* (1967).

H. Mayhew, *London Labour and the London Poor* (London, 1861–62).

E. C. Midwinter, *Social Administration in Lancashire, 1830–1860* (London, 1969).

E. C. Midwinter, *Victorian Social Reform* (London, 1968).

S. Mitchell (ed.), *Victorian Britain* (London, 1988).

G R. J. Morris and R. Rodger (eds.), *The Victorian City: A Reader in British Urban History, 1820–1914* (London, 1993).

F. Neal, *Sectarian Violence: The Liverpool Experience* (Manchester, 1987).

E. R. Norman, *Anti-Catholicism in Victorian England* (London, 1968).

G. O'Tuathaigh, *Ireland before the Famine, 1798–1848* (Dublin, 1972).

G. Parsons (ed.), *Religion in Victorian Britain*, Vol.1, *Traditions* (Manchester, 1988).

D. G. Paz, *Popular Anti-Catholicism in Mid-Victorian England* (Stanford, 1992).

M. Pelling, *Cholera, Fever and English Medicine, 1825–1865* (Oxford, 1978).

N. Philip and V. Neuburg (eds.), *Charles Dickens: A December Vision: His Social Journalism* (London, 1986).

D. Read, *England 1868–1914* (London, 1985).

A. Redford, *Labour Migration in England, 1800–1850* (London, 1926; revised edition, Manchester, 1964).

D. Richter, *Riotous Victorians* (London, 1981).

J. Rignall, *Realist Fiction and the Strolling Spectator* (London, 1992).

J. Rowbottam, *A Social and Economic History of the English Working Classes, 1815–1945* (London, 1982).

J. Rule, *The Labouring Classes in early industrial England, 1750–1818* (London, 1991).

R. Sandall, *The History of the Salvation Army, 1865–78* (London, 1947).

M. Sanderson, *Education, Economic Change and Society in England, 1780–1870* (London, 1983).

Standing Conference on University Teaching and Research in the

Education of Adults, *Victorian Learning and Leisure; (1) The Mechanics Institutes* (Nottingham, 1982).

J. Simmons, *The Railway in Town and Country, 1830–1914* (Newton Abbot, 1986).

E. Smith, *English Parish Churches* (1976).

F. B. Smith, *The People's Health, 1830–1910* (London, 1979).

D. A. P. Stewart and E.Jenkins, *The Medical and Legal Aspects of Sanitary Reform* (New York, 1969).

R. E. Swift and S. Gilley (eds.), *The Irish in Britain, 1815–1839* (London, 1989).

R. E. Swift and S. Gilley (eds.), *The Irish in the Victorian City* (London, 1985).

B. E. Supple, 'Income and Demand, 1860–1914', in R. C. Floud and D. McCloskey (eds.), *The Economic History of Britain since 1700*.

F. M. L. Thompson (ed.), *The Cambridge History of Britain, 1750–1950* (Cambridge, 1990).

J. Walvin, *Victorian Values* (London, 1987).

K. Williams, *From Pauperism to Poverty* (London, 1981).

B. R. Wilson (ed.), *Patterns of Sectarianism* (London, 1967).

J. Wintle, *Makers of Nineteenth Century Culture* (1982).

Ll. Woodward, *The Age of Reform, 1815–1870* (Oxford, 1962).

E. A. Wrigley (ed.), *Nineteenth Century Society: Essays in the use of Quantitative Methods for the study of social data* (Cambridge, 1972).

[ii] *Articles*

A. Briggs, 'Cholera and Society in the Nineteenth Century', *Past and Present*, 19 (1961).

A. P. Conley, 'Mid-Nineteenth Century Ormskirk: Disease, Overcrowding and the Irish in a Lancashire Market Town', *T.H.S.L.C.*, vol. 139 (1990).

K. J. Dodds, 'Cholera, Local Politics and Public Health in Nineteenth-Century Reading', *The Local Historian*, vol. 121, no. 4 (1991).

T. Kelly, 'The Origins of Mechanics Institutes', *British Journal of Education Studies*, vol. 1 (Nov. 1952).

J. Langton, 'The industrial revolution and the regional geography of

England', *Transactions of the Institute of British Geographers*, NS9 (1984).

N. H. Murdoch, 'Salvation Army Disturbances in Liverpool, England, 1879–1887', *Journal of Social History*, 25, 8 (Spring 1992).

M. A. G. O'Tuathaigh, 'The Irish in Nineteenth-Century Britain—problems of integration', *Trans. of the Royal Hist. Society*, xxxi (1981).

R. Perren, 'Structural change and market growth in the food industry: flour milling in Britain, Europe and America, 1850–1914', *Economic History Review*, 2nd. series, xliii (1989).

J. H. Raleigh, 'The Novel and the City: England and America in the Nineteenth Century', *Victorian Studies*, 11 (1968).

C. Richardson, 'The Irish in Victorian Bradford', *Bradford Antiquary*, ix (1976).

E. D. Steele, 'The Irish presence in the North of England, 1850–1914', *Northern History*, xii (1976).

R. E. Swift, 'Another Stafford Street Row: Law, order and the Irish presence in mid–Victorian Wolverhampton', *Immigrants and Minorities*, vol. 3, no. 1 (March 1984).

R. E. Swift, 'The Outcast Irish in the British Victorian City: Problems and Perspectives', *Irish Historical Studies*, no. 99 (May 1987).

J. Treble, 'The attitude of the Roman Catholic Church towards trade unionism in the north of England, 1833–42', *Northern History*, v (1970).

J. M. Werly, 'The Irish in Manchester, 1832–49', *Irish Historical Studies* (1973).

H. Williams, 'Public Health and Local History', *The Local Historian*, vol. 14 (1980–81).

J. G. Williams, 'The Impact of the Irish on British Labour Markets during the Industrial Revolution', *Journal Econ. Hist.*, xcvi (1986).

Theses

C. Armour, 'The Trade of Chester and the state of the Dee navigation, 1600–1800' (University of London PhD thesis, 1956).

G. Davies, 'The Impact of the Railways on Chester, 1837–1870' (Chester College of Higher Education BEd project, 1981).

D. A. Halsall, 'The Chester and Holyhead Railway and its Branches: A Geographical Perspective' (University of Liverpool PhD thesis, 1976).

J. Herson, 'Why the Irish went to Stafford: A Case Study of Irish Settlement in England 1830–1871' (London School of Economics MSc thesis, 1986).

F. Jackson, 'Police and Prisons in Chester, 1830–1850' (University of Manchester BA thesis, 1966).

M. J. Kingman, 'Chester 1801 to 1861' (University of Leicester MA thesis, 1969).

S. I. Mitchell, 'Urban Markets and Retail Distribution, 1730–1815, with particular reference to Macclesfield, Stockport and Chester' (University of Oxford DPhil thesis, 1974).

R. E. Porter, 'Agricultural change in Cheshire during the Nineteenth Century' (University of Liverpool PhD thesis, 1974).

W. T. R. Pryce, 'The Social and Economic Structure of North-East Wales, 1750–1890' (Manchester Polytechnic PhD thesis, 1971).

D. A. Savage, 'Working-Class standards of Living in the City of Chester, 1870–1914' (University of Durham BA dissertation, 1990).

M. J. Tebbutt, 'The Evolution of Ethnic Stereotypes: An examination of stereotyping with particular reference to the Irish in Manchester during the late nineteenth and early twentieth centuries' (University of Manchester MPhil thesis, 1982).

E. M. Willshaw, 'The Inns of Chester, 1775–1832' (University of Leicester MA thesis, 1979).

Index